Construction Design
for Landscape Architects

Construction Design
for Landscape Architects

Albe E. Munson, P.E., L.A.

Fellow Emeritus, American Society of Landscape Architects

McGRAW-HILL BOOK COMPANY

New York   St. Louis   San Francisco   Auckland   Düsseldorf
Johannesburg   Kuala Lumpur   London   Mexico   Montreal
New Delhi   Panama   Paris   São Paulo   Singapore
Sydney   Tokyo   Toronto

Library of Congress Cataloging in Publication Data

Munson, Albe E
   Construction design for landscape architects.

   1. Landscape architecture.   2. Civil engineering.
3. Building sites.   I. Title.
SB472.M84   624'.15   74-13526
ISBN 0-07-044046-8

*The editors for this book were Jeremy Robinson, Stanley
E. Redka, and Lester Strong, the designer was
Naomi Auerbach, and the production supervisor was
George E. Oechsner.   It was set in Caledonia by Bi-Comp, Inc.*

It was printed and bound by The Kingsport Press.

Contents

Preface   ix

Chapter 1.   Property Descriptions **1**

1.1   The Survey System—Locating Parcels   1
1.2   Closing a Traverse   4
1.3   Calculating Areas   10

Chapter 2.   Topography **12**

2.1   Contours and Elevations   12
2.2   Reading Contour Maps   19

Chapter 3.   Site Layout **21**

3.1   General   21
3.2   Coordinates   23
3.3   Stationing   24

Chapter 4.   Site Grading **28**

4.1   Grading Considerations   28
4.2   Grading-Study Procedure   29

4.3 Grading Criteria   30
4.4 Site-grading Drawings   33

Chapter 5.   Road Layout **34**

5.1 Horizontal Alignment   34
5.2 Vertical Alignment   41
5.3 Finding the High or Low Point of a Vertical Curve   46
5.4 Solving Parabolic Cross Sections   48
5.5 Parking Areas   49

Chapter 6.   Designing Dams and Retaining Walls **52**

6.1 General   52
6.2 Procedure for the Design of Dams   56
6.3 Procedure for Retaining-Wall Design   63
6.4 Earth-retaining Walls of Timber Construction   73

Chapter 7.   Earthwork Calculations **79**

7.1 General   79
7.2 Cross-Section Method   81
7.3 Grid Method   85
7.4 Contour-Planes Method   88
7.5 Method of Parallel Planes   93

Chapter 8.   Utilities **99**

8.1 General   99
8.2 Water Distribution   100
8.3 Sanitary-Sewer Lines   102
8.4 Storm Sewers   103

Chapter 9.   Storm Drainage **104**

9.1 Storm Runoff   104
9.2 Selecting the Size of Pipe   108
9.3 Swales and Ditches   113

Chapter 10.   Sprinkler Irrigation Systems **119**

10.1 Selecting the Type of System   120
10.2 Selecting Sprinkler Heads   121
10.3 Arrangement and Spacing of Sprinkler Heads   122
10.4 Dividing the System into Sections   123
10.5 Total Pressure Loss for the System   126
10.6 Sizing the Pipe   133
10.7 Pressure Losses in Loops   135
10.8 Pump and Pump Intake   136
10.9 Appurtenances   136

Chapter 11.   Wood Construction **138**

11.1   Wood as a Construction Material   138
11.2   Calculation of Live and Dead Loads   141
11.3   Determining Beam Sizes   143

Appendix A.   Mathematics **157**

A.1   Basic Algebra   157
A.2   Logarithms   159
A.3   Trigonometric Functions   161
A.4   Circular Measure   163
A.5   Squares, Cubes, Square Roots, and Cube Roots   164
A.6   Miscellaneous Area and Volume Formulas   179
A.7   Miscellaneous Trigonometric Formulas   181
A.8   Tables of Arc Lengths—Radius Equals 1 Ft   183

Appendix B.   Mathematical Devices **185**

B.1   Architect's and Engineer's Dimensioning Systems   185
B.2   Verniers   187
B.3   The Planimeter   189
B.4   The Slide Rule   192
B.5   Calculators and Desk-Top Computers   195

Appendix C.   Weights and Measures **197**

C.1   Weights   197
C.2   Liquid Measure   198
C.3   Dry Measure   198
C.4   Linear Measure   199
C.5   Square Measure   199
C.6   Cubic Measure   200
C.7   Land and Sea Measure   200

Appendix D.   Conversion Factors **201**

D.1   Conversion Factors—Miscellaneous   201
D.2   Conversion Factors—U.S. to Metric   203
D.3   Conversion Factors—Metric to U.S.   203

Index   205

Preface

This book is intended as a ready reference in the construction design of site improvements. The ability of landscape architects and their staffs to efficiently prepare workable, safe, and economical construction drawings is necessary for the success of any office. The infrequent occurrence of some types of problems tends to leave the practitioner "rusty" and slow in the solution of these problems when they do occur. It is the intention of this book to provide an easy-to-understand ready reference that will rapidly recall the basic methods and formulas for solving such problems.

This book is not intended to be a compendium of all the methods that may be used in solving a problem, nor is it intended to provide a text explaining the technical theory and mathematics underlying the application of the formulas. In general, this book shows one or two simple ways of arriving at a safe and reasonable answer to a problem. In some instances a specialist in a specific area would be able to produce a more economical solution by the use of more sophisticated formulas and methods, but in most cases in the field of site construction the saving thus made would be negligible in relation to the cost of the project as a whole.

Each type of problem is first treated in a brief summary form, followed by a solution to a typical problem, with a detailed explanation of the solution method where it was felt this would be beneficial. This presentation sequence was selected so that those needing only a brushup to recall the method of solving the problem could obtain this by reading the first few paragraphs, whereas those needing more help could follow the steps shown in solving a typical problem and, if necessary, by further reading, obtain a detailed explanation of the solution method.

Every effort has been made to keep this book from becoming dated. Cost figures, which are constantly changing, are avoided. Materials, which are also constantly being improved and changed, are mentioned only in a general sense. No actual construction practices are mentioned since these too are rapidly changing as new improved materials and equipment become available. Only the basic fundamentals for solving problems are covered, and these must be augmented with current manufacturer's literature, product catalogs, equipment catalogs, and the latest applicable codes and testing classifications.

Grateful acknowledgment and thanks are given to M. Boylan, J. Campbell, A. Miller, J. Rogers, and those of my former students who assisted with review and comment in the preparation of this book. Appreciation and thanks are extended to the many individuals, firms, and associations who responded so well to my requests. I wish particularly to thank my good wife, Dorothy, for her patient typing.

Albe E. Munson

Construction Design
for Landscape Architects

CHAPTER ONE

Property Descriptions

In order for landscape architects to read and understand property descriptions, they must have a rudimentary knowledge of the U.S. survey system.

In 1784 the U.S. system of public lands surveys was inaugurated. Twenty-eight years later, in 1812, the General Land Office was established for the purpose of directing public lands surveys. Since that date most of the country has been surveyed into rectangular control tracts. Variations from this rectangular control pattern occur where private claims and other land grants had prior title by descriptions based on some other system. Other variations occur where settlement and development preceded the establishment of the control system. Even where the control system had been established, local customs and rules, as well as changes in detailed survey instructions, have caused somewhat different standards and methods of land platting in certain sections of the country.

1.1 THE SURVEY SYSTEM—LOCATING PARCELS

In general, the survey system is based on a division of lands into 24-mile control "squares" (Fig. 1.1). The north-south lines of the squares follow

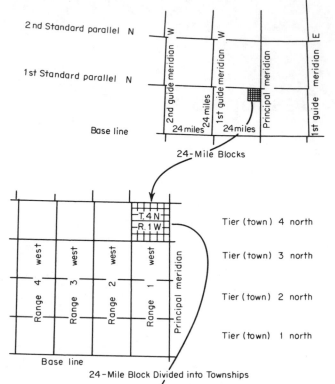

2nd Standard parallel N

1st Standard parallel N

Base line

24-Mile Blocks

T.4 N
R.1 W

Tier (town) 4 north

Tier (town) 3 north

Tier (town) 2 north

Tier (town) 1 north

Base line

24-Mile Block Divided into Townships

6	5	4	3	2	1
7	8	9	10	11	12
18	17	16	15	14	13
19	20	21	22	23	24
30	29	28	27	26	25
31	32	33	34	35	36

Township Divided into Sections

Fig. 1.1 Twenty-four-mile block divided into sections.

the longitudinal lines of the earth, and therefore the squares are not true squares, due to the convergence of the longitudinal lines as they approach the pole. In order not to accumulate this difference, a correction is made on the south line of each 24-mile tier, to bring it back to its full 24-mile dimension. The east-west lines follow the lines of latitude and are, theoretically, consistently 24 miles apart.

It must be noted that convergence of longitudinal lines, accepted lines of occupancy, and other peculiarities in section dimensions cause survey lines rarely, if ever, to measure out to the exact theoretical distances of 5,280, 2,640, 1,320, 660, and 330 ft that would obtain ideally.

Each of the so-called 24-mile control squares is further divided into 16 towns, or townships, as near 6 miles square as possible. Generally, this is the basic unit with which the landscape architect is concerned. These towns (townships) are numbered consecutively north and south from established east-west base lines, and consecutively east and west from established north-south base lines, referred to as *meridians*. Each township is approximately 6 miles square, and is further divided into 36 one-mile squares, called *sections*, each containing 640± acres. The sections of a township are numbered 1 to 36, commencing with section 1 in the northeast corner of the township, proceeding west along the northernmost tier of sections through section 6, dropping down one tier to section 7, and proceeding to the right. This process is continued, ending with section 36 in the southeast corner of the township.

The sections can be further subdivided into quarters by east-west and north-south centerlines, and these quarters can be further subdivided in a similar manner. The centerlines of a section are referred to as *quarter lines*, and the centerlines of the quarters are referred to as *eighth lines*. The intersection of the quarter lines marks the center of the section and is generally referred to as the *center post*. The intersections of the quarter lines with the bounding section lines are referred to as the *south quarter post*, the *north quarter post*, the *west quarter post*, or the *east quarter post*, depending upon which section boundary is intersected.

Property descriptions vary in phraseology, but typically, a description of rural property may read as follows: Land in Clinton Township, T.2N, R.13E, County of Macomb, State of Michigan, being more particularly described as: The SW¼ of the NE¼ Section 32, containing 40± acres.

The T.2N tells us that the land being described is in tier 2 north, the second tier of 6-mile squares north of the base line. In practice it is common to use the word *town* in place of the word *tier*. The R.13E tells us that this land is in the thirteenth range east of the meridian. Section 32 tells us that it is the second section from the west in the southernmost tier of sections in this township. The description then proceeds to locate the property more specifically within this said section 32 by telling us that it is the 40± acres in the southwest quarter of the northeast quarter of that section. Section 32 contains 640± acres, and the northeast quarter of the section contains 160± acres. The southwest quarter of this 160 acres contains the 40± acres referred to in the land description.

Ordinarily, when most land was first surveyed, it was plentiful and inexpensive, and so costly meticulous surveys were not the order of the day. As the land became more intensively used, it became more valuable, and increasingly careful surveys were required. With this progression, the lands described above would in time be more carefully located, and the descriptions changed to traverse descriptions showing taped boundary lengths and bearings. As land use changes from rural to urban, the sizes of the tracts and parcels per building site are generally reduced. The subdivision of lands into suburban or city lots requires a calculated plat wherein all control corners are marked with monuments and all lines are given bearings and dimensions to two decimal places. The manner of platting and recording subdivisions is stipulated by state plat laws and local ordinances. Any reference to the detailed records of the lot lines is simplified by the recording of the plat drawing showing all the required data, and thereafter simply referring to it by the subdivision name and lot number as shown on the recorded plat. Figure 1.2 shows a portion of a subdivision plat.

Each subdivision plat is captioned with an approved name and shows the location of the subdivision by the name of the political unit in which it is located, the town, range, section, and location within the section. Most communities have plat books which may be viewed, and in most instances photostats of any of these sheets may be purchased.

1.2   CLOSING A TRAVERSE

It is customary for an owner to supply the landscape architect with a property-line survey and topographic map of the property being developed. Before proceeding very far with the assignment, the landscape architect should check the survey to make sure it closes.

First, the bearings of the lines should be examined to see if the sum of the deflection angles is equal to 360°. This can be quickly done by adding the deflections algebraically, right deflections being considered positive, left deflections negative, starting at any selected side, going completely around the traverse and returning to the beginning side. If this is found to be grossly incorrect, the survey should be returned to the owner for correction.

If the angular error is minor, or even if the sum of the deflection

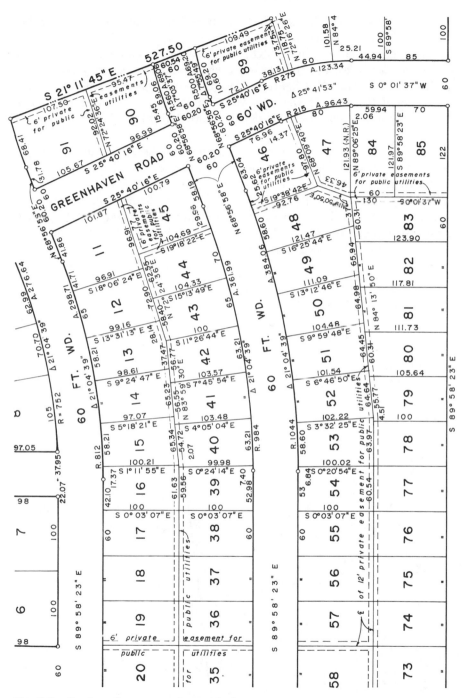

Fig. 1.2 Portion of a surveyor's record plat.

5

angles equals 360°, the lengths and bearings of the lines should be further checked for closure by using the north-south and east-west components of the survey lines. The north-south components of the lines are called *latitudes,* and the east-west components are called *departures.*

It is obvious that if a figure is closed, the sum of the east departures must equal the sum of the west departures and the sum of the north latitudes must equal the sum of the south latitudes. See Figs. 1.3 to 1.6.

The field party making the survey attempts to obtain as much accuracy as possible in all their measurements of distances and angles. In many cases there may be a measurement for a distance or an angle that was difficult to make in the field due to steep gradients, trees, water, or other obstacles, and any errors of closure would be likely to fall in that line. In other instances all lines of the traverse may be of equal diffi-

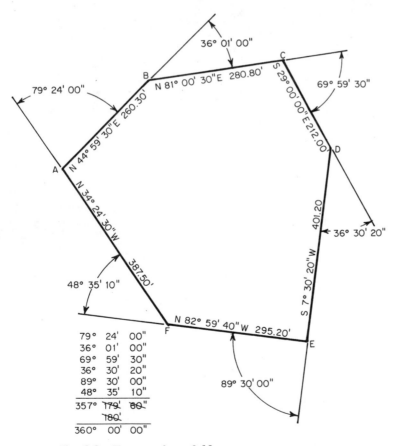

Fig. 1.3 Traverse from field survey.

| | | | Latitude | | Departure | | Correction | | | | Corrected | | | |
| | | | | | | | Latitude | | Departure | | Latitude | | Departure | |
Line	Bearing	Distance, ft	N (+)	S (−)	E (+)	W (−)	N	S	E	W	N (+)	S (−)	E (+)	W (−)
AB	N44°59′30″E	260.30	184.08	......	184.03	......	0.07	......	0.02	......	184.01	......	184.01	......
BC	N81°00′30″E	280.80	43.89	......	277.35	......	0.07	......	0.03	......	43.82	......	277.32	......
CD	S29°00′00″E	212.00	......	185.42	102.78	......	......	0.06	0.02	......	......	185.48	102.76	......
DE	S7°30′20″W	401.20	......	397.76	......	52.41	......	0.11	......	0.04	......	397.87	......	52.45
EF	N82°59′40″W	295.20	36.00	......	......	293.00	0.08	......	......	0.03	35.92	......	......	293.03
FA	N34°24′30″W	387.50	319.70	......	......	218.58	0.10	......	......	0.04	319.60	......	......	218.61
Totals		1,837.00	583.67	583.18	564.16	563.99					583.35	583.35	564.09	564.09

583.67
583.18
0.49

564.16
563.99
0.17

583.18
0.49
$\dfrac{0.49}{1,837} = 0.0002667$

563.99
0.17
$\dfrac{0.17}{1,837} = 0.0000925$

Correction per foot:

	583.35	564.09
	583.35	564.09
	xxxxxx	xxxxxx
	check	xxxxxx

Calculations:

Line	Angle	Distance, ft	cos	sin	Latitude	Departure
AB	44°59′30″	260.30	0.70720962	0.70700393	184.08	184.03
BC	81°00′30″	280.80	0.15629081	0.98771108	43.89	277.35
CD	29°00′00″	212.00	0.87461971	0.48480962	185.42	102.78
DE	7°30′20″	401.20	0.99143220	0.13062232	397.76	52.41
EF	82°59′40″	295.20	0.12196558	0.99253433	36.00	293.00
FA	34°24′30″	387.50	0.82503132	0.56408701	319.70	218.58

Latitude = distance × cos of bearing angle
Departure = distance × sin of bearing angle

Fig. 1.4 Tabular computation for correcting latitudes and departures.

culty, and in such cases any error should be spread proportionately among all the sides of the traverse.

There are two methods or rules for allocating the error proportionately around the traverse. These are the so-called *transit rule* and *compass rule*. The latter rule assumes the error to be due as much to direction as to distance and is the method commonly used to balance a survey.

Compass Rule: The correction to be applied to the latitude or departure of any course is to the total error in latitude or departure as the length of the course is to the perimeter of the field.

A survey that returns mathematically to the starting point will have the sum of the northing latitudes equal to the sum of the southing

Corrected bearings:

$$\tan \beta = \frac{\text{departure}}{\text{latitude}}$$

Line

AB $\tan \beta = \dfrac{184.01}{184.01} = 1.0000000$ $\beta = 45°$

BC $\tan \beta = \dfrac{277.32}{43.82} = 6.328617$ $\beta = 81°01'15''$

CD $\tan \beta = \dfrac{102.76}{185.48} = 0.5540219$ $\beta = 28°59'14''$

DE $\tan \beta = \dfrac{52.45}{397.87} = 0.1318269$ $\beta = 7°30'36''$

EF $\tan \beta = \dfrac{293.03}{35.92} = 8.157850$ $\beta = 83°00'41''$

FA $\tan \beta = \dfrac{218.61}{319.60} = 0.6840112$ $\beta = 34°22'21''$

Corrected distances:

$$\text{Distance} = \frac{\text{departure}}{\text{sin bearing}} = \frac{\text{latitude}}{\text{cos bearing}}$$

Line	Bearing	cos	sin	Lat./cos	Dep./sin (check)
AB	45°00'00''	0.7071068	0.7071068	260.23	260.23
BC	81°01'15''	0.1560753	0.9877452	280.76	280.76
CD	28°59'14''	0.8747278	0.4846146	212.04	212.04
DE	7°30'36''	0.9914221	0.1306992	401.31	401.31
EF	83°00'41''	0.1216720	0.9925704	295.22	295.22
FA	34°22'21''	0.8253846	0.5645709	387.21	387.21

Fig. 1.5 Tabular computation for length and bearing.

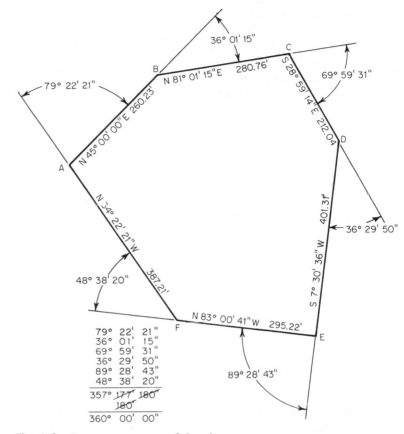

Fig. 1.6 Traverse as corrected for closure.

latitudes and the sum of the easting departures equal to the sum of the westing departures. If the survey does not close, the amounts by which they fail to balance are the latitude and departure of the *line of closure*.

After all the N and S latitudes and the E and W departures have been found, they should be examined to see that no large mistake has been made in the fieldwork. If a large discrepancy is discovered, the calculations should be rechecked thoroughly to be absolutely certain that the error is in the fieldwork and not in the calculations themselves. If the error cannot be found in the calculations, the fieldwork will have to be rechecked.

When calculating corrections using the compass rule, divide the total error in latitude or departure by the perimeter to obtain a per-foot correction constant for each. If the constant is multiplied by the distances of each line in succession, the corrections for each line are determined. The corrections so determined are applied so as to diminish the sum of the latitude or departure column which is too large and increase the sum in the column which is too small. The example shown in Figs. 1.3 and 1.4 should clarify this procedure.

Bear in mind that the numbers we are dealing with, whether they be distances or latitudes or departures of those distances, are all in feet. The determination of any of these footages to three decimal places is academic in that it is virtually impossible to measure as close as even the nearest hundredth of a foot in the field. In many cases arbitrary horse-sense distribution of a few tenths or hundredths of a foot may be as accurate as any distribution formula could be.

Once the corrected latitudes and departures are established, as in the example of Fig. 1.4, the length and bearing can be determined by using the following relationships:

$$\tan \text{bearing} = \frac{\text{departure}}{\text{latitude}}$$

$$\text{Distance} = \frac{\text{departure}}{\sin \text{bearing}} = \frac{\text{latitude}}{\cos \text{bearing}}$$

$$\text{Distance} = \sqrt{\text{latitude}^2 + \text{departure}^2}$$

1.3   CALCULATING AREAS

Appendix Sec. B.3 explains the use of the planimeter as a measuring device to determine areas of irregular plane figures. An area that is enclosed by straight lines can be computed precisely by mathematics.

When an area enclosed by a traverse consisting of straight lines is to be found, the traverse must first be closed and then the balanced latitudes and departures for each line obtained. Once this has been done, it is a matter of extending the computation to obtain the area by the *double meridian distance method*. In this method:

1. The sums of the areas found are double areas and hence must be divided by 2 to obtain the actual area.

2. The double areas are found by multiplying the DMD (double meridian distance) of each course by the latitude of that same course.

3. The DMD of the first course equals the departure of the course itself.

4. The DMD of any other course equals the DMD of the preceding course plus the departure of the preceding course plus the departure of the course itself.

5. The DMD of the last course should be numerically equal to its departure but of opposite sign.

Line	Bearing	Distance, ft	Balanced	
			Latitude	Departure
AB	N45°00'00"E	260.23	+184.01	+184.01
BC	N81°01'15"E	280.76	+ 43.82	+277.32
CD	S28°59'14"E	212.04	−185.48	+102.76
DE	S7°30'36"W	401.31	−397.87	− 52.45
EF	N83°00'41"W	295.22	+ 35.92	−293.03
FA	N34°22'21"W	387.21	+319.60	−218.61

Compute the DMDs for each line from the above balanced departures:

AB	BC	CD	DE	EF	FA
184.01	+ 184.01	+ 645.34	+1,025.42	+1,075.73	+730.25
	+184.01	+ 277.32	+ 102.76	− 52.45	−293.03
	+277.32	+ 102.76	− 52.45	− 293.03	−218.61
	+645.34	+1,025.42	+1,075.73	+ 730.25	+218.61

Fig. 1.7 Computing DMDs for each line of traverse.

Using the same survey as in Figs. 1.4 to 1.6, we have the computations shown in Figs. 1.7 and 1.8.

Compute double areas by multiplying the DMD of each course by the latitude of that course:

Line	Latitude	DMD	Double area	
			+	−
AB	+184.01	+ 184.01	33,859.68	....
BC	+ 43.82	+ 645.34	28,278.80	....
CD	−185.48	+1,025.42	....	190,194.90
DE	−397.87	+1,075.73	....	428,000.69
EF	+ 35.92	+ 730.25	26,230.58	....
FA	+319.60	+ 218.61	69,867.76	....
Totals			+158,236.82	−618,195.59

Then area equals:
   $(−618,195.59) + (+158,236.82) = 459,958.77$
   $459,958.77 \div 2 = 229,979.38$ sq ft
   $229,979.38 \div 43,560 = 5.280$ acres (1 acre = 43,560 sq ft)

Fig. 1.8 Computing area from DMD.

Notice that the sign may be either positive or negative in the final result; however, the sign is of no consequence as far as the area is concerned.

CHAPTER TWO

Topography

The instruments commonly used in site-survey work are the surveyor's transit and level. In certain types of work the plane table is an excellent tool. The transit is primarily designed for measuring angles. It can be used for taking levels, but it is not as convenient nor as accurate as the surveyor's level for that purpose. The principle of the level is simply that of striking a level line of sight from which vertical measurements are made to determine the elevation of selected objects or locations above or below this level line of sight. It is obvious that the elevation of the reference plane (the horizontal line of sight) must be known. This is accomplished by measuring the height of that line above a known datum.

2.1 CONTOURS AND ELEVATIONS

The known datum is referred to as a *bench mark*. The elevation of the bench mark may be selected arbitrarily to be used for one site without reference to any elevation available from other bench marks. The U.S. Geological Survey has established bench marks throughout the country based on a datum of mean sea level being at 00.00 elevation. In some areas these bench marks are relatively far apart. Consequently, many cities and counties have established their own system of bench marks. Sometimes these are based on an arbitrary datum, and sometimes they are an extension of the USGS system of bench marks.

Since site work is generally local in nature, arbitrary benches are often established for a job. It is advisable to use USGS or other locally adopted datum where possible.

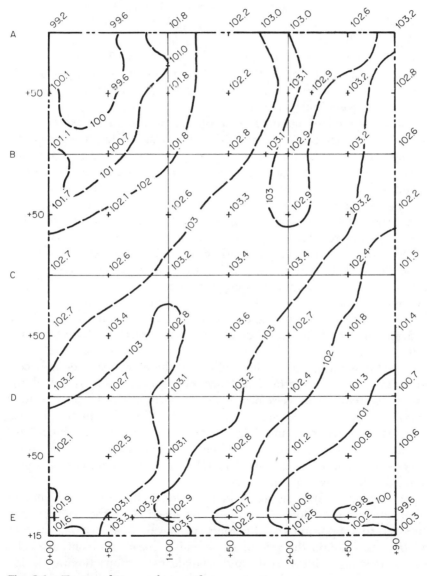

Fig. 2.1   Topographic map from grid survey.

Ordinarily, the owner supplies the landscape architect with property-line and topographical maps. The topographical map, or "topo," may be supplied either as a pattern of spot elevations or as a contour map. In some instances landscape architects will want to take their own topos or check the supplied topos in the field or do some part of the site in more detail than was furnished.

The most commonly used method of taking topography is to establish temporary stakes on a 100-ft-grid pattern and shoot the grade at each of these stakes. Often the 50-ft grid is paced to provide more shots. Breaks in grade, ditches, roads, and other features are always shot and usually located by chaining along the grid lines. In taking grades for topographic mapping, it is important to obtain grades 50 or 100 ft beyond the property lines in order to know how the proposed grading will fit the surrounding property.

Another method of taking topography is by the *stadia method*. In this method it is usual to establish a traverse within the property, locating corners of the traverse at logical locations for instrument setup. The traverse is closed, and the elevations of the stakes at the corners of the traverse are established. In this method the transit is used rather than the level, and the rod is held at such selected points as will provide the necessary data for properly mapping the topography of the site. The distance to the rod location is determined by the stadia interval, and the elevation is determined by reading the rod on the center cross hair of the instrument. On rugged and densely wooded sites this is often the best method of obtaining topographic data.

When the fieldwork is plotted on the plan, the result is a series of spot elevations. From these spot elevations, contour locations can be determined and drawn to create a graphic picture of the ground's form.

A *contour* is an imaginary line following the earth's surface at a constant elevation. The *vertical* distance between contours is called the *contour interval*. This is selected on the basis of need. The contour intervals commonly used are 1, 2, and 5 ft, the 1-ft contour interval providing most accuracy and detail. In relatively flat land, 1-ft contours are almost necessary in order to obtain a usable graphic presentation. Larger contour intervals are used in hilly or rugged land and for maps intended to be drawn to a small scale.

The elevations taken in the field are seldom, if ever, exactly on the actual contour elevation. To obtain the location of the contour it is necessary to proportion the difference in elevation to distance in feet, and from this obtain the rate of slope and so locate the contour. This can be done by using a scale and triangle as a proportioning device, or a rubber band marked off in equal divisions, or a slide rule. Most

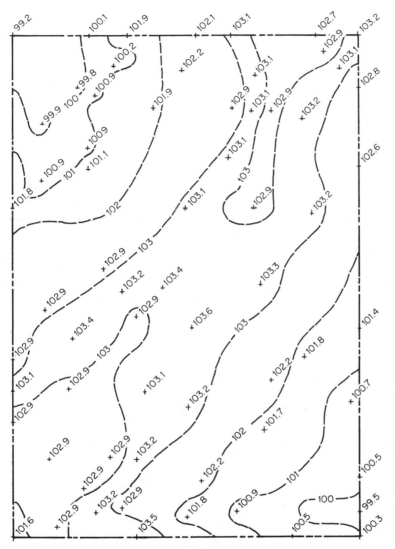

Fig. 2.2 Topographic map from stadia survey.

professionals soon attain enough proficiency to abandon these mechanical
devices and do the proportioning by eye, with only an occasional
mechanical check to verify their judgment from time to time as they
proceed. Remember that land forms are usually graceful undulating
gradients, whereas mathematical proportioning assumes a straight-line
gradient between any two elevations, and from that standpoint the locating of contours by judgment may in many cases be more true than
the mathematical or mechanical method.

The process of locating whole-foot contours first requires a visual inspection of two adjacent spot elevations to see if there will actually be a whole-foot contour at either one of the elevations or on the gradient between them. The gradient between them is considered to be a straight-line slope, and it is necessary to find the total difference between the two elevations. Once this is done, there are several ways to work out the contour location.

Slide-Rule Method

If the distance between the two elevations is 50 ft (as it might be in a grid topo) and the difference in elevation between the two spot elevations is eleven-tenths and the whole-foot contour elevation is three-tenths higher than the lower spot elevation as shown in Fig. 2.3, place the hairline over 11 on the A scale and move the slide to position 50 on the B scale at the hairline opposite 11. Move the hairline to 3 on the A scale and read 13.6 on the B scale. Scale from spot elevation 13.6 along the grid line connecting the two spot elevations and mark. Contour 101 crosses the grid line at this location. To avoid confusion and inverting scales, mark the A scale with *elev*. and the B scale with

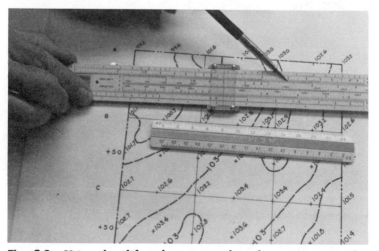

Fig. 2.3 Using the slide rule to interpolate the contours. In this photograph the zero of the 40 scale is at elevation 100.7. Fifty feet to the right the spot shows an elevation of 101.8. This is a difference of eleven-tenths. The slide rule is set to show 11 on the A scale over 50 on the B scale. The even-foot contour, 101.0, is three-tenths higher than the low elevation of 100.7. The pencil points to 3 on the A scale. Immediately below this, read 13.6 on the B scale. The 101 contour will then cross the grid line on the topographic map at about 13½ ft on the 40 scale.

feet. If these terms are printed in ink and covered with clear nail polish, the labeling will last and proportioning should be rapid. This same relationship can also be set up on the C and D scales.

Rubber-Band Method

Use a rubber band that is about ⅛ in. wide and has fairly uniform stretch characteristics. Turn the band inside out and stretch over a 6-in. scale. Opposite the scale graduations mark off equal division marks on the rubber band with India ink. The spacing of the division marks will vary with the scale of the survey map. A little experience will soon enable the operator to select a comfortable scale to use. The band is then placed over the thumb and forefinger and stretched between the two given elevations to show the number of units of elevation difference (Fig. 2.4). In this stretched position, the number of units to the whole-foot contour can be counted off and marked on the plan to show the contour location. Select a rubber band that is not too strong, since this can be very tiring on the fingers.

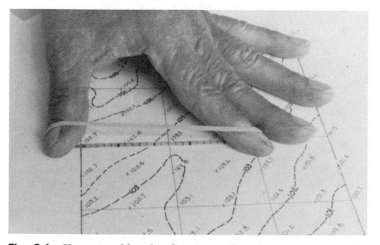

Fig. 2.4   Using a rubber band to interpolate for contours. In this picture elevation 103.2 is 6 tenths above 102.6, and the whole-foot contour, 103, is 4 tenths above 102.6. Stretch the rubber band to show six divisions between 102.6 and 103.2. Mark the 103 contour at the fourth division mark above 102.6 (the second division below 103.2).

Triangle-and-Scale Method

Any scale can be selected since it is used only for proportioning and not for measuring. The scale is placed on the plan with its zero mark on either of the two given spot elevations. A right triangle is butted

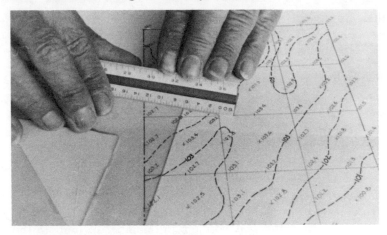

(a)

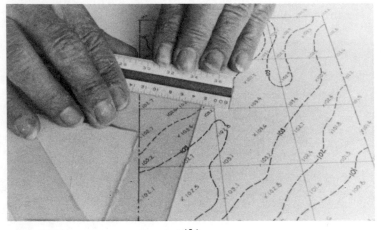

(b)

Fig. 2.5   Using a scale and triangle to interpolate for contours.

to the scale, and the perpendicular side of the triangle is set along
the scale opposite the number of units of difference between the two
elevations.   The scale selected should be such that this length is equal
to, or slightly less than, the distance on the drawing separating the
two elevations.   If the scale is less than the distance between the two
elevations, the scale and triangle should be swung as a unit until the
perpendicular side of the triangle intersects the second elevation, with
the zero mark of the scale still on the first spot elevation.   The scale
is held firmly in this position while the triangle is slid along the scale
the required number of units to reach the whole-foot contour.   A mark

is placed where the triangle crosses the line between the two elevations. See Fig. 2.5.

2.2   READING CONTOUR MAPS

The accuracy of a topographic map is determined largely by the accuracy and detail supplied by the field survey crew. The field crew must always determine that a uniform slope exists between any two adjacent spot elevations. Where this is not true, the field crew must pick out the grade change or breakpoints and record them in their data.

It is important to be able to read contour maps so well that one can visualize in three dimensions what is shown on the map. In reading a topographic map, the first thing that must be observed is where the high and low spots occur on the map. Whether reading or plotting contour maps, bear in mind: ·

1. Closely spaced contours indicate steeper slopes. Widely spaced contours indicate flatter slopes. Evenly spaced contours indicate uniform slopes.

2. Concentric contours indicate a pot hollow or peak mound. For ready identification of the landform, the bottom contour in a depression is drawn with inward (downhill) hachure marks and the top contour on a peak is drawn with hachure marks on the downhill side of the contour line.

3. Every contour is a continuous line that closes upon itself somewhere on the earth's surface, not necessarily within the limits of the drawing. In the drawing the contour forms a complete loop or runs out at the limit of the drawing. It cannot be a single line terminating within the drawing.

4. Except in the case of a vertical or overhanging face, contour lines never cross each other. Along a stream the contour line follows the valley upstream, crosses the stream at right angles, and returns downstream along the opposite valley side.

5. A contour never splits. This could occur only if the crest or valley were knife-edged and continuous exactly at a constant level at the elevation of the contour.

6. Land shapes are usually smooth and undulating and hence develop graceful contour lines. Where steep slopes, erosion, or rock outcroppings interfere with this normal smoothness, contours will cease to be lines of smooth-flowing alignment.

A slope in the long dimension of a right-of-way, street, ditch, or walk is referred to as a *longitudinal slope,* or *grade* (*gradient*).

A slope across the short dimension (i.e., at right angles to the longitudinal slope) is referred to as the *transverse slope,* or *grade* (*gradient*). Slopes and/or gradients are called out as:

Degree of Slope $0°$ = horizontal; $90°$ = vertical.

Rate of Slope   The ratio between the horizontal and vertical units; i.e., a 3 to 1 slope means three horizontal units for each 1 unit of rise. The horizontal distance is known as *run,* and the vertical distance is known as *rise.*

Percent of Slope   The rise in feet per hundred feet of run.   This is most commonly used in landscape architectural work.

Horizontal Equivalent   The number of feet of run per foot of contour interval.

CHAPTER THREE

Site Layout

The design scheme establishes the policy and theme for development of the site. The construction drawings establish the controls, locations, dimensions, and elevations for the physical development of the site. Sometimes these vertical and horizontal dimension controls are incorpo- rated in one plan, but often this becomes too confusing, and so the information is covered by two plans, the *staking plan* and the *grading plan*. This chapter covers the staking plan.

3.1 GENERAL

The layout, or staking plan, should clearly show where exact dimensions are required and where some variances will be permitted. If the site is large, the overall plan may be drawn on a small scale, for example, 1 in. = 100 ft. Generally, this scale will be too small to show enough detailed dimensioning, and the overall plan must be divided into blocks that can be blown up to 40 scale or larger on individual sheets. These individual large-scale sheets are keyed to each other and to the overall plan by base lines and match lines. Accurate location of all buildings, roads, walks, paved areas, and features such as sculptures, walls, pools, etc., must be accomplished by either complete chains of dimensions,

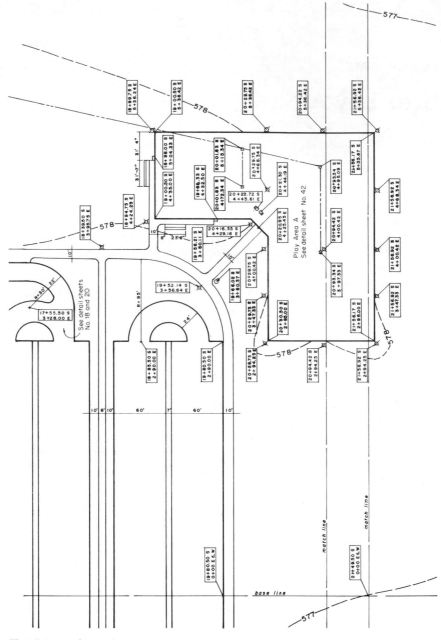

Fig. 3.1 Staking plan.

22

coordinates, or stationing. The many dimension lines required for locating all these items of site construction by chains of dimensions tend to confuse the plan. To avoid this, coordinates and stationing systems are used for primary locations, and dimensions and dimension lines for secondary measurements. See the example shown in Fig. 3.1.

All roads should be horizontally aligned, with both a coordinate and a station point correct to one-hundredth of a foot at each road intersection, point of curvature, and point of tangency. The bearings and distances on all property lines, and coordinates on all property corners, should also be shown correct to the nearest hundredth of a foot. Where possible, road centerlines should be completed as a closed traverse, and sufficient curve data given for all horizontal curves to enable staking the curve in the field as well as closing the traverse. Minimum curve data would be radius, tangent, central angle, and length of arc.

Buildings must be located by two coordinates or by dimensions from road centerlines, or from specially computed base lines that will not be obstructed during construction. It should be made clear what point of the building is being located, i.e., finished face, foundation line, or column centerline.

Usually, the sanitary sewers, storm sewers, electric lines, and water- and gas-line layouts are shown on a separate *utility* sheet. However, all visible appurtenances, such as manholes, cleanouts, lamp holes, valve boxes, catch basins, etc., are shown in the staking plan, and the center points of these are located to the nearest hundredth of a foot by dimensions or coordinates or by stationing along road centerlines.

Other features such as retaining walls, dams, bridges, decks, etc., that are located by grading or grading considerations must be shown on the staking plan and precisely located by either dimensions or coordinates.

3.2   COORDINATES

In the coordinate system the position of a point is identified by giving two dimensions, each being perpendicularly measured from each of two base lines which intersect at right angles. Generally, these base lines run north-south and east-west. They are perpendicular to each other and for convenience can be oriented in directions other than true N-S and E-W, but nominally will be called out as the N-S and the E-W base lines. Whatever their orientation, they must be able to be located in the field and should be located on the site in such a place that construction will not obstruct them. The advantage of the coordinate system is that it eliminates dimension lines on the drawings, and each pair of coordinates locates a point by reference to the base lines and is not dependent on the proper position of any other point or points in the field.

All corners of a survey, road centerline, building, or other feature can thus be located by stating the x and y dimensions from the base lines of the system. Coordinates are easier to work with if the entire site is in one quadrant of the intersecting base lines. This is seldom possible because it is advisable to establish the base lines within the site. In such cases all points east of the N-S base line are positive ($+$); all points west of the N-S base line are negative ($-$); all points north of the E-W base line are positive ($+$); and all points south of the E-W base line are negative ($-$).

Coordinates are written in various ways. Whatever the system adopted, it must be consistent throughout the construction set.

Example 3.1

$$A + \begin{array}{|c|} \hline 12 + 74.03\text{N} \\ 9 + 22.17\text{E} \\ \hline \end{array}$$

$$B + \begin{array}{|c|} \hline 11 + 26.01\text{N} \\ 11 + 20.19\text{E} \\ \hline \end{array}$$

In this example, point A is 1,274.03 ft north of the E-W base line and 922.17 ft east of the N-S base line. Point B is 1,126.01 ft north of the E-W base line and 1,120.19 ft east of the N-S base line. In each case the coordinate is placed in a standard-sized rectangular box, with a tag line from the box to the point being identified. The N-S coordinate is the upper figure, and the E-W coordinate the lower figure in the box in each instance. The order and the presentation method should be consistent throughout the plan. Note that the hundreds are set apart by a $+$ sign in the same manner as is done in stationing.

In the above example, point A is 148.02 ft north of point B and 198.02 ft west of point B.

$$\begin{array}{r} 1{,}274.03'\text{N} \\ -1{,}126.01'\text{N} \\ \hline 148.02' \end{array} \qquad \begin{array}{r} 1{,}120.19'\text{E} \\ -\ \ 922.17'\text{E} \\ \hline 198.02' \end{array}$$

3.3 STATIONING

Stationing is normally used in positioning linear construction such as road and sewer centerlines. The progression in stationing is from $0 + 00$ at the commencement point, proceeding in the direction that construction would take place or in a direction that would otherwise be logical. Stationing is generally used for traverses that do not close; in other words, for traverses that do not return to the starting point.

The starting point of the traverse is called station 0; the next station,

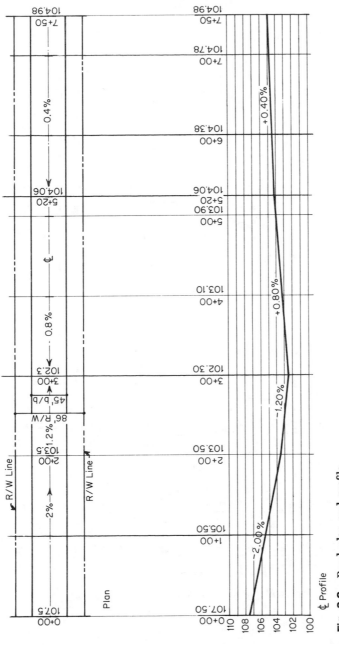

Fig. 3.2 Road plan and profile.

25

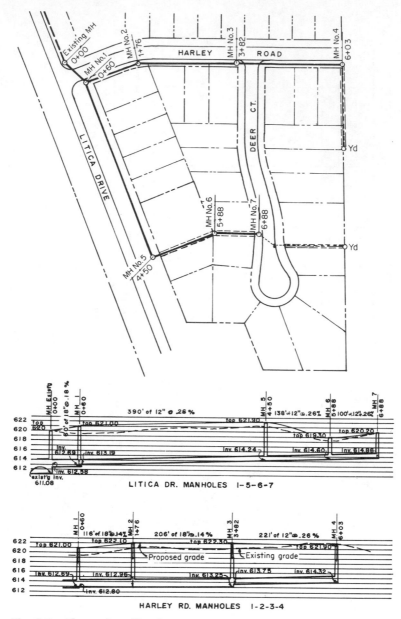

Fig. 3.3 Plan and profile of storm sewer.

100 ft away, is called station 1; the next, station 2; etc. Every 100 ft is a full station, and any fractional distance is called a *plus*. See Figs. 3.2 and 3.3.

Stationing roads consists in stationing along the centerline of the road; giving stations every 100 ft and at gradient change points, centerline intersection points, and at all PCs (points of curvature); and continuing measurements around the arc (not out to the point of intersection) to establish a station at the PT (point of tangency). Chapter 5 discusses the details of road layout and profiling.

Stationing sewers is done by calling the outlet end of the pipe or the centerline of the collector pipe station 0 +00. Proceed up the sewer centerline, giving stations every 100 ft, at all manhole centers and at wye-branch centerline intersections, ending the stationing at the centerline of the last manhole or other terminal appurtenance.

CHAPTER FOUR

Site Grading

A site plan that is not well adapted to the existing topography may result in costly grading and in extra cost in building foundations and utilities and, more than likely, will produce a project that has a forced appearance. Even though designers constantly visualize grades and grading as they develop their plans, the design should not be "frozen" until the grading design is completed.

4.1 GRADING CONSIDERATIONS

The grading scheme is normally developed as a whole, structure elevations being adjusted and readjusted until a balance of all potential site requirements is achieved. The starting point is usually the established grades of the existing boundary streets and walks. Finished grades should attempt to conform as nearly as possible to the grades of existing trees and other permanent site features. Besides visualizing the site grading as they develop their design plans, landscape architects must also visualize the site drainage and project sewers that grading will necessitate.

The preferred drainage plan is one in which no swales are required. However, it is practically impossible to avoid swales completely, especially where there are several closely spaced structures on the site. Any storm wash from adjacent properties onto the site should be diverted at the boundary of the site whenever possible. Where it is necessary to have steep banks on the site, the banks should be given smooth well-rounded sections and the surface water should be diverted back from the top of the slope unless the drainage area is very small. Terraces should be graded to prevent accumulated water from rushing from the higher level down over the bank to the lower level.

In most situations the landscape architect should strive for a reasonable balance of earthwork cut and fill. Included in the earthwork calculations should be basement excavation from buildings; cubic yards of displacement derived from surfacing materials for roads, walks, etc., brought onto the site; and hauled-in backfill sand and gravel, as well as hauled-in topsoil for lawn and planting areas.

4.2 GRADING-STUDY PROCEDURE

To do the grading study, the landscape architect should have:

1. An accurate survey showing property lines, existing utilities, other existing site features, and existing topography
2. Bordering grades, including existing street data
3. Information on the location, size, capacity, and invert elevations of existing drainage facilities
4. High-water and flood data in reference to the site
5. Data on rainfall intensity and frequency for the project area
6. Surface- and subsurface-soil characteristics
7. Information on any storm runoff shedding onto the site from adjacent property
8. Data on any basement, crawl space, etc., that may need drainage

Before proceeding beyond the most preliminary grading studies, the landscape architect should determine:

1. Typical cross sections for proposed roads and parking areas
2. The minimum elevation on site that will allow the use of available storm sewers and/or drainage ditches

The next steps are as follows: On most sites begin the grading study at the fixed controls (i.e., bounding streets, etc.); then grade the roads; next proceed up the approach walks to the building or buildings, and determine the first-floor elevation. At this point check the elevations against the storm drainage outlet to make sure nothing can be impounded to a danger point. Always design the grading so that there is an escape for the storm water before it reaches a depth where it will cause damage.

Basically, storm water may be carried away either over the surface or underground in pipes. Where storm water must be carried across the site for some distance, the best method is by underground pipes when an outlet is available. It is generally preferrable to locate roads and drives in valleys rather than on ridges since storm structures will be too costly if sized for the maximum rainfall and in this location the road itself can act as an emergency drainage channel. Where positive drainageways exist in the valleys on either side of a ridge, the drive or road can be placed on the ridge when the land falls away from the road on both sides.

From time to time, as the grading study proceeds, visually recheck the grading against the topo map to see if the cut and fill appear to balance. Time and experience will help the designer in making this determination.

4.3 GRADING CRITERIA

Every site is a separate grading design problem. Nevertheless, there are certain criteria that serve as guidelines in developing the grading plan.

Sidewalks along streets are generally cross-pitched ¼ in. per ft (2 percent) toward the road. Hence there need not be any particular concern about the longitudinal gradients except in problem situations. Approach walks, on the other hand, are generally not cross-pitched but are drained longitudinally. An ideal gradient for approach walks is 2 percent. If approach walks exceed this gradient, they should be given an ogee profile so that the walk gradient at the step will not exceed 2 percent.

In any region having relatively flat ground with winter snow and ice, do not exceed longitudinal gradients of 7 percent. Steep gradients of this nature are most likely to develop in approach walks to units in long rowhouses. It is better to add extra steps at the building to avoid these steep grades. Steps may also be required at steep banks or slopes. Keep steps together. Never place a single riser alone in a walk. On longer runs where the gradient is excessive, perrons may be used.

Avoid abrupt changes in grade on walks as well as on streets. On streets the profile will incorporate vertical curves at these points. On walks, it is more practical to simulate vertical curves by using short stationing lengths of increasing or decreasing gradients. Avoid wavy profiles.

Longitudinal grades for streets with curb and gutter should not be less than 0.30 percent for concrete pavements and not less than 0.40 percent for bituminous pavements. Gradients can be less for streets not having curb and gutter which are drained by swales and ditches running alongside the road.

When water is collected at a circulation or collector walk, it is better to cross-pitch the walk and use a swale parallel to the walk on the low side. This swale should parallel the walk several feet away and should be so shaped as to be mowable if in grass. If there are more than a few approach walks coming into the collector walk, the use of a swale is seldom satisfactory. In such cases it is better to use the low side of the collector walk as the gutter valley.

Generally, a gradient of 2 to 4 percent is used for ground areas for the first 10 or 20 ft around buildings to ensure runoff away from the building. A grade of 1 percent is a minimum to carry sheet runoff over unpaved areas, and 0.5 percent is a minimum over paved areas. On sandy land use flat grades to minimize erosion. Heavier soils can stand steeper gradients without eroding. The greater the watershed being collected by a swale or ditch, the more susceptible it is to erosion. Swales may start with a gradient of 1 percent, reduced to 0.5 percent, and even to 0.25 percent, as the watershed becomes larger. Drainage ditches may be reduced to a gradient as low as 0.15 percent. For the most part the gradients thus far mentioned are minimums. It is better to use gradients greater than the minimum wherever possible in order to absorb minor inaccuracies in construction. Ditches having gradients of 2 percent or more should be sodded on both slopes and bottom. Ditches having gradients in excess of 5 percent should be constructed with grouted rip-rap. Note the following guidelines for outdoor gradients:

3%   This is a slope of approximately ⅜ in. per ft. It is *very noticeable* in relation to level construction.

2.5%   This is a slope of approximately ⁵⁄₁₆ in. per ft. It is *quite noticeable* in relation to level construction. It is a good *maximum* to strive for in parking-area grading.

2%   This is a slope of approximately ¼ in. per ft. It is *noticeable* in relation to level construction and should be considered a good *maximum* for terrace and patio paving. It is an *ideal* gradient for grass, tanbark, and wood-chip areas.

1.5%   This is a slope of approximately ³⁄₁₆ in. per ft. It is considered a good *minimum* gradient for moderately rough paving.

1%   This is a slope of approximately ⅛ in. per ft. It is considered a good *minimum* for most paving, such as brick, smooth flagging, wood block, etc.

0.5%   This is a slope of approximately ¹⁄₁₆ in. per ft. For all intents and purposes it is flat and should only be used on the smoothest types of paving surfaces.

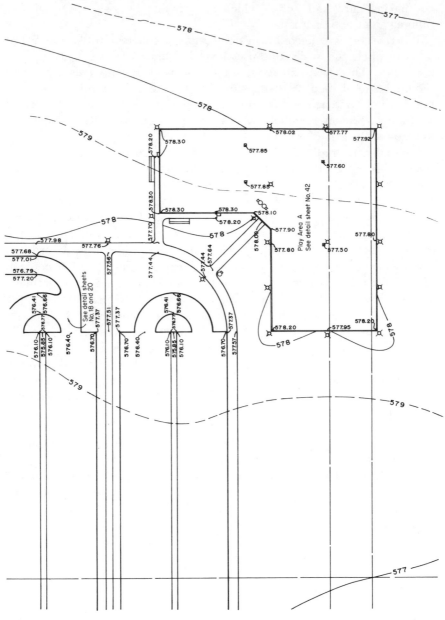

Fig. 4.1 Grading plan.

4.4   SITE-GRADING DRAWINGS

The drawings that portray the site grading include the grading plan, showing the existing and proposed shape of earth and surfaced areas, plus the plan and profile of roads and other profiled pavements.   The amount of information on the plan can become overwhelming unless the method of portrayal is well thought out and systematized.   The following stipulations cover the needs in most situations:

1. Show grades at corners of buildings, step landings, and first-floor elevations.   Indicate the number of risers at all outside steps.

2. Show finished grades at the edges of surfaced areas and at such interior points as necessary to show the shaping of the area.

3. Show the proposed road centerline elevation at 100-ft stations and at all breaks in grade, points of curvature, points of tangency, and points of intersection.

4. Show top-of-curb grades at all connecting walks, curb returns, and all catch-basin locations.

5. Show spot elevations to indicate and control the shape for all warped surfacing.

6. Show spot elevations along swale lines, using arrows to show direction of flow.   Show gradients.

7. Show top elevation of all storm- and sanitary-sewer manholes and other appurtenances.

8. Lawn and earth grades can be shown by proposed contours and by spot elevations where necessary.

9. Existing contours are usually shown by broken lines; finished contours by solid lines over lawn and earth areas.   Do not run finished contours through paved areas.   Depend on profiles, cross sections, and spot elevations to control the grading of paved areas.

CHAPTER FIVE

Road Layout

In the design phase of the site plan, the major features of the development were given their place in the scheme of things. Now it becomes necessary to fix these locations by measurement so they can be field staked, bid-priced, and constructed. Roads and drives are probably among the most difficult of these features to locate and shape.

5.1 HORIZONTAL ALIGNMENT

To begin with, design schemes are often freehand layouts, or if mechanically drawn, they are often laid out with french curves. In either case the construction drawing must convert this to a mathematical equivalent. The french curve has no consistent radius and should be converted to a circular arc, a series of circular arcs of varying radii, or a circular arc having spiral approaches. Most site work involves slow-speed rather than high-speed roads. The spiral curve is essential on high-speed roads, but it is not necessary on low-speed roads, and unless there are good reasons to the contrary, the curve should be reduced to a circular arc. The differences between a spiral and a circular curve are not visible, nor are they sensed at the scale and travel speed of most site developments.

The first step is to overlay the designed centerline alignment with straight lines, omitting any curves. These straight sections of the road are called *tangent sections*. The tangent sections will meet at points of intersection. Circular arcs should then be swung from tangent line to tangent line at all curves. The radius will be selected by trial and error to develop an arc that overlays the design curve as closely as possible. Once this is done, all fixes (controls) must be established and the road centerline mathematically located to meet the requirements of the controls. Where possible the road alignment should be developed as a closed traverse and calculated for closure, as described in Sec. 1.2. Note that the circular curves are omitted from these calculations, all distances and bearings being carried to the points of intersection.

Once the alignment of the tangent sections is correct and satisfactory, the circular curves are inserted as required to fit the alignment. Two characteristics of a curve must be given to identify it. The deflection angle ($\angle DCF$ in Fig. 5.1) is equal to the central (interior) angle ($\angle BAD$). Thus, this is a given characteristic of the curve once the tangent lines of the road alignment have been established. The radius which was selected by trial can be measured by scaling, or the tangent distance from the point of curvature to the point of intersection can be measured and called good. Once these two characteristics have been set, any other relationship for the curve can be mathematically determined. Four characteristics are generally given for each curve in order to simplify layout in the field. These are:

Radius
Tangent
Interior angle
Arc length

If only one of these is known, one other assumption must be made, usually by scaling, before the other parts of the curve can be determined.

In Fig. 5.1 note that:

Tangent $T = BC = CD$
Radius $R = AB = AE = AD$
Interior or central angle I or $\triangle = \angle BAD$
Arc length $A = BED$
Chord $C = BGD$

Point B, entering the curve from the tangent, is called the *point of curvature* (PC).

Point D, leaving the curve to the tangent, is called the *point of tangency* (PT).

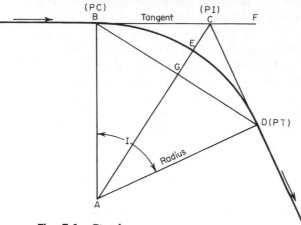

Fig. 5.1   Circular curve.

Point C, at the intersection of the tangents, is called the *point of intersection* (PI).

Note the following relationships:

CBA and CDA are right angles.
$\triangle ABC$ and $\triangle ADC$ are identical right triangles.
BC and CD are always equal.
AB, AE, and AD are radii and therefore equal.
$BG = DG$
$\angle FCD = \angle BAD$
$\angle BAC = \angle DAC = \frac{1}{2}I$
$\angle CBD = \angle CDB = \frac{1}{2}I$
$$\tan \tfrac{1}{2}I = \frac{CD}{AD}$$

(This last relationship is used a great deal in the solution of circular curves.)

The length of the arc BED can be obtained by using Appendix Table A.8, Arc Lengths—Radius Equals 1 Ft. Find the length of arc for the interior angle if the radius is 1 ft and multiply this finding by the length of the radius.

Example 5.1   Find the length of arc of a circular curve whose interior angle is $42°22'15''$ and radius is 640 ft.

1. Turn to the table of Appendix Sec. A.8 and find:

$$
\begin{aligned}
42° &= 0.7330383 \\
22' &= 0.0063995 \\
15'' &= 0.0000727 \\
\hline
\text{Total} &= 0.7395105
\end{aligned}
$$

The arc length for this angle would be 0.7395 ft if the radius of the curve were 1 ft.

2. Since there is a constant relationship between the arc and the radius of a circle, this length of arc for a 1-ft radius can be multiplied by the actual radius to obtain the length of the arc:

$$
\begin{array}{r}
0.7395105 \\
\times 640 \\
\hline
473.286720000
\end{array}
$$

The length of the arc is 473.29 ft.

In some instances it is convenient to know the following:

Long chord $= BGD = c$
Middle ordinate $= EG = m$
External distance $= CE = e$

$$\text{Degree of curve} = \frac{5{,}729.57795}{R} = \frac{5{,}730}{R} = D$$

The *degree of curve* is used by most highway departments to designate the curvature of a circular arc. It is the angular measurement of the interior angle in units of the angle that subtends an arc of 100 ft.

The following are additional equations for the solution of circular curves:

$$T = \text{tangent} = R\left(\tan\frac{I}{2}\right)$$

$$= e\left(\cot\frac{I}{4}\right)$$

$$= \frac{c}{2\cos\dfrac{I}{2}}$$

$$m = \text{middle ordinate} = R - \left(R\cos\frac{I}{2}\right)$$

$$= R\left(\text{vers}\frac{I}{2}\right)$$

$$= e\left(\cos\frac{I}{2}\right)$$

$$I = \text{interior angle} = \frac{180°A}{\pi R}$$

$$= \frac{57.2957795°A}{R}$$

$$= \text{deflection angle}$$

$$A = \text{arc length} = 0.01745329R(I)$$

$$= 100\frac{I}{D}$$

$$= \frac{\pi R I}{180}$$

$$c = \text{chord length} = 2R\left(\sin\frac{I}{2}\right)$$

$$= 2T\left(\cos\frac{I}{2}\right)$$

$$e = \text{external distance} = R\left(\text{exsec}\frac{I}{2}\right)$$

$$= T\left(\tan\frac{I}{4}\right)$$

$$= \frac{R}{\cos I/2} - R$$

$$R = \text{radius} = 57.2957795\frac{A}{I}$$

$$= T\left(\cot\frac{I}{2}\right)$$

$$= \frac{c}{2(\sin I/2)}$$

When compound curves are used, the two curves have a common point on the arc where the curvature changes from one radius to another. This point is called the *point of compound curvature* (PCC). The radii for each of the curves at the PCC must have the same alignment

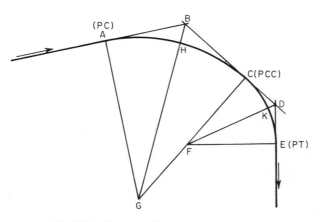

Fig. 5.2 Compound curve.

even though their lengths are not the same (see Fig. 5.2). In this figure *AHCKE* is a compound curve consisting of arc *AHC* of one radius and arc *CKE* of a much shorter radius. The center of the second curve, *CKE*, will lie somewhere on radius line *GC* of the larger curve. If this were not true, the curves would not meet and be tangent at the PCC.

Example 5.2 In this example the bearings of the two tangents are given and the radius of the circular arc is scaled as being 600 ft. (Fig. 5.3.)

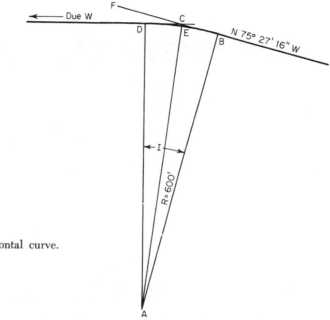

Fig. 5.3 Horizontal curve.

1. Find the interior angle *I*. We know this is equal to the deflection angle.

$$89°59'60''$$
$$(-) \quad 75°27'16''$$
$$\angle FCD = \overline{14°32'44''}$$

$$\angle FCD = \angle DAB$$
$$\text{and } \angle DAB = I \qquad \text{therefore} \qquad I = 14°32'44''$$

2. Calculate the length of the tangents. Both tangents are of equal length. Solve for either one of them. Use the formula

$$\tan\frac{I}{2} = \frac{CD}{AD}$$

CD is the tangent length we are solving for. AD is the radius. We know it is 600 ft long. Then

$$CD = 600\left(\tan\frac{I}{2}\right)$$
$$= 600\ (\tan 7°16'22'')$$

From natural function tables tan 7°16'22" is 0.12762; so

$$CD = 600(0.12762) = 76.57 \text{ ft}$$

3. Find the length of arc. This is done by using the table of Appendix Sec. A.8, Arc Lengths—Radius Equals 1 Ft.

$$14° = 0.2443461$$
$$32' = 0.0093084$$
$$44'' = \underline{0.0002133}$$
Total $= 0.2538678$ (arc length for 1-ft radius)
0.2538678×600-ft radius $= 152.32$ ft
Arc length $= 152.32$ ft

4. Then the data for the curve are

$$\triangle = 14°32'44''$$
$$R = 600.00 \text{ ft}$$
$$T = 76.57 \text{ ft}$$
$$A = 152.32 \text{ ft}$$

In some situations it becomes necessary to use a reverse-curve type of alignment. This should be avoided because the driver of a car has no time to reverse his steering wheel from one direction to the other in an abrupt curve reversal. There should be some room between the two curves. The length of the tangent between the two curves should be greater on higher-speed than on lower-speed roads, and in any case should be at least equal to the length of a car or bus. The shorter the radii of the two curves, the more recovery time necessary between curves, and hence a longer tangent length is needed between curves with shorter radii.

In some cases, where traffic is slow-speed and the curve radii long, where a reverse curve can make a bike path more interesting, or where a pedestrian path is being laid out precisely, it may be convenient to use the following reverse-curve formulas.

1. Connecting parallel tangents:

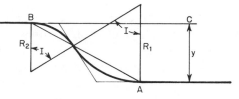

Fig. 5.4 Reverse curve with parallel tangents.

$$\angle ABC = \frac{I}{2}$$

$$\text{vers } I - \frac{y}{R_1 + R_2}$$

$$AB = \sqrt{2y(R_1 + R_2)}$$

If both curves have the same radii, then

$$\text{vers } I = \frac{y}{2R} \quad \text{and} \quad AB = 2\sqrt{yR}$$

2. Connecting nonparallel tangents:
GIVEN: T_1, I_1, R_1, R_2.
FIND: I_2, I_3, and T_2.

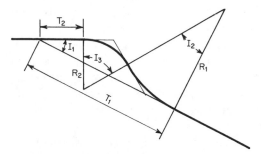

Fig. 5.5 Reverse curve with nonparallel tangents.

$$I_2 = I_3 - I_1$$

$$\text{vers } I_3 = \frac{(R_1 \text{ vers } I_1) + (T_1 \sin I_1)}{R_1 + R_2}$$

$$T_2 = (T_1 \cos I_1) + (R_1 \sin I_1) - (R_1 + R_2) \sin I_3$$

GIVEN: T_2, I_1, R_1, R_2.
FIND: I_2, I_3, and T_1.

$$I_3 = I_2 + I_1$$

$$\text{vers } I_2 = \frac{(R_2 \text{ vers } I_1) + (T_2 \sin I_1)}{R_1 + R_2}$$

$$T_1 = (T_2 \cos I_1) + (R_2 \sin I_1) + (R_1 + R_2) \sin I_2$$

5.2 VERTICAL ALIGNMENT

Once the horizontal alignment is established, the existing topography along the centerline of the road should be plotted as a profile. Usually, the vertical scale of the profile is exaggerated at a 10 to 1 ratio; e.g., if the horizontal scale is 50 ft to the inch, the vertical scale will be 5 ft to the inch, and if 40, the vertical scale will be 4, etc. The centerline of the road is plotted on the existing grade in straight lines at reasonable gradients. If reasonable gradients can be maintained without excessive cut and fill, the horizontal alignment can be accepted as satisfactory and vertical alignment can be refined. The centerline gradient will intersect at points where gradients change. These intersections are referred to as *points of vertical intersection* (PVI), and vertical curves should be inserted at these points when:

1. The difference between the tangent gradients exceeds 0.5 percent on major streets and higher-speed roads.

2. The difference between the tangent gradients exceeds 1.0 percent on less important and slower-speed roads.

The purpose of the vertical curve is to make a safer, smoother ride. The amount of the gradient change, the site distance, and the relative speed of the traffic determine the length of the vertical curve. However, in site work, room is often limited, and the length of the vertical curve is most often determined by the amount of space available.

In Fig. 5.6 *AV* and *BV* are tangent lines having gradients of -2 and $+1$ percent, respectively. The negative percentage indicates a downhill gradient, and the positive percentage indicates an uphill gradient. The PVI is *V*, and the change in gradients is 3 percent. A 200-ft vertical curve is to be inserted at this PVI. The 200-ft length is a purely arbitrary determination.

Figure 5.7 is a plan and profile of a road showing three vertical curves.

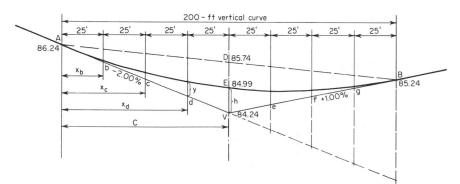

Fig. 5.6 Vertical curve.

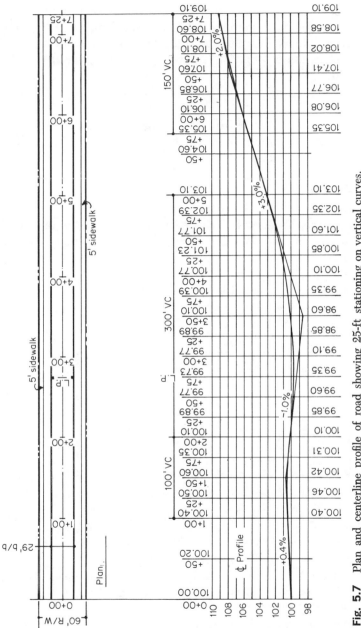

Fig. 5.7 Plan and centerline profile of road showing 25-ft stationing on vertical curves.

43

The following rules hold true for all vertical curves (see FIG. 5.6):

1. The centerline of the vertical curve is established through the vertex V, and points A (the beginning of the vertical curve) and B (the ending of the vertical curve) are equidistant from the PVI (vertex V).

2. The elevation of point D is always halfway between the elevation of A and B.

3. The elevation of point E is always halfway between the elevations of points D and V.

4. The vertical offset y from the tangent line for any point on a parabolic curve is proportional to the square of its distance from the point of tangency. Hence

$$\frac{y}{h} = \frac{x^2}{C^2}$$

where x is the horizontal distance from the point of tangency A to the desired point, and C is the horizontal distance from A to the PVI (one-half the length of the vertical curve).

5. The vertical offsets from the tangent line for the second half of the curve are identical with the first half but in reverse order.

Station	% grade	Distance from PVC or PVT	Tangent elev.	Offsets from tan		V C elev.
				+	−	

Fig.   5.8 Tabular   form   for   setting   up   vertical-curve computations.

Figure 5.8 shows a convenient tabular form for setting up vertical curve computations.

Example 5.3   In Fig. 5.6 the gradients of the two tangents are known, the elevation 84.24 of the PVI is known, and the length of the vertical curve has been selected as 200 ft.

1. Find the elevation at points A and B.

$$\text{Elev. at } A = 84.24 + (100 \times 0.02)$$
$$= 84.24 + 2.00 = 86.24$$
$$\text{Elev. at } B = 84.24 + (100 \times 0.01)$$
$$= 84.24 + 1.00 = 85.24$$

2. Find h.

The elevation of point D is halfway between the elevation of points A and B:

$$\text{Elev. of point } D = \frac{86.24 + 85.24}{2} = 85.74$$

and the elevation of point E is halfway between the elevations of point D and point V (the PVI):

$$\text{Elev. of point } E = \frac{85.74 + 84.24}{2} = 84.99$$

Then

$$h = 84.99 - 84.24 = 0.75 \text{ ft}$$

3. Determine the tangent elevations at:

$$b = 86.24 - (25 \text{ ft at 2 percent}) = 86.24 - 0.50 = 85.74$$
$$c = 86.24 - (50 \text{ ft at 2 percent}) = 86.24 - 1.00 = 85.24$$
$$d = 86.24 - (75 \text{ ft at 2 percent}) = 86.24 - 1.50 = 84.74$$
$$v = 86.24 - (100 \text{ ft at 2 percent}) = 84.24 = 84.24 \text{ (CHECK)}$$
$$e = 84.24 + (25 \text{ ft at 1 percent}) = 84.24 + 0.25 = 84.49$$
$$f = 84.24 + (50 \text{ ft at 1 percent}) = 84.24 + 0.50 = 84.74$$
$$g = 84.24 + (75 \text{ ft at 1 percent}) = 84.24 + 0.75 = 84.99$$
$$B = 84.24 + (100 \text{ ft at 1 percent}) = 85.24 = 85.24 \text{ (CHECK)}$$

4. Find the offsets from the tangent line.

$$\frac{y}{h} = \frac{x^2}{C'^2}$$

$$\frac{y_b}{0.75} = \frac{25 \times 25}{100 \times 100}; \qquad \frac{y_b}{0.75} = \frac{1 \times 1}{4 \times 4}; \qquad 16y_b = 0.75;$$

$$y_b = 0.047 \qquad \text{(call it 0.05 ft)}$$

$$\frac{y_c}{0.75} = \frac{50 \times 50}{100 \times 100}; \qquad \frac{y_c}{0.75} = \frac{1 \times 1}{2 \times 2}; \qquad 4y_c = 0.75;$$

$$y_c = 0.19 \text{ ft}$$

$$\frac{y_d}{0.75} = \frac{75 \times 75}{100 \times 100}; \qquad \frac{y_d}{0.75} = \frac{3 \times 3}{4 \times 4}; \qquad 16y_d = 6.75;$$

$$y_d = 0.42 \text{ ft}$$

5. In a summit curve the curve is below the tangent lines and the offsets must be subtracted from the tangent elevation to obtain the arc elevation.

In a sag curve the curve is above the tangent lines and the offset is added to the tangent elevation to obtain the arc elevation.

Since this is a sag curve, add offsets to tangent elevations:

Elev. of arc at A = 86.24 + 0.00 = 86.24
Elev. of arc at b = 85.74 + 0.05 = 85.79

—(from step 4)
—(from step 3)

Elev. of arc at c = 85.24 + 0.19 = 85.43
Elev. of arc at d = 84.74 + 0.42 = 85.16
Elev. of arc at V = 84.24 + 0.75 = 84.99
(this is a check on step 2)

The rest of the curve can be figured in the same manner by extending the entering tangent to the end of the curve and figuring the offsets using the distance from BVC in each case. However, note that the offsets for the second half of the curve are identical with the offsets for the first half but in reverse order, thus:

Elev. of arc at e = 84.49 + 0.42 = 84.91
Elev. of arc at f = 84.74 + 0.19 = 84.93
Elev. of arc at g = 84.99 + 0.05 = 85.04
Elev. of arc at B = 85.24 + 0.00 = 85.24

Solving vertical curves on a slide rule:

1. On the A scale, mark the algebraic difference of tangent gradients.
2. Set the B scale with 2 times the length of the vertical curve opposite the mark on the A scale.
3. On the C scale, select the distance from BVC or EVC and read the vertical offset from the tangent line on the A scale.

5.3 FINDING THE HIGH OR LOW POINT OF A VERTICAL CURVE

The high point of a summit curve or the low point of a sag curve would occur at the PVI station only if both tangents were opposed at the same gradient. The location of a high point in a summit curve is of importance in figuring sight distances, and the low point of a sag curve is of importance in locating catch basins.

Landscape architects usually work with low-speed roads and normally any sight distance problems are corrected in the design stage but they must be able to locate the drainage basins or runoff swales at the low point of a sag curve.

If the horizontal distance from *BVC* to the low (high) point of the vertical curve is called l_1, then:

$$l_1 = \frac{lg_1}{g_1 - g_2}$$

where l = total length of vertical curve
$\quad g_1$ = gradient of tangent entering curve
$\quad g_2$ = gradient of tangent leaving curve

Note that the low (high) point is in that half of the vertical curve opposite the steepest tangent.

When l_1 has been found, the elevation of the low point (LP) and high point (HP) of the curve can be determined thus:

$$\text{Elev. of LP} = \text{elev. of } BVC - l_1\left(\frac{g_1}{2}\right)$$

or

$$\text{Elev. of HP} = \text{elev. of } BVC + l_1\left(\frac{g_1}{2}\right)$$

This can be checked by using *EVC*, thus:

$$\text{Elev. of LP} = \text{elev. of } EVC - l_2\left(\frac{g_2}{2}\right)$$

or

$$\text{Elev. of HP} = \text{elev. of } EVC + l_2\left(\frac{g_2}{2}\right)$$

where l_2 is the distance from *EVC* to the low (high) point.

Another check can be made using the formula

$$\frac{y}{h} = \frac{x^2}{C^2}$$

using l_1 or l_2 for x and adding or subtracting the offset thus found to or from the elevation of the tangent at the low-(high-)point station.

Example 5.4   Find the low point in the vertical curve of Fig. 5.6.
1. Find the distance to the low point:

$$l_1 = \frac{lg_1}{g_1 - g_2}$$

$$= \frac{200(-2)}{(-2) - (+1)} = \frac{-400}{-3}, \text{ or } 133.33 \text{ ft}$$

Then $l_1 = 133.33$ ft   and $l_2 = 66.67$ ft

2. Find the elevation of the low point.

$$\text{LP elev.} = BVC \text{ elev.} - \left(\frac{g_1}{2}\right) l_1$$

$$= 86.24 - \left(\frac{0.02}{2}\right) \times 133.33$$

$$= 86.24 - 1.33 = 84.91$$

CHECK:

$$\text{LP elev.} = EVC \text{ elev.} - \left(\frac{g_2}{2}\right) l_2$$

$$= 85.24 - \left(\frac{0.01}{2}\right) \times 66.67$$

$$= 85.24 - 0.33 = 84.91$$

5.4   SOLVING PARABOLIC CROSS SECTIONS

Transverse slopes on roads are usually made parabolic in shape on straight-aways and warped into a banked or superelevated cross section at curves. In the computation of a parabolic cross section the tangent to the curve at the centerline is used instead of the tangent at the beginning or end of the curve (Fig. 5.9).

The vertical offset from the tangent is still proportional to the square of the distance from the point of tangency, and so the same formula is used:

$$\frac{y}{h} = \frac{x^2}{C^2}$$

Generally, the overall crown for typical site-development roads with curb and gutter will approximate a 2 percent differential from the center-line crown grade to the gutter grade at the inside of the curb.

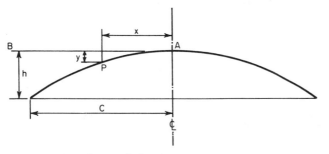

Fig. 5.9   Parabolic cross-section.

NOTE: In solving parabolic sections, express all dimensions in the same unit, i.e., feet and decimals of a foot. *Do not confuse feet and inches.*

5.5 PARKING AREAS

Figures 5.10 to 5.13 are layouts for typical parking areas. Dead-ended parking bays are satisfactory for long-time and all-day parkers but are not very suitable for use by short-time parkers. In such bays the parking must be at 90° and there must be backaround space provided for the two end parking stalls. It is poor economy to crowd cars into narrower parking stalls (that is, 8 ft 6 in. is a *minimum*) or to reduce the width of the travel lanes to anything less than shown on these layouts. It is also inadvisable to establish parking-stall widths that are too wide (i.e., over 10 ft) since experience shows that when drivers have too much room they become careless and soon do not follow the stall lines, and parking becomes very haphazard.

The grading of the parking lot will be largely determined by the topography and the type of surfacing. Most parking lots will have hard surfacing of either concrete or asphalt. The gradient on which the car is parked should ideally have a slope of 2 to $2\frac{1}{2}$ percent, shedding surface water either toward the bumper curb or toward the driveway. There is the advantage in tilting the parking bay forward toward the bumper curb that a car parked inadvertently out of gear without the brakes set will not gravitate out into the travelway where it may cause an accident or otherwise impede the flow of parking-lot traffic. There is a disadvantage in areas of snow and ice since it may be difficult to back upgrade from a dead start under slippery conditions. In a grading arrangement where the drainage is toward the bumper curb, more footage of drain pipe is generally required than when the grading is toward the center, using an inverted crown on the travelway.

When a large, controlled, field-type parking area is being developed, the parking plan and stall arrangement should be first worked out to ensure efficient use of the area. Once this design is determined, the grading should be planned. If asphalt surfacing is being used, the minimum gradient should be $1\frac{1}{2}$ percent, with $2\frac{1}{2}$ percent being considered more or less ideal. If concrete surfacing is used, the minimum gradient can be somewhat less, in the range of 1 to 2 percent. In either case, plan the grading so that the pavement can be laid by machine.

Since only a fixed cross-section shape can be placed by the paving machine in one pass, the grading should be thought out in straight lines, the paver pattern paralleling the long dimension of the parking area. Cross-slopes will be at right angles to this.

Where it is impossible or impractical to machine-pave (as in odd-

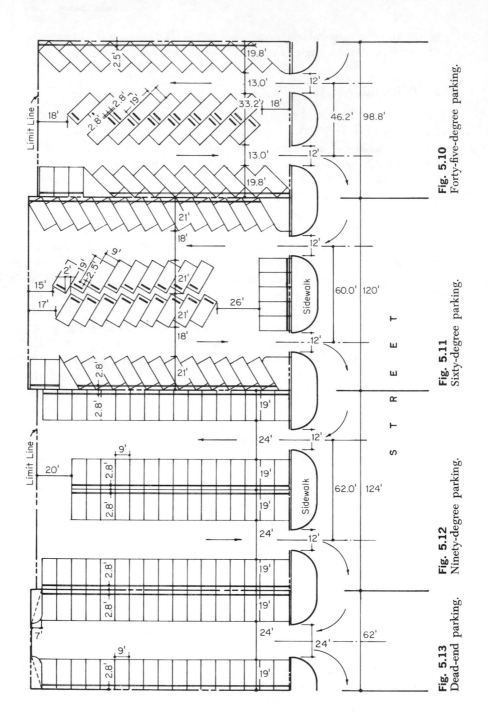

Fig. 5.10 Forty-five-degree parking.

Fig. 5.11 Sixty-degree parking.

Fig. 5.12 Ninety-degree parking.

Fig. 5.13 Dead-end parking.

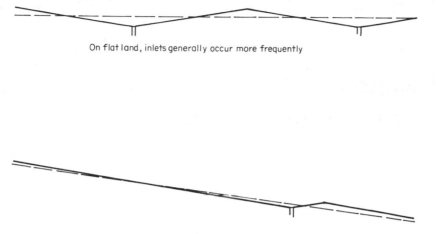

On flat land, inlets generally occur more frequently

On sloping land, inlets can generally be farther apart

Fig. 5.14 Sections showing ponding depths at drain inlets. Even though in the one case fewer inlets will work, the capacity of the grates and pipe must be sized to carry the full amount of runoff in either case.

shaped corners), the paving will have to be done by hand.   Since hand-placed paving cannot possibly be laid as true to grade as machine-laid paving, the minimum gradients in these areas should be increased to 2 to 2½ percent for concrete and 2½ to 3 percent for asphalt.

In flat land there is usually no way to shed surface runoff from large parking areas without using drain inlets and underground storm sewers. The usual grading plan conceives two rows of parking plus the travelway as a unit width.   The length of this unit width of drainage area is determined by the depth of the ponding basin developed.   The limitation of surface sag to a drain inlet is set by appearance (it shall not be aesthetically displeasing) and by the ponding depth created.   The ponding depth should never become dangerously deep if an inlet were to be accidently blocked.   For most situations this works out to provide inlets at spacings of 200 to 400 ft apart, or between 2 and 8 inlets per acre, depending on the slope of the terrain, the shape of the section, and the storm intensity (frequency of recurrence) for which the drainage system is being designed.

CHAPTER SIX

Designing Dams and Retaining Walls

Dams and retaining walls serve very similar functions. In each case the intent is to retain material at a higher level on one side of the wall than on the other. The design process is basically the same for both.

6.1 GENERAL

Certain basic rules of physics apply to the forces acting on and within both retaining walls and dams:

1. The *moment arm* of a force is the perpendicular distance from the line of action of the force to the point being acted on (i.e., its lever arm).

2. The resultant of a system of two or more forces is a force having the same effect as the several forces acting simultaneously.

3. The line of action of any system of two nonparallel forces must have a point in common, and the resultant of the two forces will pass through this common point.

4. The solution for the magnitude and the direction of the resultant can be computed mathematically, but in most cases the graphic solution is sufficiently accurate and is more easily and quickly accomplished:

   A. Any two nonparallel forces can be drawn with their lines of action intersecting, each lying in its respective direction of action. From the point of intersection, each of the respective forces can be scaled off along these lines of action at so many pounds per unit of length.

   B. A parallelogram can then be constructed with the two forces as adjacent sides. The diagonal of the parallelogram is the resultant of the two forces. Its magnitude can then be determined by scaling. The direction of the resultant line of action is graphically shown.

Once the magnitude and direction of the resultant are determined (Fig. 6.1a), another parallelogram of forces can be constructed having a rectangular shape from which can be determined the equivalent horizontal and vertical forces that would create the same resultant force (Fig. 6.1b).

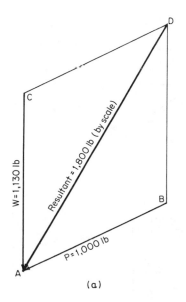

(a)

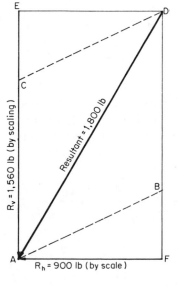

(b)

Fig. 6.1 (a) Solving for resultant by use of parallelogram of forces; (b) solving for horizontal and vertical components of resultant.

For the sake of clarity these forces are referred to as the *horizontal component* of the resultant, R_h, and the *vertical component* of the resultant, R_v.

The center of gravity of a geometrical figure is called the *centroid* of that figure. The centroid of a rectangle is located in the geometric center of the rectangle, whereas the centroid of a right triangle is located one-third of the length of the sides from the heel of the triangle in both directions.

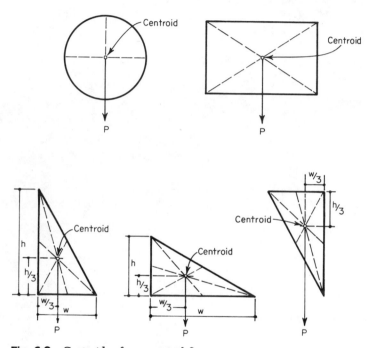

Fig. 6.2 Centroids of geometrical figures.

Dams and retaining walls are designed as either *gravity* walls or *cantilevered* walls. Gravity walls depend on their weight for their stability, whereas cantilevered walls depend on their geometry for their stability.

Gravity walls generally have a narrow top and a wide base. In most designs the wall face slopes slightly and the back of the wall is either sloped or stepped. As a general guide:

1. Width of base
   0.35 to 0.40 the height of the wall on gravel soil
   0.58 to 0.60 the height of the wall on wet sand
   0.75 the height of the wall on water-bearing soil
2. The width of the top of gravity walls
   For walls under 6 ft—generally 12 in. wide
   For walls 6 to 10 ft high—generally 18 in. wide
   For walls over 10 ft high—generally 24 in. wide

Cantilevered walls are, essentially, composed of a thin vertical slab of reinforced concrete called the *stem* and a wide horizontal slab of reinforced concrete called the *base*. The stem and the base are securely tied together with reinforcing bars. In this type of construction the weight of the fill behind the wall is utilized to oppose its own overturning pressure, thereby greatly reducing the amount of concrete needed in the wall.

In some instances a cantilevered wall will be reinforced by support walls built into the structure at spaced intervals on the back of the wall. This has the effect of reducing both the amount of reinforcing steel needed in the structure and the thickness of the stem. This is called a *counterfort* wall, but current cost of labor for the considerable forming necessary for this type of construction has practically eliminated the use of this type of wall.

The design of a cantilevered wall may be started by using the following rules of thumb:

1. Width of base
   0.45 of height for horizontal loading
   0.60 of height for surcharged loading
   0.65 of height for horizontal with road to support
2. Location of stem
   One-third point from toe usually produces the most economical structure, but other features and obstructions often dictate location, i.e., property limits, foundations, other structures, etc.
3. Stem thickness
   12 in. customarily, 8 in. minimum

All walls higher than 4 ft should be sized and shaped by mathematical design. Generally, walls under 10 ft may be either gravity or cantilevered. Above 10 ft, gravity walls generally become uneconomical, and the walls should be designed as cantilevered walls.

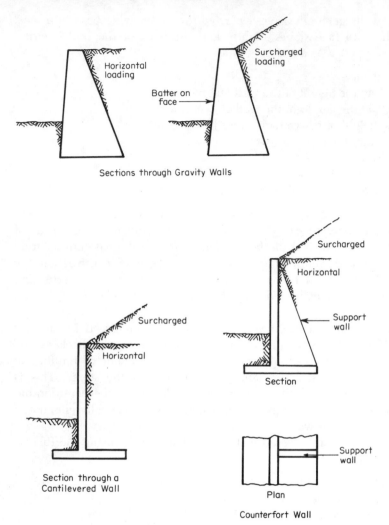

Fig. 6.3   Various kinds of retaining walls.

6.2   PROCEDURE FOR THE DESIGN OF DAMS

A dam or retaining wall may fail by:

1. Overturning
2. Settlement at the toe (crushing)
3. Sliding horizontally on its base

Any design must be checked to ensure against failure in any of these three ways.

Knowing only the purpose and the site criteria, the procedure is to select a wall cross section meeting these requirements and known from past experience to be suitable. The initial wall cross section can be designed either by using the ratios and proportions given in Sec. 6.1 or by typical standard wall sections.[1]

The selected wall should first be given a check for general stability. It has been found that a wall is generally stable if the line of action of the resultant cuts through the middle third of the base. This test is always made before proceeding with any further investigation. If the line of action of the resultant does not cut through the middle third of the base, the wall will fail in one or more of the three ways mentioned above, and a new selection should be made, or the selected section should be adjusted so as to cause the line of action of the resultant to cut through the middle third of the base.

Dam design will be considered first because it may be somewhat easier to comprehend, since the pressure of liquid is the same in all directions for any given depth and the pressure is always perpendicular to the sides (wall) of the retaining vessel (dam).

The procedure for making the test for general stability is to construct graphically a force parallelogram as mentioned in Sec. 6.1 under basic rule 4. Figure 6.4b shows this parallelogram of forces for the selected wall section (Fig. 6.4a).

Example 6.1 In Fig. 6.4a the retained water is 10 ft deep. Obviously, there is zero pressure at the top surface and maximum pressure at the base. *In investigating a design section, use a 1-ft length of the wall.* Since 1 cu ft of water weighs 62.5 lb, the pressure against this 1-ft section will be (results in pounds per square foot, abbreviated psf):

At the top: 1 ft $\times$ 0 ft $\times$ 62.5 lb = 0 psf

At the bottom: 1 ft $\times$ 10 ft $\times$ 62.5 lb = 625 psf

and the average pressure is

$$\frac{0 + 625}{2} \qquad \text{or} \qquad 312.5 \text{ psf}$$

and the total pressure is the area in square feet of water against this 1-ft strip of wall times the average pressure of water in pounds per square foot, or

10 sq ft $\times$ 312.5 lb = 3,125 lb

---

[1] Standard wall sections may be found in E. E. Seelye, "Data Book for Civil Engineers Design," 3d ed., John Wiley & Sons, Inc., New York, 1960; Charles G. Ramsey and Harold R. Sleeper, "Architectural Graphic Standards," 6th ed., John Wiley & Sons, Inc., New York, 1970; or Technical Committee, "Building Design Handbook," Wire Reinforcement Institute, Inc., Washington, D.C., 1963 reprint.

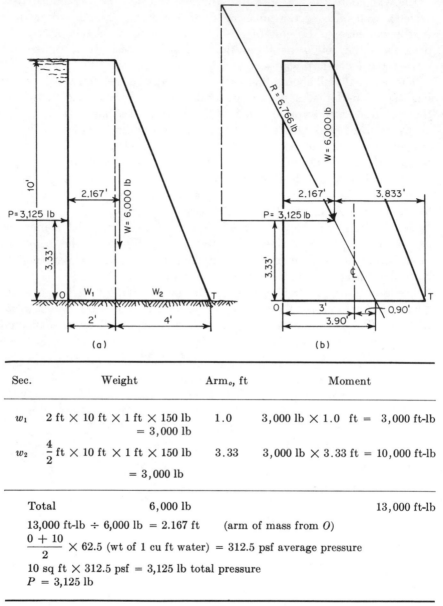

(a)   (b)

Sec.	Weight	Arm$_o$, ft	Moment
w_1	2 ft × 10 ft × 1 ft × 150 lb = 3,000 lb	1.0	3,000 lb × 1.0 ft = 3,000 ft-lb
w_2	$\frac{4}{2}$ ft × 10 ft × 1 ft × 150 lb = 3,000 lb	3.33	3,000 lb × 3.33 ft = 10,000 ft-lb

Total   6,000 lb   13,000 ft-lb

13,000 ft-lb ÷ 6,000 lb = 2.167 ft   (arm of mass from O)

$\dfrac{0 + 10}{2}$ × 62.5 (wt of 1 cu ft water) = 312.5 psf average pressure

10 sq ft × 312.5 psf = 3,125 lb total pressure

P = 3,125 lb

(c)

Fig. 6.4 (a) Section of a dam; (b) dam section showing parallelogram of forces; (c) tabular calculation for weight, moments, and moment arms.

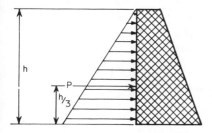

Fig. 6.5 Illustration of $h/3$ principle.

Since the water pressure increases consistently from zero pounds at the top to a maximum at the bottom, the pressures can be considered as a triangle of forces acting on the wall (see Fig. 6.5).

The total of this triangle of forces can be resolved as being equivalent to a single force acting through the centroid (center of gravity) of the triangle and therefore through a point one-third of the height above the base, or 3.33 ft ($10 \div 3 = 3.33$ ft) above the base in this example. Then a horizontal force of 3,125 lb is acting against the wall at a point 3.33 ft above the base. The other force is the downward force caused by the weight of the wall itself. Again, a 1-ft strip of the wall is used in calculating this. The cross section of the wall is divided into geometric figures whose volume can be readily solved.

> **Example 6.2** In Fig. 6.4a we have section w_1, a rectangle, and w_2, a triangle. The weight of reinforced concrete is considered to be 150 pcf (pounds per cubic foot). The rectangular section is 1 ft long × 2 ft wide × 10 ft high, or 20 cu ft. Then
>
> 20 cu ft at 150 pcf = 3,000 lb
>
> The triangular section w_2 is 1 ft long × 4 ft base × 10 ft high, and its volume is 1 ft × ½ ft × 10 ft = 20 cu ft. Then
>
> 20 cu ft at 150 pcf = 3,000 lb
>
> The sum of the two components $w_1 + w_2$ makes up the total weight of the 1-ft strip of wall, 6,000 lb.

This force (the total weight of the mass) is equivalent to a single force acting through the centroid (center of gravity) of the mass. Since the moment of the whole is equal to the moment of its parts, this line of force through the centroid can be located by finding the moments of each of the subsections, adding them together, and dividing by the total weight of the mass. The moment arms may be taken from either the heel, point O, or the toe, point T.

> **Example 6.3** In Fig. 6.4b, using point O as a point of rotation, the downward force of 3,000 lb for the rectangle is acting on an arm of

1 ft, and the downward force of 3,000 lb for the triangle is acting on an arm of 3.33 ft ($2 + \frac{1}{3} = 3.33$ ft). These data are recorded in tabular form as shown in Fig. 6.4c. Referring to this tabular form, the sum of the moments for all the parts of the mass is a total of 13,000 ft-lb. Since the total weight of the mass is 6,000 lb, the moment arm of the mass is 13,000 ft-lb divided by 6,000 lb, or 2.167 ft from point O.

We now know the force of the retained material acting on the wall and where it is acting. We also know the amount and location of the downward force of the wall. Knowing these facts, we can construct the parallelogram of forces as in Fig. 6.4b and draw in the diagonal resultant. This diagonal can be scaled to determine its magnitude. The direction of this force is shown graphically. By extending this line of force, we can find where its line of action cuts the base.

> **Example 6.4** The dam in Fig. 6.4b has been drawn to some scale. Using this same scale, measure in the location of the horizontal and vertical forces that have just been determined. From the point of intersection of these two lines, scale the force acting in each direction. Use a scale of so many pounds per inch, for example, 1 in. = 2,000 lb. Select as large a scale as is convenient. It has no relationship to the scale that was used for the drawing of the dam.
>
> Complete the parallelogram and draw in the diagonal. The diagonal represents the resultant of the horizontal and vertical forces acting simultaneously. The magnitude of the resultant can be found by scaling the length of the diagonal, using the scale for measuring the forces. It is scaled as 6,750 lb (6,766 lb, actually), and its line of action cuts through the base at a point 3.90 ft from O (by scaling, using the scale of the drawing). The middle third of the base occurs between 2 and 4 ft from point O, and therefore the resultant cuts through the base within the middle third, and the dam can be considered generally stable.

Having found the structure to be generally stable, the investigation must be continued to make certain the structure will not fail by:

Overturning
Crushing
Sliding

Overturning

If the dam were to be overturned, it would revolve about its toe (point T). The force tending to overturn the structure is P, the horizontal component of the resultant (also called R_h), multiplied by its moment arm from T. The force resisting this tendency to overturn is the weight of the structure, W, the vertical component of the resultant (also called R_v), multiplied by its moment arm from T. A safety factor of 2 is desirable.

Example 6.5   In Fig. 6.4b the force tending to overturn the wall is P, 3,125 lb, multiplied by its moment arm from T, 3.33 ft:

$$3,125 \text{ lb} \times 3.33 \text{ ft} = 10,416 \text{ ft-lb}$$

The force resisting the overturning is the weight of the structure, 6,000 lb, multiplied by its arm from T, 3.83 ft:

$$6,000 \text{ lb} \times 3.83 \text{ ft} = 23,000 \text{ ft-lb}$$

A safety factor of 2 is required:

$$23,000 \div 10,416 = 2.2 \quad \text{(therefore acceptable)}$$

Crushing

The tendency to overturn may cause excessive pressures on the foundation bed at the toe of the structure. The soil-bearing capacity must be determined. For important work, test borings and load tests should be made at the site. An experienced testing laboratory should be employed for this work. For lesser work, Table 6.1 may be used.

The toe pressure of the structure in pounds per square foot must be less than the bearing capacity of the soil expressed in pounds per

TABLE 6.1 Approximate Bearing Capacities of Various Soils and Rock

	Tons per sq ft	Lb per sq ft
Alluvial soil	½	1,000
Soft clay	1	2,000
Firm clay	2	4,000
Wet sand	2	4,000
Sand and clay mixed	2	4,000
Fine dry sand	3	6,000
Hard clay	4	8,000
Coarse dry sand	4	8,000
Gravel	6	12,000
Gravel and sand well cemented	8	16,000
Hard pan or hard shale	10	20,000
Medium rock	20	40,000
Hard rock	80	160,000

square foot. The pressure at the toe can be determined by using the following formula:

$$f = \frac{R_v}{A}\left(1 + \frac{6e}{d}\right)$$

where f = pressure, psf at toe

R_v = downward force, lb (weight or vertical component of resultant)

A = area of base

e = eccentricity (distance from centerline of base to point where line of force of resultant cuts base)

d = full width of base from heel to toe

Example 6.6 The investigation of the toe pressure for the structure shown in Fig. 6.4b is as follows:

$$f = \frac{R_v}{A}\left(1 + \frac{6e}{d}\right)$$
$$= \frac{6,000}{6}\left(1 + \frac{6 \times 0.90}{6}\right)$$
$$= 1,000\ (1 + 0.90)$$
$$= 1,900\ \text{psf}$$

With reference to Table 6.1, a structure of this design could not be used on alluvial soil since that soil has a bearing capacity of only 1,000 psf. It could be used on soft clay (bearing capacity 2,000 psf), but this would be inadvisable because 1,900 lb is extremely close to the 2,000 lb bearing capacity of soft clay. The structure would be safe on the other soils with higher bearing capacities.

Horizontal Sliding

The force tending to cause horizontal sliding is the horizontal component of the resultant, R_h. The force resisting sliding is the weight of the structure or the vertical component of the resultant, R_v, multiplied by the coefficient of friction between the concrete and the type of soil on which the structure is resting. The following table gives average coefficients of friction:

TABLE 6.2   Average Coefficients of Friction for Concrete on Various Foundation Beds

Foundation bed	Coefficient of friction
Gravel	0.6
Dry clay	0.5
Sand	0.4
Wet clay	0.3

A safety factor of at least 1.5 must be attained to be acceptable. The factor of safety against sliding is the resisting force divided by the force that tends to cause sliding.

Example 6.7 In Fig. 6.4b the force that tends to cause sliding is P, 3,125 lb. Assume the foundation bed is gravel. Then

W × coefficient = 6,000 × 0.6 = 3,600 lb
3,600 ÷ 3,125 = 1.15

This is less than the 1.5 safety factor and is not acceptable. See the following paragraph.

Other slide-resisting factors occur where the dam must be constructed deep enough into the ground to prevent underwashing of the footing and, in the case of a retaining wall, where the footing must be deep enough to be below the frost line. A rough bottom in the footing excavation will also increase the friction coefficient. A transverse key formed in the foundation bed or a sloped bottom requiring the structure to slide uphill is often used to counteract the sliding force. See Figs. 6.6 and 6.7.

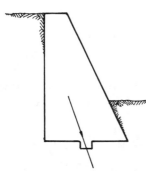

Fig. 6.6 Section showing key to prevent sliding.

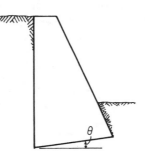

Fig. 6.7 Section showing sloping bottom to prevent sliding.

6.3 PROCEDURE FOR RETAINING-WALL DESIGN

Retaining walls are designed in the same manner as dams, except that earth pressure differs from water pressure in that earth piles up whereas water levels out. Pressure in water at any given depth is the same in all directions, and its force is always perpendicular to any retaining structure. Earth, on the other hand, is composed of particles which develop friction between each other, so that various kinds of soils have various angles of repose.

Angles of repose vary with each type of soil, but for purposes of simplifying our problem, we will consider that, for all conditions, retained soil will have a slope of 1½ to 1, which is an angle of approximately 33°40′.

Although there are many formulas for designing walls for different loading situations and soil types, landscape architects will be able to satisfy most of their wall-designing requirements by using one or the other of the two following situations:

1. For walls retaining soil level with the top of the wall, the direction of P (pressure of the earth against the wall) is parallel with the surface and hence is horizontal, as shown in Figs. 6.8 and 6.10. P acts at a point $h/3$ above the base of the structure, and its magnitude is only 0.286 of its weight because of the friction between the particles of soil. Hence, use the formula

$$P = 0.286 \frac{wh^2}{2}$$

where P = magnitude of earth pressure, lb
$\quad\;\; w$ = weight of retained material, pcf
$\quad\;\; h$ = height of retained material, ft (measured from bottom of wall footing)

2. For walls retaining a surcharge of soil, as in Fig. 6.9, assume the surcharge is at a safe maximum angle of repose of 1½ to 1, regardless

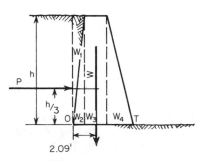

Fig.   6.8 Horizontally   loaded gravity wall.

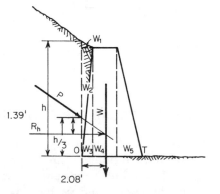

Fig. 6.9 Surcharged gravity wall.

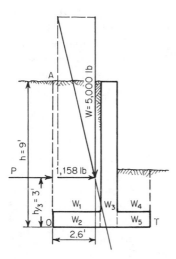

Fig. 6.10 Horizontally loaded cantilevered wall.

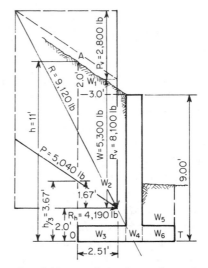

Fig. 6.11 Surcharged cantilevered wall.

of the actual slope of the retained soil from the top of the wall. The direction of P in this case is also parallel to the surface, and therefore acts at a point $h/3$ above the base, but at an angle of $1\frac{1}{2}$ to 1. In this case use the formula

$$P = 0.833 \frac{wh^2}{2}$$

where P = magnitude of earth pressure, lb
w = weight of retained material, pcf
h = height of retained material, ft (measured from bottom of wall footing)

In a cantilevered wall, h is measured vertically from the end of the heel to the surface of the soil. In a surcharged situation, as shown in Fig. 6.11, h will be greater than the height of the wall, and the point of application of pressure, P, will be one-third of this h, rather than one-third the height of the wall. Everything resting on the footing is considered a part of the wall. In Fig. 6.11, line OA is considered to be the back of the structure and w_1, w_2, and w_5 are included in the weight of the structure even though they are earth. A wall with a batter on the back of the wall develops this same situation. See Fig. 6.9.

When using a facing of stone, brick, or other material, investigate the design, as is normally done.   When the design investigation is completed and acceptable, add 20 percent to the thickness of the wall to compensate for the weakness inherent in the nonintegral facing.   This thickness dimension includes the facing.   However, in no case shall the final dimension be such that the integrally poured wall will be less than 8 in. in thickness for a reinforced wall or less than 12 in. in thickness for a nonreinforced wall.

Dams are constructed with their footings at sufficient depth below grade to prevent underwashing and frost action.   Walls are also constructed with their footings below the frost line.   This is usually considered to be $3\frac{1}{2}$ ft deep in the North Central states, but the depth will vary, depending on climate.   *The soil on the low side does develop counter loads and resistant reactions to overturning and sliding, but they are so minor that it is not necessary to consider them in any wall or dam calculations that a landscape architect will encounter.*

Examples of four wall-design investigations follows.   Each is of a different wall situation.

1. A horizontally loaded gravity wall
2. A surcharged gravity wall
3. A horizontally loaded cantilevered wall
4. A surcharged cantilevered wall

Sandy clay soil @ 100 lb per cu ft
Concrete @ 130 lb per cu ft

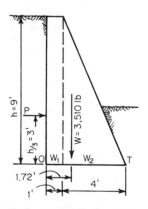

Fig.   6.12   Horizontally   loaded gravity wall.

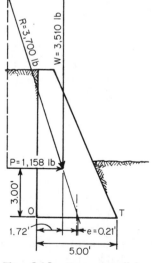

Fig.   6.13   Force   parallelograms.

Example 6.8 Figure 6.12 shows a horizontally loaded gravity retaining wall. Test this design for (1) general stability, (2) overturning, (3) crushing, and (4) sliding.

1. *General Stability*

Sec.	Weight, lb	Arm$_o$, ft	Moment, ft-lb
w_1	$1 \times 1 \times 9 \times 130 = 1,170$	0.50	585
w_2	$1 \times \dfrac{4}{2} \times 9 \times 130 = 2,340$	2.33	5,452
Total	3,510		6,037

6,037 ft-lb ÷ 3,510 lb = 1.72 ft   (arm from O)
5.00 − 1.72 = 3.28 ft   (arm from T)

$$P = 0.286 \frac{wh^2}{2}$$

$$= 0.286 \times \frac{100 \times 9^2}{2} = 0.286 \times 4,050 = 1,158 \text{ lb}$$

The middle third of the base extends from 1.67 ft from O to 3.33 ft from O. The line of action of the resultant cuts the base 2.71 ft from O and thus falls within the middle third of the base, and the wall can be considered generally stable. This can be determined accurately enough if it is done by scaling the drawing.

2. *Overturning.* The force tending to overturn the wall is P acting at $h/3$ above the base. Any overturning of the wall would rotate the wall about its toe, point T, and the moment arm would be the perpendicular distance from the force P to the point T.

$$1,158 \text{ lb} \times \frac{9 \text{ ft}}{3} = 3,474 \text{ ft-lb} \qquad \text{(overturning force)}$$

The force resisting overturning is the weight of the structure rotating on an arm from T. The arm from T is the whole width of the base less the arm from O, or 3.28 ft.

$$3,510 \text{ lb} \times 3.28 \text{ ft} = 11,513 \text{ ft-lb}$$

$$\frac{\text{force resisting rotation}}{\text{force tending to rotate}} = \frac{11,513 \text{ ft-lb}}{3,474 \text{ ft-lb}} = 3.31 \text{ safety factor}$$

Since this exceeds the desired safety factor of 2, this wall will not overturn.

3. *Crushing*

$$f = \frac{R_v}{A}\left(1 + \frac{6e}{d}\right)$$

$$= \frac{3{,}510}{5}\left(1 + \frac{6 \times 0.21}{5}\right) = 702 \times 1.25 = 878 \text{ psf}$$

Sandy clay has a bearing capacity of 4,000 psf; so this is acceptable.

4. *Sliding.* The force tending to cause sliding is P. P has a force of 1,158 lb.

At the force tending to resist sliding is the weight of the structure multiplied by the coefficient of friction for concrete on sandy clay (from Table 6.2). A safety factor of 1.5 is desired.

$$3{,}510 \text{ lb} \times 0.4 = 1{,}404 \text{ lb} \qquad \text{(force resisting sliding)}$$

$$\frac{\text{force resisting sliding}}{\text{force tending to cause sliding}} = \frac{1{,}404 \text{ lb}}{1{,}158 \text{ lb}} = 1.21$$

This is less than the 1.5 safety factor desired and is not acceptable.

The simplest way to correct this condition would be to dig a trench about 10×10 in. (a shovel wide and a shovel deep) in the bottom of the footing excavation centered under the line where the line of action of the resultant will cut the base, Fig. 6.6. This excavation should be rough. In fact, the whole footing excavation should be rough in order to increase the friction factor.

Example 6.9   Assume the same wall as in Example 6.8 but in a surcharged condition, Figs. 6.14 and 6.15.

Sec.	Weight, lb	Arm_o, ft	Moment, ft-lb
w_1	$1 \times 1 \times 9 \times 130 = 1{,}170$	0.50	585
w_2	$1 \times \dfrac{4}{2} \times 9 \times 130 = 2{,}340$	2	5,452
Total	3,510		6,037

6,037 ft-lb ÷ 3,510 lb = 1.72 ft   (arm from O)
5.00 − 1.72   = 3.28 ft   (arm from T)

$$P = 0.833\frac{wh^2}{2}$$

$$= 0.833 \times \frac{100 \times 9^2}{2} = 3{,}374 \text{ lb}$$

1. *General Stability.* The resultant cuts the base 2.74 ft from O. The middle third of the base extends from 1.67 ft from O to 3.33 ft from O. Therefore the line of action of the resultant cuts the base within the middle third of the base, and the wall can be considered generally stable.

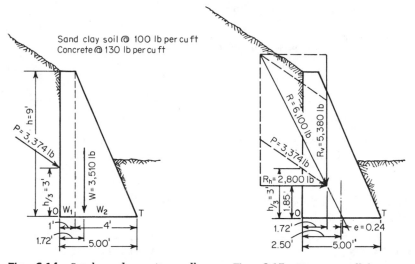

Fig. 6.14 Surcharged gravity wall.   **Fig. 6.15** Force parallelograms.

2. *Overturning.* The force tending to overturn the wall is the horizontal component of the resultant, R_h.

$R_h = 2,800$ lb acting on a 1.85-ft arm from T

The force tending to resist overturning is the vertical component of the resultant, R_v, acting on a 3.28-ft arm from T.

$R_v = 5,380$ lb acting on a 3.28-ft arm from T

$$\text{Safety factor} = \frac{\text{force resisting overturning}}{\text{force tending to overturn}}$$

$$= \frac{5,380 \times 3.28}{2,800 \times 1.85} = \frac{17,646 \text{ ft-lb}}{5,180 \text{ ft-lb}} = 3.41$$

3.41 exceeds the desired safety factor of 2 and is therefore acceptable.

3. *Crushing*

$$f = \frac{R_v}{A}\left(1 + \frac{6e}{d}\right)$$

$$= \frac{5,380}{5}\left(1 + \frac{6 \times 0.24}{5}\right) = 1,076 \times 1.288 = 1,386 \text{ psf}$$

Sandy clay has a bearing capacity of 4,000 psf, and therefore this is acceptable.

4. *Sliding.* The force tending to cause sliding is the horizontal component of the resultant.

$R_h = 2,800$ lb

The force tending to resist sliding is the vertical component of the resultant multiplied by the coefficient of friction for concrete on sandy clay.

$$R_v \times 0.4 = 5{,}380 \times 0.4 = 2{,}152$$

$$\text{Safety factor} = \frac{\text{force resisting sliding}}{\text{force tending to cause sliding}}$$

$$= \frac{2{,}152}{2{,}800} = 0.77$$

A safety factor of 1.5 is desirable.   Therefore 0.77 is not acceptable and redesign will be necessary in order to make this wall acceptable.

Example 6.10   Investigate this horizontally loaded cantilevered wall constructed of reinforced concrete.

Sandy clay soil @ 100 lb per cu ft

Concrete @ 150 lb per cu ft

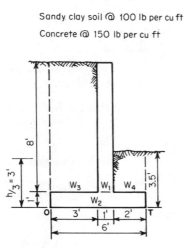

Fig.   6.16 Horizontally   loaded cantilevered wall.

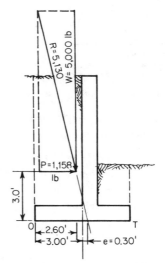

Fig. 6.17 Force parallelograms.

Sec.	Weight, lb		Arm$_0$, ft	Moment, ft-lb
w_1	$1 \times 1 \times 8 \times 150$	$= 1{,}200$	3.5	4,200
w_2	$1 \times 1 \times 6 \times 150$	$= 900$	3.0	2,700
w_3	$1 \times 3 \times 8 \times 100$	$= 2{,}400$	1.5	3,600
w_4	$1 \times 2.5 \times 2 \times 100 =$	500	5.0	2,500
Total		5,000		13,000

13,000 ft-lb ÷ 5,000 lb = 2.60 ft   (arm from O)
6.00 − 2.60   = 3.40 ft   (arm from T)

$$P = 0.286 \frac{wh^2}{2}$$

$$= 0.286 \frac{100 \times 9^2}{2} = 1{,}158 \text{ lb}$$

1. *General Stability.* The resultant cuts the base 3.30 ft from O and therefore falls within the middle third of the base, and the wall can be considered generally stable.
2. *Overturning.* The force tending to overturn the structure is the horizontal component of the resultant, R_h, which in the case of horizontally loaded walls is equal to P.

$$R_h = P = 1{,}158 \text{ lb acting on an arm of 3.0 ft}$$
$$1{,}158 \times 3 = 3{,}474 \text{ ft-lb} \quad \text{(overturning force)}$$

The force resisting overturning is the vertical component of the resultant, R_v, which in the case of horizontally loaded walls is equal to the weight of the structure, W.

$$R_v = W = 5{,}000 \text{ lb acting on an arm of 3.4 ft}$$
$$5{,}000 \text{ lb} \times 3.4 \text{ ft} = 17{,}000 \text{ ft-lb} \quad \text{(resisting overturn)}$$

$$\text{Safety factor} = \frac{\text{force resisting overturning}}{\text{force tending to overturn}}$$
$$= \frac{17{,}000 \text{ ft-lb}}{3{,}474 \text{ ft-lb}} = 4.89$$

4.89 exceeds the desired safety factor of 2. Therefore this is acceptable.

3. *Crushing*

$$f = \frac{R_v}{A}\left(1 + \frac{6e}{d}\right)$$
$$= \frac{5{,}000}{6}\left(1 + \frac{6 \times 0.30}{6}\right) = 833.3 \times 1.3 = 1{,}083 \text{ psf}$$

Sandy-clay soil has a bearing capacity of 4,000 psf. Therefore this is acceptable.

4. *Sliding*

$$\text{Safety factor} = \frac{\text{force resisting sliding}}{\text{force tending to cause sliding}}$$
$$= \frac{5{,}000 \times 0.4}{1{,}158} = 1.73$$

1.73 exceeds the desired safety factor of 1.5. Therefore this is acceptable.

Example 6.11 Use the same wall as in Example 6.10, except that it will have surcharged loading, Figs. 6.18 and 6.19.

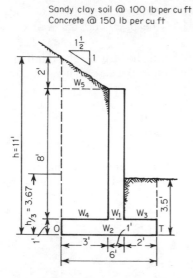

Sandy clay soil @ 100 lb per cu ft
Concrete @ 150 lb per cu ft

Fig. 6.18 Surcharged cantilevered wall.

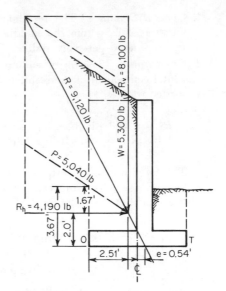

Fig. 6.19 Force parallelograms.

Sec.	Weight, lb		Arm$_0$, ft	Moment, ft-lb
w_1	$1 \times 1 \times 8 \times 150$	$= 1,200$	3.5	4,200
w_2	$1 \times 1 \times 6 \times 150$	$= 900$	3.0	2,700
w_3	$1 \times 2 \times 2.5 \times 100$	$= 500$	5.0	2,500
w_4	$1 \times 3 \times 8 \times 100$	$= 2,400$	1.5	3,600
w_b	$1 \times \dfrac{3}{2} \times 2 \times 100$	$= 300$	1.0	300
Total		5,300		13,300

13,300 ft-lb ÷ 5,300 lb = 2.51 ft   (arm from O)
6.00 − 2.51   = 3.49 ft   (arm from T)

$$P = 0.833 \frac{wh^2}{2}$$

$$= 0.833 \times \frac{100 \times 11^2}{2} = 5,040 \text{ lb}$$

1. *General Stability.* The resultant cuts the base 3.54 ft from O. The middle third of the base extends from 2 to 4 ft from O. Therefore the line of action of the resultant cuts the base within the middle third of the base, and the wall can be considered generally stable.

2. *Overturning.* The force tending to overturn is the horizontal component of the resultant, R_h, 4,190 lb, acting on an arm from T of 2.00 ft.

The force tending to resist overturning is the vertical component of the resultant, R_v, 8,100 lb, acting on an arm from T of 3.49 ft.

$$\text{Safety factor} = \frac{8,100 \times 3.49}{4,190 \times 2.00} = \frac{28,269}{8,380} = 3.37$$

3.37 exceeds the desired safety factor of 2. Therefore this is acceptable.

3. *Crushing*

$$f = \frac{R_v}{A}\left(1 + \frac{6e}{d}\right)$$

$$= \frac{8,100}{6}\left(1 + \frac{6 \times 0.54}{6}\right) = 1,350 \times 1.54 = 2,079 \text{ psf}$$

Sandy clay has a bearing capacity of 4,000 psf. Therefore this is acceptable.

4. *Sliding*

$$\text{Safety factor} = \frac{8,100 \times 0.4}{4,190} = \frac{3,240}{4,190} = 0.77$$

This is less than the desired safety factor of 1.5 and is therefore not acceptable.

6.4 EARTH-RETAINING WALLS OF TIMBER CONSTRUCTION

Timber is often used for retaining earth embankments. It is a material that fits with the natural landscape and when treated with preservatives will last a long time. Three types are in common use: (1) sheet-pile wall held in place, with alignment by guide piles and heavy timber wales, (2) retaining walls of horizontal planking held in place by posts or timber piles, and (3) cribbing and retaining walls composed of railroad ties, without guide piles or vertical posts.

Railroad ties are usually laid up in a manner similar to brick. The component ties are held in place with 6- and 10- or 12-in. spikes, and the whole wall is given a batter of about 1 to 1½ in. per ft of height. Where corners and returns do not provide the necessary resistance to overturning, anchors and deadmen are planted behind the wall at horizontal intervals of about 10 or 15 ft. These are repeated at staggered locations every 3 or 4 ft of vertical height. The anchors and deadmen are set in undisturbed soil and are tied to the back of the wall by eyebolts and cables or rods. The tie rods and cables are usually

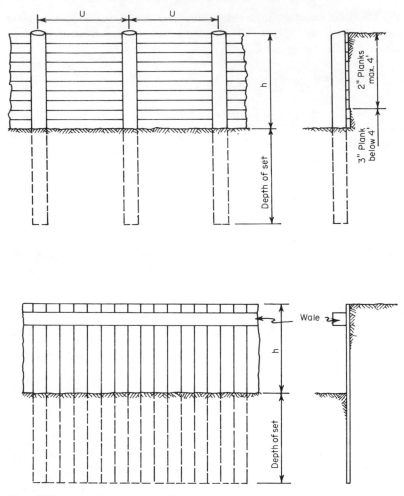

Fig. 6.20 Wood retaining walls.

equipped with turnbuckles to remove all slack between the wall and the anchor.

Walls of the other two types, Fig. 6.20, can be constructed up to 7 ft high without tiebacks or brace posts if the guide piles or support posts are set to the recommended depth.   Walls higher than 7 ft need tiebacks or brace posts to provide the needed additional support.   Walls of either type will not succeed in poor soils having no lateral support.

It is normally impractical to obtain an exact determination of the lateral pressures that the retained earth will develop.   Experiments have shown that these lateral pressures can vary as much as 30 percent above and below the average because of the seasonal changes during a year.   It is also difficult to determine the exact lateral support to the guide piles and support posts by the soil in which they are set. The time and expense involved in the soil testing and the elaborate calculations needed for sizing the posts, timbers, and planks of a wood bulkhead can be justified only in very special cases and where wall heights exceed 10 ft. In those cases it is advisable to seek the assistance of an engineer with experience in this type of construction. Generally, it is recommended that wood retaining walls be limited to 10 ft in height.

The indefiniteness of soil characteristics makes precise calculations impractical. Experience indicates that:

1. The *depth of set* for guide piles and support posts shall be equal to the height of the wall above grade for average soil conditions. Under excellent conditions this depth can be reduced by 10 percent, and for poor soil the depth must be increased by at least 40 percent. Under very poor conditions the depth of set should be increased by a full 100 percent to a depth of set equal to twice the height of the wall above the ground.

TABLE 6.3

Height of wall, ft	Spacing of posts, c-c, ft	Diameter of posts, in.	Depth of set, ft		
			Good soil*	Avg soil†	Poor soil‡
3	6	6	3.5	4.5	6.0
	4	6	4.0	5.0	6.5
4	4	6	4.0	5.0	6.5
	6	8	4.0	4.5	6.5
5	4	8	4.0	5.0	6.5
	5	8	4.5	5.5	...
	5	9½	...	...	7.5
6	4	9½	5.5	7.0	9.5
	5	9½	6.0	8.0	....
	5	10½	...	...	11.0

* Good soil is well drained and in a well-drained location. It is composed of compact sand, gravel, hard clay, broken rock, or a well-graded mixture of these.

† Average soil is soil that drains well enough so that no water stands on the surface. It is composed of compact fine sand, medium clay, well-drained sandy loam, and loose coarse sand and gravel.

‡ Poor soil refers to soils in low-lying areas where water stands in wet seasons. The soil itself is poor-draining and retains large amounts of moisture. It is composed of poorly compacted sand, soft clay, and soils containing large amounts of silt or organic matter.

Railroads use 12- and 14-in.-diameter pile posts, but for most site-improvement work the dimensions shown in Table 6.3 should be satisfactory for retaining walls constructed of post piling and horizontal planks.

Since precise and complicated design formulas are unrealistic, the following easy-to-use formulas will provide sufficiently accurate solutions for figuring post and plank sizes.

2. A safe answer to the *horizontal pressure of the retained earth* can be obtained by using the following variations of the Parker adaptation of the Rankine formula:

For horizontally loaded walls: $P = 0.286 \dfrac{wh^2}{2}$

For surcharged retaining walls: $P = 0.694 \dfrac{wh^2}{2}$

The latter formula is based on a 1½ to 1 sloped surcharge. Some adjustment downward toward the horizontally loaded (0.286) wall can be made if the slope of the retained material has a relatively flat angle above the top of the wall.

3. The size of guideposts and timber pilings, when set at depths recommended in rule 1 above, can be determined by the following formula:

$$S = \frac{2UPh}{f}$$

where S = section modulus S_{y-y}
   U = distance vertical pile posts are set c-c, ft
   P = total horizontal pressure on wall, lb (from rule 2, above)
   h = wall height above lower ground elevation, ft
   f = extreme allowable fiber stress (Select f from Table 11-5 for type and grade of wood being used. If round posts are being used, the allowable fiber stress can be increased by 18 percent as a standard "form" allowance.)

Select a *square* timber having a section modulus equal to or greater than the calculated section modulus. The square timber is used because it has the depth to resist the bending and also has the face width to present to the embedding earth, resisting the tendency to rotate. If a round post is used, select one with a minimum cross-section area equal to that of the square timber. Always set the round post with its minimum diameter uppermost.

4. Select vertical planking in sheet-pile walls (held in place and alignment by guide piles and heavy timber wales) by using the

following formula:

$$S = \frac{1.54Ph}{f}$$

where S, P, h, and f have the same meaning as in rule 3, above.

Select a plank from Table 11.6 with a section modulus S_{y-y} at least equal to the calculated section modulus S.

5. Determine the thickness of the horizontal planking (in retaining walls of horizontal planking held in place by posts or timber piles) by the use of the following formula:

$$t = 3U \sqrt{\frac{wd}{fb}} \qquad \text{(for horizontally loaded walls)}$$

where t = required thickness of plank, in. (actual)
U = distance between support posts, ft, c-c
w = weight per cubic foot of retained material
d = distance from the surface of retained material (top of wall) to centerline of plank in question
b = width of plank, in. (actual)
f = allowable extreme fiber stress for kind and grade of lumber being used

Add 20 to 30 percent to thickness of plank for surcharged walls.

Example 6.12 A wall 4 ft high, horizontally loaded, posts 4 ft c-c, earth average at 100 pcf, $f = 1,700$.

(a) Average soil, depth of set 4 ft.

(b) $P = 0.286 \dfrac{wh^2}{2} = 0.286 \times \dfrac{100 \times 4 \times 4}{2} = 229$ lb

(c) Size of guideposts:

$$S = \frac{2UPh}{f} = \frac{2 \times 4 \times 229 \times 4}{1,700} = 4.31$$

Therefore use 4 × 4-in.-square or 5-in.-diameter round posts.

(d) Thickness of lowest horizontal plank:

$$t = 3U \sqrt{\frac{wd}{fb}}$$

$$= 3 \times 4 \sqrt{\frac{100 \times 4}{1,700 \times 6}}$$

$$= 12 \sqrt{\frac{1}{25.5}} = 12 \sqrt{0.0392} = 12 \times 0.198 = 2.38 \text{ in.}$$

Therefore use a 6-in. plank at least 2.4 in. thick (for example, 3 × 6 in.).

(e) If vertical sheet piling and wales are used, vertical planks will be

$$S = \frac{1.54Ph}{f}$$

$$= \frac{1.54 \times 229 \times 4}{1,700}$$

$$= \frac{1,411}{1,700} = 0.83 \qquad S_{y-y} = 0.83$$

Therefore use 1 × 10 in. or 2 × 4 in. as minimum.

Example 6.13   A wall 6 ft high, surcharged loading, posts 5 ft c-c, earth average at 100 pcf, $f = 1,700$.

(a) Depth of set for average soil is 6 ft.

(b) $P = 0.693\dfrac{wh^2}{2} = 0.693\dfrac{100 \times 6^2}{1,700} = 1,247$ lb

(c) Size of guideposts:

$$S = \frac{2UPh}{f} = \frac{2 \times 5 \times 1,247 \times 6}{1,700} = 44.01$$

Therefore use 8 × 8-in.-square or 10-in.-diameter round posts.

(d) Thickness of lowest horizontal plank:

$$t = 3U\sqrt{\frac{wd}{fb}}$$

$$= 3 \times 5\sqrt{\frac{100 \times 6}{1,700 \times 10}}$$

$$= 15\sqrt{0.353} = 15 \times 0.188 = 2.82 \text{ in.}$$

For surcharged wall add 20 to 30 percent. $2.82 + 25\% = 3.52$ in The nearest available size would be 4 × 10 in.

(e) If vertical sheet piling is used,

$$S = 1.54\frac{Ph}{f}$$

$$= \frac{1.54 \times 1,247 \times 6}{1,700} = \frac{11,522}{1,700} = 6.78 \qquad S_{y-y} = 6.78$$

Therefore use 3 × 8 in. minimum for vertical planks.

CHAPTER SEVEN

Earthwork Calculations

One of the basic elements in the implementation of the landscape architect's design is the movement of earth. In most situations the volume
of cut and the volume of fill are expected to be equal in amount so
as to provide a balance of cut and fill. The landscape architect must
make allowances for the volume of all materials being brought onto
the site from off-site, such as road and walk materials, backfill sand
and gravel, topsoil brought in from off-site, etc. These items provide
a fill figure that must be determined and accounted for in the calculations. Basement and pool excavations provide quantity displacements
that must also be taken into consideration when figuring earthwork
quantities.

7.1 GENERAL

Landscape architects must usually make these mathematical determinations as part of their services to their clients. Earthwork computation
is a tedious, time-taking job, and it behooves landscape architects to
develop a judgment sense as to earth balance so that they will not
have to perform this mathematical determination more than once. This

is not an easy facility to acquire. It takes time to acquire the essential experience. In the early years of practice, landscape architects must mathematically check their work from time to time as they develop the grading plan. As they become more proficient, they are able to rely more and more on judgment, reducing the mathematical checks to parts or areas that are difficult to visualize and estimate. Ultimately, they become sure enough of their earthwork estimating judgments to be able to complete the grading plan to its final stage before calculating the earthwork. If, at this time, there is a small imbalance, the project elevations can be adjusted up or down one- or two-tenths over the whole or a part of the project area to refine the earth balance.

In making this kind of adjustment, it is necessary to make certain that no water pockets are being created or gradients developed above or below the recommended maximums or minimums in meeting points of fixed (nonadjustable) elevation.

Earth movement, as opposed to the amount of cut and fill, is not generally a consideration in site development. However, if the landscape architect is doing highway work or extensive areas or long narrow areas, earth movement (length of haul) does become an important factor, and for such cases the landscape architect has access to reference books on highway work. The text in this chapter concerns itself only with earthwork-quantity calculations.

In estimating cut, the difference between the original and the final ground elevations will provide a quantity figure of *in-place* compacted earth. In preparing *unit-price* specifications, specify all quantities, either cut or fill, as in-place quantities. Bulking, expansion, shrinkage, and other losses in moving earth around are the contractor's concern. The landscape architect, however, will be concerned about the earthwork-volume losses and gains when figuring earthwork balance. The in-place volume of cut will yield less than that volume of fill by 15 or 20 percent. The shrinkage and expansion of the soil will vary with the type of soil. Gravel will provide the least variation (12 percent), organic topsoil the greatest (24 percent), with sandy and clayey soils falling in between these extremes. At best, the computation for the earthwork cannot be completely precise, and the use of a 15 or 20 percent allowance for shrinkage should be sufficiently accurate. *The important thing to remember is that the on-site in-place cut must be 15 to 20 percent greater than the on-site in-place fill figure in order to end up with an earth balance on the site.*

There are several methods of figuring earthwork. The four most common methods used by landscape architects are cross-sectioning, grid method, contour planes, and parallel planes. Each has its distinctive advantage, and no one method is superior to the others in all situations.

Most landscape architects develop their own procedure for calculating earthwork and use one method in preference to the others for most of their earthwork calculating. However, there is a distinct advantage in each method under certain circumstances, and the landscape architect should be thoroughly familiar with all four methods.

7.2   CROSS-SECTION METHOD

Cross-sectioning is the most commonly used method of measuring earthwork volumes. It is particularly applicable to areas without basement excavations. It is the easiest method for determining earthwork quantities for street and highway work.

Cross sections, as the word implies, are sections through the project, transverse to a stationed base line. Parallel section-location lines are drawn across the plan at selected locations or predetermined intervals. The intervals are generally equal, but they can be varied, depending on the character of the site and the desired accuracy of the final result.

Accuracy is increased by increasing the number of cross sections. The cross sections should be parallel to each other and perpendicular to the longitudinal stationing line. A profile is drawn of each of the parallel section-location lines showing the existing grade superimposed by another profile showing the proposed grades. These are the cross sections and are usually drawn with the vertical dimension exaggerated five or ten times the horizontal scale. Each cross-section area is measured and its area recorded (usually in square feet). This is called the *end area*. The average of two adjacent end areas multiplied by the distance between them will give the volume for that increment. In each case the *fill* areas are kept separate from the *cut* areas.

The area of a cross section (end area) can be measured by dividing the cross section into its component geometric subareas for calculating and adding these subareas together to obtain the total area of the cross section, or by overlaying with a grid and tabulating the grid squares, or by measuring the end areas with a planimeter. The planimeter method is the quickest, easiest, and generally the most accurate.

The cross-section method can produce inaccurate results if care is not taken to select locations for the cross sections that most truly reflect the warping of the topography. The results can also be incorrect where basement excavations are involved. More accurate results are obtained if the basements or similar excavations are figured separately and the cross sections are selected at locations where they do not go through basements, swimming pools, etc.

Example 7.1   Figure 7.1 shows a 325- × 450-ft parcel of irregular ground which is to be reshaped into a smoother plane having a finished grade

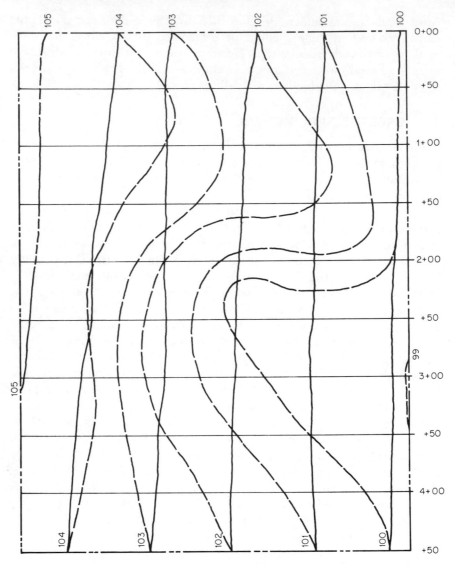

Fig. 7.1 Topographic map showing location of cross-section lines. - - - Existing contour; —— proposed contour; — - - — existing contour to remain.

of approximately 1.6 percent slope. Cross-section location lines are shown at 50-ft intervals, and Fig. 7.2 shows the cross sections as they occur at these 50-ft stations. These cross sections are drawn at a 10 times exaggeration, using a horizontal scale of 1 in. = 50 ft and a vertical scale of 1 in. = 5 ft. No cross sections were required for stations 0 + 00 and 4 + 50 because these are at the limits of the grade change and there is no cut or fill at either of these stations.

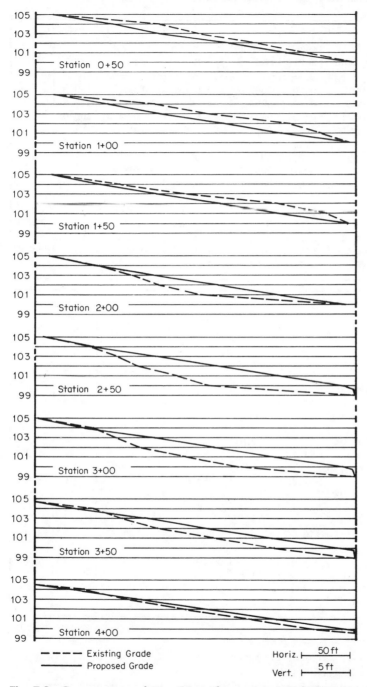

Station 0+50

Station 1+00

Station 1+50

Station 2+00

Station 2+50

Station 3+00

Station 3+50

Station 4+00

- - - - Existing Grade
——— Proposed Grade

Horiz. 50 ft
Vert. 5 ft

Fig. 7.2 Cross sections of Fig. 7.1 as they occur at 50-ft stations.

Plane or station	First reading	Second reading	Average reading	Correction factor	Corrected reading, sq in.	Area, sq ft	
						Cut	Fill
0 + 50	0060	0120	0060 ✗	1.006 =	0.604 ✗⁹⁰≥	150.9	.....
1 + 00	0086	0175	0087	1.006	0.875	218.8	.....
1 + 50	0064	0132	0066	1.006	0.664	166.0	.....
2 + 00	0001	0002	0001	1.006	0.010	2.5	.....
2 + 50	....	....	......	.....	......	0.0	.....
3 + 00	0005	0009	0004.5	1.006	0.0453	11.3	.....
3 + 50	0003	0007	0003.5	1.006	0.0352	8.8	.....
4 + 00	0002	0004	0002	1.006	0.020	5.03	.....
2 + 00	0068	0136	0068	1.006	0.684	......	171.0
2 + 50	0154	0307	0153.5	1.006	1.544	......	386.0
3 + 00	0126	0253	0126.5	1.006	1.273	......	318.2
3 + 50	0082	0165	0082.5	1.006	0.830	......	207.5
4 + 00	0037	0073	0036.5	1.006	0.367	......	91.8

Station	Cut	Average cut	Fill	Average fill	Dist., ft	Volume, cu ft	
						Cut	Fill
0 + 00	0.0						
		75.45		....	50	3,773	......
0 + 50	150.9		.....				
		184.85		....	50	9,243	......
1 + 00	218.8		.....				
		192.4			50	9,620	......
1 + 50	166.0		0.0				
		84.25		85.5	50	4,212	4,275
2 + 00	2.5		171.0				
		1.25		278.5	50	63	13,925
2 + 50	0.0		386.0				
		5.65		352.1	50	282	17,605
3 + 00	11.3		318.2				
		10.05		262.85	50	502	13,142
3 + 50	8.8		207.5				
		6.92		149.65	50	346	7,483
4 + 00	5.03		91.8				
		2.52		45.9	50	126	2,295
4 + 50	0.0		0.0				

Total = 28,167   58,725

Fill = 58,725 cu ft, or 2,175 cu yd
Cut = 28,167 cu ft, or 1,043 cu yd
Balance = 1,132 cu yd fill

Fig. 7.3 Calculations for earthwork by cross-section method.   The horizontal and vertical scales are shown in Fig. 7.2.

Following the cross sections are the earthwork computations. The upper chart is a record of the planimeter work using a tabular form similar to the one suggested in the article on the planimeter (Appendix Sec. B.3). The lower chart follows the tabular form shown in Fig. 7.4. The square-foot end areas calculated from the planimeter readings are used to compute the cubic-foot volumes of cut and/or fill for each segment between stations. Two adjacent end areas are averaged, and this average is multiplied by the distance between the two end areas to obtain the volume in each segment. The volumes of the segments are added together to obtain the total amounts of cut and fill. These amounts are in cubic feet and must be divided by 27 to obtain cubic yards.

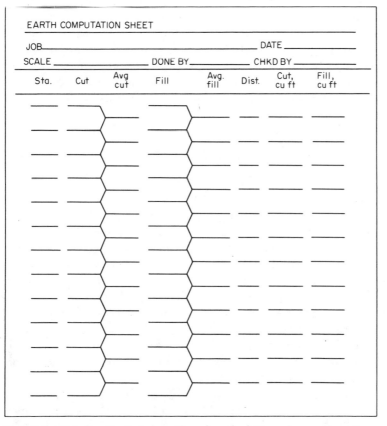

Fig. 7.4 Tabular form for earthwork calculations by cross-section method.

7.3 GRID METHOD

Basements and other sharply defined and limited excavations are best calculated as separate items. If we know the elevations of the existing topography and the elevation of the bottom of the excavation, the depth of the cut at each of the four corners of the excavation can be determined. The average of these four depths of cut multiplied by the area of the excavation will give the volume of the cut.

A more accurate calculation, and one that is useful for larger areas and those of a more complicated nature, may be accomplished by breaking the area into small identical squares.

In Fig. 7.5, label all the corners that pertain to a single square a; all corners that pertain to two squares b; all corners that pertain to three squares c; and all corners that pertain to four squares d. Then determine the depth of cut or fill at each of these corners. Add all the a depths together. Add all the b depths together and use twice this sum (since each b corner pertains to two squares). Add all the c depths together and use three times this sum (since each c corner pertains to three squares). Add all the d depths together and use four times this sum (since each d corner pertains to four squares). Add these four total sums together and divide by 4 (since each square has four corners) to determine the average depth. Multiply this answer by the area of one small square to obtain volume in cubic units. This process can be expressed by the formula

$$\text{Volume} = \frac{a + 2b + 3c + 4d}{4} \times A$$

where A is the area of one small square, a is the sum of all the a depths, b the sum of all the b depths, c the sum of all the c depths, and d the sum of all the d depths. If all the dimensions have been in feet, the answer will be in cubic feet. Divide this by 27 to obtain cubic yards.

This is a laborious process, but it is the most accurate process for such volumes as basements, geometrically shaped pools, etc.

Since most topographic surveys are taken on a grid system, intermediate elevations can be interpolated and the existing and proposed elevations obtained for relatively small squares (for example, 10 ft, 25 ft, etc.), and the volumes then obtained by punching these numbers into a programmed computer. This method may come into much more use than it is at present because it is probably the easiest to program for a computer. The disadvantage is that the answer is the earth balance for the site and the quantities of cut and fill are not shown separately. The answer shows only the shortage or overage of cut or fill.

Example 7.2 Figure 7.5 shows an L-shaped basement excavation staked out on an irregular piece of topography. The excavation area is sub-

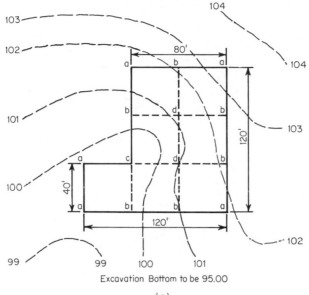

Excavation Bottom to be 95.00

(a)

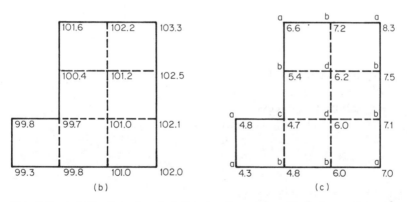

(b)   (c)

Fig. 7.5 (a) Earthwork calculation by the grid method shows the grid layout; (b) interpolated existing elevations at grid corners; (c) depths of cut at each corner of grid.

divided into 40-ft squares, and the corners of the squares are labeled *a*, *b*, *c*, and *d*, depending on the number of squares each corner pertains to. The bottom of the excavation is to be at elevation 95.00. Figure 7.5*b* shows the existing elevations of the earth surface obtained by interpolating between the contours. Figure 7.5*c* shows the depth of cut at each of the corners, obtained as follows:

a corners

101.6	103.3	99.8	99.3	102.0
−95.0	−95.0	−95.0	−95.0	−95.0
6.6	8.3	4.8	4.3	7.0 = 31.0 total cut

b corners

102.2	100.4	102.5	102.1	99.8	101.0
−95.0	−95.0	−95.0	−95.0	−95.0	−95.0
7.2	5.4	7.5	7.1	4.8	6.0 = 38.0 total cut

c corners

99.7
−95.0

4.7 = 4.7 total cut

d corners

101.2	101.0
−95.0	−95.0
6.2	6.0 = 12.2 total cut

Then, using the formula

$$\text{Volume} = \frac{a + 2b + 3c + 4d}{4} \times A$$

where A = a 40- × 40-ft square, or 1,600 sq ft.   Then

$$\text{Volume} = \frac{31.0 + 2(38.0) + 3(4.7) + 4(12.2)}{4} \times 1,600$$

$$= \frac{31.0 + 76.0 + 14.1 + 48.8}{4} \times 1,600$$

$$= \frac{169.9}{4} \times 1,600 = 67,960 \text{ cu ft}$$

$$\frac{67,960}{27} = 2,517 \text{ cu yd}$$

7.4   CONTOUR-PLANES METHOD

Contours are a simple way of showing the shape of the ground. A comparison of existing and proposed contours will disclose the amount of cut or fill required in an area. This is accomplished by first defining a line of *no-cut no-fill* within which earthwork consists of either cut or fill but *not* both. See Fig. 7.6.

The spread between existing and proposed locations of a contour line amounts to a horizontal cross section. The vertical distance between contours, the contour interval, will be the distance between these hori-

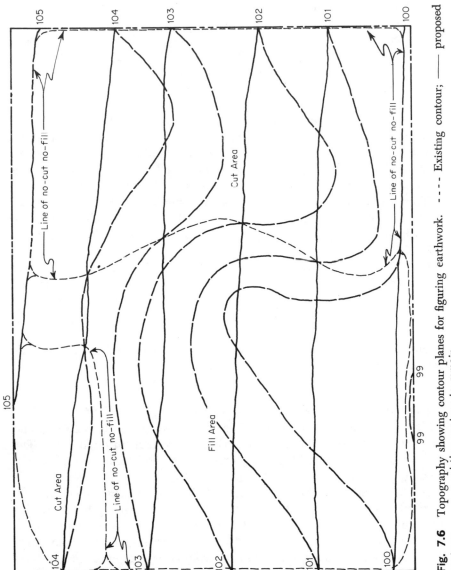

Fig. 7.6 Topography showing contour planes for figuring earthwork. ---- Existing contour; —— proposed contour; —·—·— existing contour to remain.

89

zontal cross sections. Each such horizontal cross section is measured and recorded. Within each cut or fill area the sum of all these area measurements multiplied by the contour interval will give the volume of cut or fill in cubic feet. Volumes in cubic feet must be divided by 27 to obtain cubic yards.

The first step of defining the line of no-cut no-fill is to draw a line surrounding a cut or a fill area where the cut or fill runs out and there is no change in grade from the original topography. At such locations the elevations of the existing and the proposed ground are exactly the same.

Wherever a proposed contour crosses an existing contour of the same elevation, there is a point of no-cut no-fill. Connect all such adjacent points with a line to form an enclosed area. Within such an enclosed area the proposed contours will represent a fill over or a cut from the original contourage.

The second step is to measure the horizontal area of the change at each contour plane within the limits of the no-cut no-fill line. The easiest, and in most cases the most accurate, way to measure these areas is by means of a planimeter. Add these areas together and multiply by the contour interval to obtain the total cut or fill within the no-cut no-fill limits. This can be expressed by the following formula:

$$\text{Volume} = i\,(A + B + C + \cdots)$$

where i is the contour interval expressed in feet, and A, B, C, etc., represent the area of each respective contour plane. The answer will be in cubic feet. Divide by 27 to obtain cubic yards.

PROOF $\text{Volume} = i(A + B + C + \cdots)$

The lower drawing in Fig. 7.7 is a plan showing the existing and proposed contours. The upper drawing is a section through FF'. The geometrical equivalent for each increment of the section is shown immediately above the section.

At the upper and lower reaches of the fill (or cut) area, the fill (or cut) tapers to meet the existing grade. At the points where the fill (cut) meets the existing grade, the fill (cut) becomes zero. Thus it can be seen that the volume of these two end segments will approximate the shape of a pyramid, and the volume is computed as one-third of the base area multiplied by the altitude. The base area is the area between the existing and proposed contour, and the altitude is the contour interval.

The volume of the segments between the upper and lower reaches of the fill (cut) area can be determined by the same end-area method

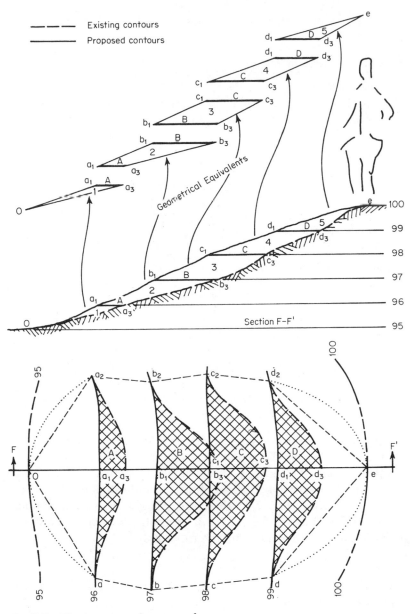

Fig. 7.7 The geometry of contour planes.

as used in the cross-section calculations; i.e., the volume between A and B is

$$\frac{\text{Area of } A + \text{area of } B}{2} \times \text{distance between } A \text{ and } B$$

The distance between A and B is the contour interval. Thus, in Fig. 7.7, if the contour interval is called i, then

$$\text{Volume of increment No. 1} = i\left(\frac{A}{3}\right)$$

$$\text{Volume of increment No. 2} = i\left(\frac{A + B}{2}\right)$$

$$\text{Volume of increment No. 3} = i\left(\frac{B + C}{2}\right)$$

$$\text{Volume of increment No. 4} = i\left(\frac{C + D}{2}\right)$$

$$\text{Volume of increment No. 5} = i\left(\frac{D}{3}\right)$$

The volume within the no-cut no-fill line will be

$$\text{Volume} = i\left(\frac{A}{3}\right) + i\left(\frac{A + B}{2}\right) + i\left(\frac{B + C}{2}\right) + i\left(\frac{C + D}{2}\right) + i\left(\frac{D}{3}\right)$$
$$= i(\tfrac{1}{3}A + \tfrac{1}{2}A + \tfrac{1}{2}B + \tfrac{1}{2}B + \tfrac{1}{2}C + \tfrac{1}{2}C + \tfrac{1}{2}D + \tfrac{1}{3}D)$$
$$= i(\tfrac{5}{6}A + B + C + \tfrac{5}{6}D)$$

Since the actual earthwork shape tends to flow in curves rather than along the straight lines of the geometrical figures used in the mathematical calculations, and the taper in the terminal increments (Nos. 1 and 5) is more apt to approach a curved line (as indicated by the dotted lines in the plan view, Fig. 7.7) than the straight lines of a pyramid (shown by broken lines in Fig. 7.7), it is probably more accurate to change the 5/6 to 6/6, thus resolving the formula to

$$\text{Volume} = i(A + B + C + D)$$

where i is the contour interval, and A, B, C, and D are the areas of the respective contour planes.

Example 7.3   Figure 7.6 shows the same parcel of land with the same topographical reshaping as was shown in Fig. 7.1. The lines of no-cut no-fill are shown, and the areas between the existing and proposed contours of the same elevation are measured with a planimeter and recorded on a typical form for planimeter work. These areas are then used in the volume formula to obtain separate figures for each area of cut and/or fill. The totals so obtained are converted to cubic yards by dividing by 27. These computations are shown in Fig. 7.8.

Plane or station	First reading	Second reading	Average reading	Correction factor	Corrected reading, sq in.	Area, sq ft	
						Cut	Fill
			Left Cut Area				
104	0068	0134	0067	1.006	0.674	1,685	
			Right Cut Area				
101	0249	0496	0248	1.006	2.495	6,237.5	
102	0289	0577	0288.5	1.006	2.902	7,255	
103	0232	0464	0232	1.006	2.330	5,825	
104	0238	0476	0238	1.006	2.394	5,985	
			Fill Area				
100	0743	1485	0742.5	1.006	7.47	....	18,675
101	0684	1367	0683.5	1.006	6.88	....	17,200
102	0615	1230	0615	1.006	6.19	....	15,475
103	0284	0566	0283	1.006	2.85	....	7,125
104	0006	0011	0005.5	1.006	0.055	....	138

Volume $= i(A + B + C + \cdots)$ $(i = 1 \text{ ft})$

Left cut area:

Volume $= 1 \times 1,685 = 1,685$ cu ft cut

Right cut area:

Volume $= 1 \ (6,237.5 + 7,255 + 5,825 + 5,985) = 25,302$ cu ft cut

Fill area:

Volume $= 1 \ (18,675 + 17,200 + 15,475 + 7,125 + 138) = 58,613$ cu ft fill, or 2,171 cu yd fill

1,685 cu ft cut

25,302 cu ft cut

26,987 cu ft cut, or 1,000 cu yd cut

Fig. 7.8 Calculations for earthwork by contour-planes method. Scale: 1 in. = 50 ft; 1 sq in. = 2,500 sq ft.

7.5 METHOD OF PARALLEL PLANES

This method differs from the contour-planes method in that the areas measured are horizontal projections of warped surfaces rather than horizontal planes (see Fig. 7.9). In this method smaller contour intervals give greater accuracy, and in most instances 1-ft contours are necessary in order to make this method work. Lines of no-cut no-fill are first

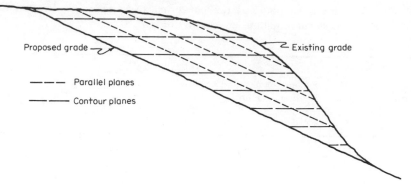

Fig. 7.9 An exaggerated section showing typical parallel planes as compared with typical contour planes.

drawn by connecting points where existing and proposed contours of the same elevation cross each other. At these points there is no change in grade, i.e., no fill, no cut. The line connecting these points cannot cross any contour line, existing or proposed, except where existing and proposed contour lines of the same elevation cross each other. This line will close upon itself to form a complete enclosure within which the earthwork is either all cut or all fill, but never both. See Fig. 7.10.

If the cut (fill) is deep enough, existing and proposed contours will cross with a 1-ft differential between the existing and proposed. Again, these points are connected to form an enclosed area, and this line is referred to as the 1 line. If the cut (fill) is deep enough, areas enclosed by lines showing 2- and 3-ft, even 4- or 5-ft, differential are drawn in. At the very top or bottom of the fill or cut there will usually be a spot that is less than a full contour interval above or below the last enclosing plane. This depth must be ascertained and used in calculating the volume of the earthwork.

It is often necessary to interpolate between the contours to obtain the location of the point of maximum cut or fill or the line enclosing a plane. This situation occurs adjoining structures, slabs, etc., and at places where it is difficult to visualize exactly where the whole-foot differential occurs. In doing such interpolation, it is necessary to interpolate the tenth-foot intervals for both the existing and the proposed topographic grade to find where the proper differential occurs. Figure 7.10 shows both existing and proposed contours at 1-ft intervals. Notice that in the interpolation process the space between two adjacent existing contours is divided into 10 equal parts, each representing a rise in elevation of 0.1 ft. Similarly, the space between two adjacent proposed contours in the same vicinity is also divided into 10 equal parts, each representing a rise in elevation of 0.1 ft. By comparing these tenth-foot

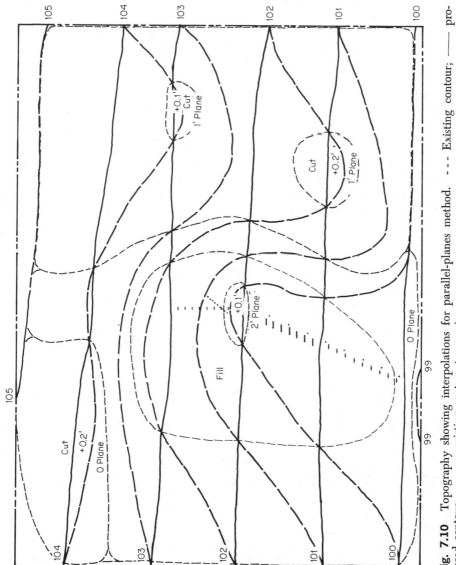

Fig. 7.10 Topography showing interpolations for parallel-planes method. - - - Existing contour; ———— proposed contour; —·—·— existing contour to remain.

95

elevations, existing and proposed, it is not too difficult to locate exactly where there is a differential of 0, 1, 2, or 3 ft or other precise amount. This same method of showing tenth-foot contour locations will locate the peaks of fill (cut) and their vertical distance above or below the last whole-foot plane.

After each of the planes has been outlined, their respective enclosed areas can be measured with a planimeter. Keep the cut areas separated from the fill areas. Average plane area 0 and plane area 1 and multiply this average by the contour interval. Average planes 1 and 2, planes 2 and 3, etc. In each instance multiply by the contour interval to obtain the volume in each increment. The peak in each cut or fill area is 0 sq ft in area and is averaged against the next preceding plane's area and multiplied by the vertical distance (less than a contour interval). Record these areas in tabular form such as Fig. 7.11. Note that a separate tabular form is used for each cut and each fill area. Add all the fill increments together and divide by 27 to obtain cubic yards of fill. Add all the cut increments together and divide by 27 to obtain cubic yards of cut.

Earthwork computation

Plane	Area	Average	Int.	Volume	Plane	Area	Average	Int.	Volume

Plane	Area	Average	Int.	Volume	Plane	Area	Average	Int.	Volume

Fig. 7.11 Tabular form for earthwork computation by parallel-planes method.

Example 7.4 Figure 7.10 shows both existing and proposed contours at 1-ft intervals. This is the same topo map used in Figs. 7.1 and 7.6, only this time the earthwork is to be calculated by the use of the parallel-planes method. The lines of no-cut no-fill are first drawn in. These are the base planes of the parallel-planes method. They are called 0 planes. Within each 0 plane area, find the points of intersection of the existing and the proposed contours where there is a 1-ft differential. Connect these points to form an enclosed area. This is plane 1. Remember that the line enclosing any of these planes cannot cross either an existing or proposed contour except where they themselves cross each other at the differential represented by this enclosing line.

When running the enclosing line along a route more or less parallel to and in between the contours, it may be necessary to interpolate by tenth-foot contours to determine just where this line should be located. Figure 7.10 shows how the plane lines and the peak points were located by interpolation.

After the planes have been drawn on the topo map, use the planimeter to measure these areas. Do not mix the cut areas with the fill areas. Record as shown on the earthwork computation form, Fig. 7.11. After the cut and fill areas have been worked into square feet, calculations are set up in tabular form (Fig. 7.12) and the computations for volume are made.

Plane or station	First reading	Second reading	Average reading	Correction factor	Corrected reading, sq in.	Area, sq ft	
						Cut	Fill
Left Cut Area							
0	0491	0975	0487.5	0.984	4.80	12,000	
Right Cut Area							
0	2282	4567	2283.5	0.984	22.47	56,175	
1n	0048	0094	0047	0.984	0.462	1,155	
1s	0114	0227	0113.5	0.984	1.117	2,792.5	
Fill Area							
0	2808	5612	2806	0.984	27.61	. . . .	69,025
1	1053	2106	1053	0.984	10.36	. . . .	25,900
2	0049	0097	0048.5	0.984	0.48	. . . .	1,200

Fig. 7.12 Tabulation of earthwork computations by parallel-planes method. Scale: 1 in. = 50 ft; 1 sq in. = 2,500 sq ft. (*Continued on page 98.*)

Plane	Area, sq ft	Average area, sq ft	Interval, ft	Volume, cu ft
Left Cut Area				
0	12,000			
		6,000	0.2	1,200
Peak	0			
Right Cut Area				
0	56,175			
		30,061	1.0	30,061
$1n + 1s$	3,947.5			
$1n$	1,155			
		577.5	0.1	58
$Peak_n$	0			
$1s$	2,792.5			
		1,396	0.2	279
$Peak_s$	0			

Total cut = 31,598 cu ft,
or
1,170 cu yd

Plane	Area, sq ft	Average area, sq ft	Interval, ft	Volume, cu ft
Fill Area				
0	69,025			
		47,462.5	1.0	47,462.5
1	25,900			
		13,550	1.0	13,550
2	1,200			
		600	0.1	60
Peak	0			

Total fill = 61,072 cu ft,
or
2,262 cu yd

Fill = 2,262 cu yd
Cut = 1,170 cu yd
Balance = 1,092 cu yd fill

Fig. 7.12   (*Continued*)

CHAPTER EIGHT

Utilities

The term *utilities* in its general usage refers to public services provided by the community or a public service company franchised by the community. They include:

Water supply
Sanitary sewerage
Storm sewerage
Gas
Electricity
Telephone, telegraph, and TV cable
Public transportation
Heat and steam distribution (infrequent)

8.1 GENERAL

The underground utilities are of primary concern in the development plans for a site. These include water supply, gas, and sanitary and storm sewers. Steam distribution is usually underground, but occurs so infrequently that it will not be considered here. Telephone, electricity, etc., can be either overhead or underground, but are usually sufficiently flexible so as to cause no problem. The water and sewer lines are usually quite limited as to where and how they may be located, and it is important to check all land-use proposals in relation to economical and efficient provisions for these services. The design of underground utilities is usually accomplished by a professional engineer, but for advantageous collaboration with the consultant engineer on the project, the landscape architect should understand the basics involved. Always check with local authorities relative to codes, ordinances, and other regulations concerning utilities.

8.2   WATER DISTRIBUTION

The water distribution system includes all mains, lateral lines, standpipes, reservoirs, pumping stations, gates, meters, and service connections. The reservoirs may be basins, standpipes, or storage tanks located at high elevations in the system. A service reservoir should be of sufficient capacity to hold at least one day's supply and maintain the total number of fire streams for a period of from 6 to 10 hr. Standards such as this, the minimum pipe size and pressure feeding fire hydrants, and the spacing of fire hydrants have been established for various sizes of towns and classes of insurance ratings by insurance underwriters.

Modern fire pumpers can actually pump smaller water mains dry. It is advisable to have hydrants supplied by at least 6-in. mains from two directions. Master schemes in some of the larger cities and metropolitan areas indicate 12-in. feeder mains ½ mile apart with alternating 6- and 8-in. lines cross-connecting between them.

In lieu of other underwriter standards, fire hydrants should be about 200 ft apart in heavily built-up areas such as commercial and high-rise-apartment districts. In residential one- and two-family districts, the hydrants should be about 500 or 600 ft apart. Two hydrants should be available for any fire, the longest hose run from any hydrant being not over 500 feet to reach the furthermost dwelling in any service area.

The type and extent of growth and development should be anticipated in the layout of the system so as to avoid expensive future changes. Public water mains should always be located within street rights-of-way or other accessible publicly controlled land or easements.

Waterlines must be laid at such depths as to prevent freezing. These depths are usually specified by local regulations. Since waterlines are under pressure, they can be laid uphill and downhill. They should be laid at such distances from sewer lines as to prevent possible contamination of the water. At least 10 ft of horizontal separation is recommended, and wherever possible the waterline should be at a higher elevation than the adjacent sewer.

Fundamentally, the water starts out from a municipal main, an elevated storage tank, or a pressure tank of known pressure (head). As the water moves through the pipe to its outlet point, it loses pressure counteracting friction with the interior walls of the pipe and fittings such as elbows, tees, wyes, etc. The friction loss in the pipe varies with the size of the pipe, the condition and the material of which the pipe is made, the design of the pipe, the volume and velocity of the flow in the pipe, and the length of the run of pipe. The determination of pipe size is basically a matter of selecting pipe of such size and layout that the losses in the pipe will not reduce the volume and residual pressure to less than that required to satisfy the critical need.

The losses for flow through pipes are commonly derived by using the Hazen and Williams formula

$$V = 1.318Cr^{0.63}S^{0.54}$$

where V = velocity, fps
C = coefficient of pipe smoothness
r = hydraulic radius, ft
S = hydraulic slope, ft per ft of length

This is a complicated formula to use, but the relationships have been worked into special slide rules, nomographs, and charts which greatly simplify its application.

The losses in pressure are expressed as pounds per square inch (psi) or as feet of head. They can be converted from one to the other by the following formulas:

Feet of head $\times$ 0.4335 = pounds per square inch
Pounds per square inch $\times$ 2.307 = feet of head

The feet of head refers to the height in feet of a column of water. A column of water of a certain height will always produce a pressure per square inch of 0.4335 lb for each ft of column height.

Engineering books on water supply and distribution, as well as engineering handbooks, contain curves for head losses for various flows through different kinds and diameters of pipe. These books also have charts or tables giving head losses through the various kinds of pipe fittings and valves. These head losses are expressed in terms of equivalent lengths of pipe of the same size.

The selection of pipe size in a water system is generally determined by the highest demand required of the system. In municipal work the fire demand is the critical control, and this is also often the case for country clubs, campus developments, commercial developments, and industrial sites. If the site waterlines are extensions of a municipal system, local regulations and controls should be checked. A typical requirement is a 50-psi residual pressure at the fire hydrant. Even if the water system is to be private, local regulations and controls should be followed as closely as possible; e.g., fire hydrants should open with the same wrench and direction of rotation and have the same hose thread pitch and diameter as the local fire departments use.

In other cases where buildings are minimal or where fire hazard is not a consideration, the critical demand could be for sprinkler irrigation. Chapter 10, on sprinkler irrigation, discusses the considerations and problems of water distribution for that need.

8.3 SANITARY-SEWER LINES

Sanitary-sewer lines are not under pressure and must be laid on a slope to provide gravity flow. The sewer system must be related to the slope of the basic topography since the piping could get inordinately deep if laid counter to the natural fall of the land. Standards for the design of sanitary sewers are established by state and local regulations. In the Midwest, the health departments of 10 states have joined together to set standards for sanitary sewers and sewage treatment, referred to as the "Ten States Standards." They are on file both at state health departments and other departments having jurisdiction over such matters. Usually, the state has review and approval over public improvements being done by counties, townships, and municipalities, and the local community has review and approval powers over private development.

Basically, the slope of the sanitary-sewer pipes should provide a self-cleaning velocity of $2\frac{1}{4}$ fps (feet per second). It is often impossible to avoid developing deep cuts (over $25 \pm$ ft) as a sewer is extended at self-cleaning gradients. At such points it becomes necessary to install lift (pumping) stations. Lift stations are to be avoided as much as possible because they are a continuous maintenance problem. They must be inspected and checked out regularly and should be equipped with automatic switchover standby power service and standby pumps to take care of emergencies.

The minimum depth at which sanitary sewers should be installed varies with the soil conditions, climate, and other technical considerations. A common rule is a minimum depth of $9\frac{1}{2}$ ft so as to permit the service connection from the basement of a house or other building to operate on gravity flow.

There should be no roof-runoff, surface, or other storm-drainage connections to the sanitary-sewer system. If this precaution were not observed, the size of the piping would have to be greatly increased and the volume of water going through the treatment plant would require a much larger plant and would otherwise upset the treatment process during heavy rains.

Sanitary-sewer house connections are usually 4- or 6-in.-diameter pipe. The larger size is preferable. Lateral lines should not be less than 8 in., and in many communities 10 in. is the preferred minimum size.

Note that the pipe system for sewers is called *sewerage,* and the material sewers carry is called *sewage*.

8.4   STORM SEWERS

Storm sewers are usually not under pressure and are laid at a slope to provide gravity flow. They are laid slightly steeper than sanitary sewers, i.e., a velocity of $2\frac{1}{2}$ versus $2\frac{1}{4}$ fps for sanitary sewers. Just as in designing sanitary sewers, the storm-sewer system must be related to the topography, since it could get inordinately deep if laid counter to the natural fall of the land.

Modern sewer systems do not combine sanitary and storm flows in one pipe; they are always separate piping systems. Storm sewers are designed to carry off storm water and are sized to carry the peak rate of rainfall for the design interval (frequency) selected for the location.

Landscape architects are involved in the shaping of the land and are concerned with the swales, ditches, and storm piping necessary to take care of the storm runoff developed by the shaping of the land and the site improvement. Since these items are of vital importance in the architecture of the site, Chap. 9 deals further with storm runoff and the sizing of storm piping, ditches, and swales.

CHAPTER NINE

Storm Drainage

Rainfall records have been kept for many years, and it has been found that rains of great intensity occur less frequently than rains of lesser intensity. It has also been found that the intensity of a rainfall is greatest in the early part of the rain and becomes less intense as the duration of the rainfall continues. Most large municipalities, the Weather Bureau, and the U.S. Dept. of Agriculture have records and other data available concerning the intensity, duration, and frequency of rainfall. See Figs. 9.1 and 9.2.

9.1 STORM RUNOFF

The accumulation of storm water on a site can become inconvenient, even in small quantities, if not drained away. In large quantities, accumulated storm water can make the site unusable and in flood situations can become dangerous and costly. The design of storm-water drainage is of utmost importance in any site-improvement plan.

A number of methods are used for estimating storm runoff. At best the formulas are only approximations. There are too many factors peculiar to any one piece of ground that cannot be accounted for in any formula.   All the formulas for runoff include considerations of intensity of the rainfall, duration of the rainfall, and a runoff coefficient.

Intensity is the rate at which rain falls for a given period of time.   This is expressed in inches per hour.   One inch of rainfall on one acre of ground in one hour amounts to 1.0083 cubic feet per second (cfs).   For practical purposes one inch of rainfall in one hour is considered as one cubic foot per second per acre.

Duration is the time period during which rain falls at a given rate. This is usually expressed in minutes.

Runoff coefficient refers to the percentage of the rainfall that actually reaches the drainage structure or ditch.   Not all the rain falling on the ground will reach the drainage system.   Part will be absorbed by the earth, part will be impounded by irregularities in the ground surface, and part will evaporate, cling to leaves, stems, branches, etc.   The water that does reach the drainage system is called the *runoff*.

Table 9.1 gives the average runoff coefficient for some types of surfacing.

The average period of time within which rainfall of a certain intensity and duration can be expected to recur is referred to as *frequency*, usually expressed in years.   Figure 9.2 shows typical probability curves for rainfall in the North Central United States.   Curves are shown for storms

TABLE 9.1

| | Runoff coefficient | |
Surface	Percent	As a ratio
Roofs	95	0.95
Concrete and asphalt	95	0.95
Bituminous and macadam	80	0.80
Gravel		
Loose	30	0.30
Compact	70	0.70
Land		
Unimproved	50	0.50
Barren	75	0.75
Light plant growth	60	0.60
Wooded	20	0.20
Parks, golf courses, lawns	35	0.35
Suburban residential	45	0.45
Urban dense residential	60	0.60

NOTE: These coefficients are based on 2 to 4 percent slopes.   Lesser slopes will reduce the coefficients by as much as 50 percent for pervious areas and 5 to 10 percent for impervious areas during the first hour of rainfall.

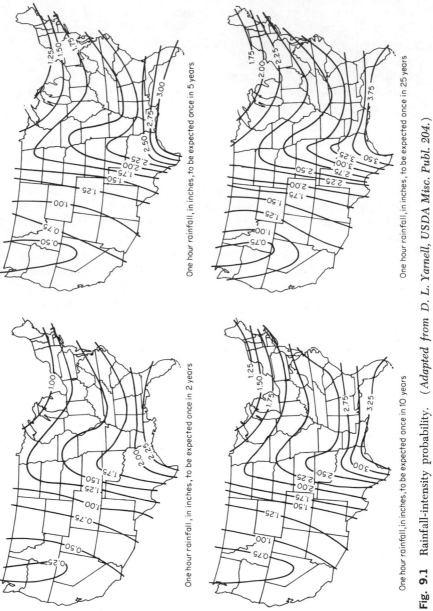

One hour rainfall, in inches, to be expected once in 5 years

One hour rainfall, in inches, to be expected once in 25 years

One hour rainfall, in inches, to be expected once in 2 years

One hour rainfall, in inches, to be expected once in 10 years

Fig. 9.1 Rainfall-intensity probability. (*Adapted from D. L. Yarnell, USDA Misc. Publ. 204.*)

recurring on an average of 1, 5, 10, 20, 50, and 100 years. The storms of 1-year frequency are of much less intensity than the storms occurring at a 10-year frequency, etc. The selection of the frequency of the storm on which the design is to be based is a matter of judgment. The cost of the larger pipes to accommodate a rainfall that will occur once in a century is justified only when there is risk of great economic loss or damage. Economics must also be considered in determining the relative merits of designing to accommodate lesser storms of 2, 5, or 10 years frequency. In many cases the municipal drain authority having jurisdiction in the area will stipulate the rainfall frequency that the drainage system must be designed to accommodate. In situations where local rainfall data are not available, the data shown in Fig. 9.1 are sufficiently accurate to meet most needs.

The problem in the design of drainage systems is not so much concerned with the total amount of water to be accommodated as with the peak rate. Drainage structures, whether pipe or ditch, must be designed to handle peak rates of runoff.

One of the basic assumptions is that the design storm selected will be of a duration great enough to allow water to be arriving at the outlet of the drainage area simultaneously from all parts of the watershed. This is called the *time of concentration* (TOC).

The time of concentration is the time interval required for water to

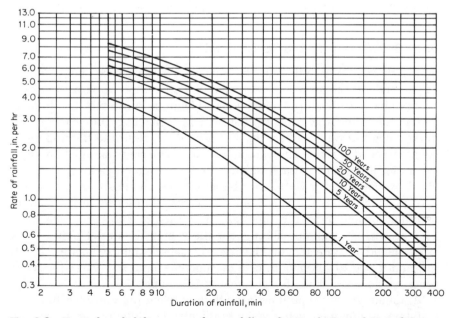

Fig. 9.2 Typical probability curves for rainfall in the North Central United States.

flow from the most remote point of the watershed to the drainage-area outlet. It is composed of the time required for the overland flow to reach the inlet (called the *inlet time*) plus the time required for the flow in the pipe to go from the inlet to the outlet.

Charts and formulas have been developed for approximating overland flow time (inlet time). One such nomograph is published in the section on drainage in E. E. Seelye's "Data Book for Civil Engineers," volume 1. This source will help in judging inlet time, but at best it is only an estimate. Considering all the indefiniteness of rainfall and runoff characteristics, *the use of 15 or 20 min inlet time will provide a satisfactory solution in most site design situations.*

The length of the pipe or ditch from the inlet point to the outlet point divided by the average velocity of the flow in the pipe or ditch will give the time of flow in the pipe or ditch. This added to the inlet time will give the time of concentration.

Whether the drainage system is to be underground (i.e., pipes) or on the surface (i.e., swales or ditches), the so-called *rational formula* is generally used to determine volume of runoff:

$$Q = CiA \qquad \text{also expressed as} \qquad Q = AiR$$

where Q = runoff, cfs

A = area drained, acres

i = intensity of rainfall, in. per hr

C or R = a coefficient expressing the ratio of runoff to rainfall

9.2   SELECTING THE SIZE OF PIPE

When the storm runoff is to be carried away in pipe, begin at the upper end of the drainage system and outline the subarea that will be draining into the uppermost inlet. Continue on down the drainage system, outlining the subarea that will be collecting into each of the inlets along the way. When this has been done, return to the uppermost subarea and determine the volume of water entering this inlet by using the rational formula. Each subarea is so computed, and the pipe is sized by the use of a Kutter or Manning pipe flow chart or nomograph.

At junction points the flow from all the contributing subareas is added together to determine the pipe size necessary to carry the total flow. This process is continued throughout the run to the outlet point. Pipe sizes should be selected on the basis of self-cleaning velocities of $2\frac{1}{2}$ fps, and $n = 0.10$ for smooth clay or concrete pipe, $n = 0.013$ for rough concrete, and $n = 0.015$ for corrugated iron pipe.

Maximum gravity pipe flows are attained when pipes are 0.8 full. To maintain an unimpeded hydraulic gradient (the slope of the upper surface of the water in the pipes), inverts (the bottom inside of the pipe) are set to maintain the 0.8 diameter of the pipe at a consistent gradient. In practice, this is accomplished by keeping the crowns of the pipes level at points where pipe size changes.

Figure 9.3 shows a catch basin and a drain inlet. The catch basin has a sump built into it that acts as a settling well. The drain inlet does not have a settling basin and allows water to flow directly into the drain line. The sump well in the catch basin will fill up with sediment and debris and must be cleaned out from time to time. It is recommended that inlets, rather than catch basins, be used in all areas that cannot be readily reached and maintained with cleaning equipment, since any sump well will soon fill up, no longer acting as a settling basin, and the debris collected in such a catch basin will have organic matter in it that will soon start to decay and give off foul odors. It is much better to use drain inlets and let the storm water carry the sediment and debris to the discharge outlet.

Pipe leads from inlets and catch basins should preferably connect to the main storm line at manholes. Manholes are usually about 4 ft in diameter, corbeled in at the top to 2 ft, and have built-in ladder steps to provide access to the sewer by workmen. Manholes are placed at all changes in sewer alignment, at all changes in pipe diameters and gradients, at all junction points, and at distances not exceeding 400 ft apart along all lines (except where pipes are large enough for workmen to get through). The 400-ft limitation is the limit of most sewer-cleaning apparatus. In some municipalities this distance may be

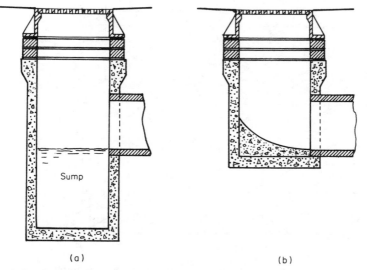

(a)   (b)

Fig. 9.3 Sections through (a) catch basin and (b) drain inlet.

reduced to 300 ft due to the limitations of the local sewer cleaning and rodding equipment.

The elevations of manhole covers and drainage grates are shown on the grading plan. These are repeated on the utility plan, which also shows the pipe diameter, length of run from center of manhole to center of manhole, pipe slope, and invert elevations. The cover and rim elevations are determined by the grading plan, and the elevations shown are those determined by the grading in the areas. It is good practice to have a general note on both the grading and the utility plan stating that catch basins and inlet grates shall be set 0.2 ft lower than the elevation called for on the plan. This is to ensure positive drainage

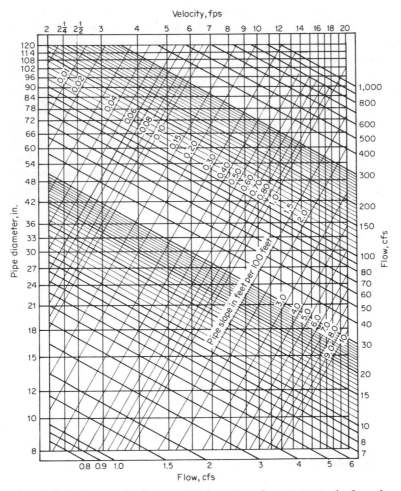

Fig. 9.4 Flow in circular sewer pipes, based on Manning's formula $n = 0.012$.

into the inlet by the warping of grassed or paved areas in the vicinity of the drain grate. This is particularly necessary in sag vertical curves in roads and parking areas where the parabolic shape inherently tends to be virtually flat at the bottom of the curve. Brass and bronze inlet covers, 8 in. and less in diameter, such as are used in terrazzo and other fine-finished mall and patio areas, and drain grates in paved play areas are usually set only 0.02 to 0.05 ft low.

The diameters and slopes of storm-drainage pipes are determined by using charts based on either the Kutter or the Manning formula. The Manning formula, being more convenient, is more generally used. Figure 9.4 is based on the Manning formula, using a pipe-smoothness coefficient of $n = 0.012$. To use the chart, enter from the lower right at the "cfs" the pipe must carry. Follow the diagonal line toward the upper left until the vertical line representing $2\frac{1}{2}$-fps velocity is reached. Select the pipe size at this intersection or the next higher on the velocity line. The slope of the pipe thus selected is shown by the line sloping toward the upper right. Smaller pipe may be selected when they can be laid at a steeper slope in order to handle the volume if there is no problem of getting too deep into the ground with the sewer line.

Example 9.1

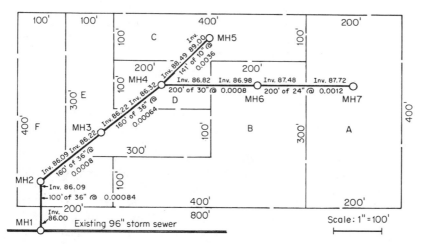

Fig. 9.5 Plan of proposed storm sewer.

1. Assume all manholes (MH) are inlet manholes with rim elevations of 100.00.
2. Assume no surface runoff either to or from adjacent property.
3. Design for a 10-year rain.
4. Minimum cover over pipe shall be 10 feet.
5. Use $n = 0.012$ and pipe slope to develop a velocity of $2\frac{1}{2}$ fps.
6. *Area A* is commercial (stores and blacktop parking) at an average

surface slope of 2.5 percent. *Area B* is multiple-family (25 percent building coverage, 25 percent streets, parking, and walks, and 50 percent lawn area) at an average surface slope of 2 percent. *Area C* is also multiple-family (same as area *B*). *Area D* is a play area (50 percent gravel, 50 percent grass) at 2 percent slope. *Area E* is parking (concrete pavement) at 3 percent surface slope. *Area F* is wooded with a surface slope of 1.5 percent.

PROBLEM: Figure runoff and size of pipe and give pipe slope and invert grades.

SOLUTION: The inlet time for area *A* works out to be about 6 min using an overland-flow time chart. Use 15 min, as suggested at the end of Sec. 9.1. Checking Fig. 9.2 for the intensity curve for a 10-year rain, find an intensity of 4.2 in. per hr for a 10-year rain after 15 min duration. Using 200×200 ft as an acre, this area is 2 acres. The coefficient of runoff for a commercial area is 0.95. Then

$$Q_A = CiA$$
$$= 0.95 \times 4.2 \times 2 = 7.98 \text{ cfs}$$

This requires a 24-in pipe at 0.0012 slope (from Fig. 9.4).

The distance from manhole 7 to manhole 6 is 200 ft. At a velocity of 2½ fps, it takes 80 sec, or 1⅓ min, time in the pipe to arrive at manhole 6.

This is 16⅓ min after the storm began.

Area *B* is multiple-family, with a runoff coefficient of 0.65 and an area of 2 acres. The intensity *i*, 16⅓ min after the storm began, is 4 in. per hr on the 10-year curve on the chart. Then

$$Q_B = CiA$$
$$= 0.65 \times 4.0 \times 2 = 5.20 \text{ cfs}$$

The pipe out of manhole 6 must carry all the water arriving from manhole 7 plus all the runoff from area *B*, that is, $7.98 + 5.20$ cfs, or a total of 13.18 cfs.

This requires a 30-in. pipe at 0.0008 slope.

This flow arrives at manhole 4 at 17⅔ min after the storm started (16⅓ min + 80 sec in pipe = 17⅔ min).

Area *D* is a playground with a runoff coefficient of 0.52 $[(0.70 + 0.35)/2 = 0.52]$ and an area of 0.5 acre. From the 10-year curve, the intensity *i* is 3.8 in. per hr at 17⅔ min into the storm. Then

$$Q_D = CiA$$
$$= 0.52 \times 3.8 \times 0.5 = 0.99 \text{ cfs}$$

But at this same time, storm water is arriving from area *C*. The length of pipe from area *C* is $140 \pm$ ft, so at a velocity of 2½ fps it took 56 sec for this water to run through the pipe from *C*. The water now arriving at *D* from *C* is rain that landed on *C* 56 sec earlier, or 16⅔ min after the storm started.

Area C is 1 acre, and the intensity i is 3.9 in. per hr at 16⅔ min into the storm. Then

$$Q_C = CiA$$
$$= 0.65 \times 3.9 \times 1 = 2.54 \text{ cfs}$$

and the pipe out of manhole 4 must carry $13.18 + 0.99 + 2.54$ cfs, or a total of 16.71 cfs. This requires a 36-in. pipe at 0.00064 slope.

The length of pipe to manhole 3 is 160± ft, which will equal 64 sec time in the pipe at a velocity of 2½ fps. This means that the flow will arrive at manhole 3 18⅔ min (17⅔ min + 64 sec = 18⅔ min) after the storm began. The intensity 18⅔ min after the storm began is 3.7 in. per hr for a 10-year storm.

Area E is parking with a runoff coefficient of 0.95. It has an area of 1¼ acres. Then

$$Q_E = CiA$$
$$= 0.95 \times 3.7 \times 1.25 = 4.39 \text{ cfs}$$

and the pipe out of manhole 3 must carry $16.71 + 4.39$ cfs, or 21.10 cfs.

This requires a 36-in. pipe at 0.0008 slope.

The 160 ft of pipe to manhole 2 will add 64 sec to the 18⅔ min to become 19⅔ min. The intensity at 19⅔ min after the storm began is 3.6 in. per hr.

Area F is wooded with a runoff coefficient of 0.20. It has an area of 1¼ acres. Then

$$Q_F = 0.20 \times 3.6 \times 1¼ = 0.90 \text{ cfs}$$

and the pipe out of manhole 2 must carry $21.10 + 0.90$ cfs, or 22 cfs.

This requires a 36-in. pipe at 0.00084 slope.

You will note that the slope of the pipe has been called out in feet of slope per foot of pipe length. For example, 24-in. pipe at 0.0008 means a 0.0008-ft drop in each foot of pipe run between manholes 6 and 4. This could also be expressed as 0.08 percent, meaning 0.08 ft of drop in each 100 ft of pipe run between manholes 6 and 4.

Figure 9.6 shows a convenient tabular form for storm sewer design calculations.

9.3 SWALES AND DITCHES

In Sec. 4.3 we discussed grading criteria for swales and ditches. The shape and size are dependent on the volume of storm water that must be accommodated. The quantity of runoff from a drainage area is figured by using the rational formula, the same as in the first step of determining the diameter of storm pipe needed.

Once the discharge requirement in cubic feet per second has been

Location			Area			Time of flow			i	Q		Design					Profile				
Area	From	To	Increment	Total	C	To inlet	In pipe	TOC		Increment	Total	Diam.	Slope	Capacity	Velocity, fps	Length, ft	Fall, ft	Other losses	Inverts In	Out

Fig. 9.6 Tabular form for storm-drainage design summary.

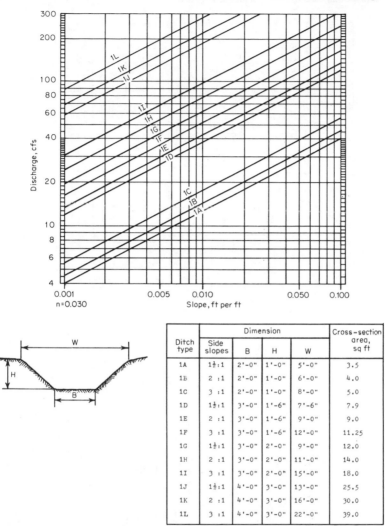

Ditch type	Dimension				Cross-section area, sq ft
	Side slopes	B	H	W	
1A	1½:1	2'-0"	1'-0"	5'-0"	3.5
1B	2 :1	2'-0"	1'-0"	6'-0"	4.0
1C	3 :1	2'-0"	1'-0"	8'-0"	5.0
1D	1½:1	3'-0"	1'-6"	7'-6"	7.9
1E	2 :1	3'-0"	1'-6"	9'-0"	9.0
1F	3 :1	3'-0"	1'-6"	12'-0"	11.25
1G	1½:1	3'-0"	2'-0"	9'-0"	12.0
1H	2 :1	3'-0"	2'-0"	11'-0"	14.0
1I	3 :1	3'-0"	2'-0"	15'-0"	18.0
1J	1½:1	4'-0"	3'-0"	13'-0"	25.5
1K	2 :1	4'-0"	3'-0"	16'-0"	30.0
1L	3 :1	4'-0"	3'-0"	22'-0"	39.0

Fig. 9.7 Ditch flow capacity.

determined, go to Figs. 9.7, 9.8, and/or 9.9, rather than Fig. 9.4, which was used for pipe sizing. Select a ditch or swale from any one of the three charts on the basis of the desired shape and the required discharge capacity.

Enter the chart with a horizontal line across the chart at the required discharge capacity in cubic feet per second. Enter from the bottom of the chart at the hydraulic slope of the ditch or swale with a vertical line. Select the ditch at or just above the point where this vertical line intersects the previously entered horizontal line.

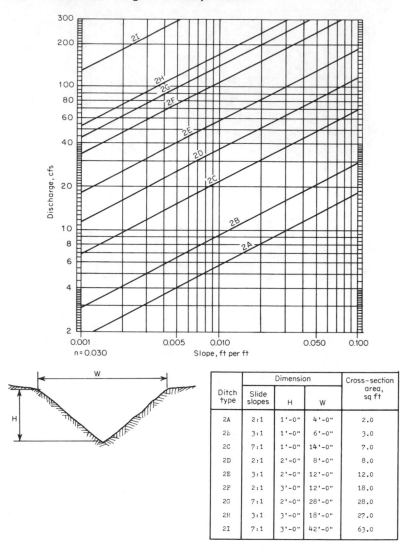

Fig. 9.8   Ditch flow capacity.

Ditch type	Slide slopes	Dimension		Cross-section area, sq ft
		H	W	
2A	2:1	1'-0"	4'-0"	2.0
2B	3:1	1'-0"	6'-0"	3.0
2C	7:1	1'-0"	14'-0"	7.0
2D	2:1	2'-0"	8'-0"	8.0
2E	3:1	2'-0"	12'-0"	12.0
2F	2:1	3'-0"	12'-0"	18.0
2G	7:1	2'-0"	28'-0"	28.0
2H	3:1	3'-0"	18'-0"	27.0
2I	7:1	3'-0"	42'-0"	63.0

The selected swale or ditch should be checked for velocity by using the formula

$$V = \frac{Q}{A}$$

where V = velocity, fps
A = cross-section area, sq ft
Q = flow, cfs

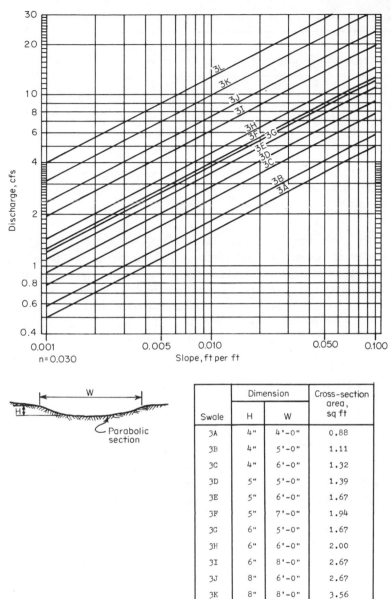

	Dimension		Cross-section area, sq ft
Swale	H	W	
3A	4"	4'-0"	0.88
3B	4"	5'-0"	1.11
3C	4"	6'-0"	1.32
3D	5"	5'-0"	1.39
3E	5"	6'-0"	1.67
3F	5"	7'-0"	1.94
3G	6"	5'-0"	1.67
3H	6"	6'-0"	2.00
3I	6"	8'-0"	2.67
3J	8"	6'-0"	2.67
3K	8"	8'-0"	3.56
3L	8"	10'-0"	4.44

Fig. 9.9 Swale flow capacity.

TABLE 9.2

Swale or ditch surfacing	Maximum allowable velocities, fps
Grassed channels	4
Ungrouted riprap	8
Grouted riprap and bituminous paving	15
Concrete and solid rock	Not limited

Excessive velocities in the swale or ditch will cause scouring and will erode the channel. Table 9.2 gives the average velocities considered safe maximums.

Earth and Turf Channels

The capacities of the swales and ditches in these charts are based on smooth mowed grass or clean smooth earth at $n = 0.030$. If some weeds or stones are expected to be present or the ditch or swale not maintained in good condition ($n = 0.040$), assume that it will carry about 75 percent as much volume. In other words, start out your calculations by adding 33 percent to the discharge-volume requirement.

Rubble-lined Channels

If the ditch is lined with dry rubble, it will carry only about 90 percent of the volume on the chart; so start your calculations by adding 11 percent to the discharge-volume requirement.

Concrete-lined Channels

If the ditch is lined with smooth concrete or asphalt ($n = 0.015$), it will carry about twice as much as the volume shown on the chart; so start your calculations using 50 percent of the discharge-volume requirement.

CHAPTER TEN

Sprinkler Irrigation Systems

Landscape-maintenance labor costs have risen to a point where underground sprinkler irrigation systems are the most economical method of landscape irrigation. The designing of such systems has become a part of the landscape architect's work.

The sprinkler-irrigation designer proceeds by first drawing an accurately scaled plan of the site showing:

1. All property lines—north point, scale, etc.
2. Contours and elevations
3. Structures, including buildings, decks, patios, pools, drives, walks, and fences
4. Area uses
5. Vegetation—trees, shrubs, hedges, planters, gardens, lawns, etc., noting water requirements
6. Utility locations—water, gas, sewer, telephone, electricity, etc.
7. Any other pertinent on-site or off-site structures or conditions

It is also necessary to know:

1. Soil character—particularly the porosity of the soil and the water-retention characteristics

2. Climate
   A. Prevailing winds—direction and velocity
   B. Humidity and rainfall characteristics
3. Water supply
   A. Source—well, reservoir, lake, pond, or municipal supply
   B. Available flow and pressure
4. Owner's requirements and desires

These items are all essentials necessary to the process of designing any sprinkler irrigation system.

10.1 SELECTING THE TYPE OF SYSTEM

In a broad sense there are three basic design concepts for sprinkler irrigation systems:

1. The *quick-coupling system,* where all the underground lines are under pressure and sprinkler heads or hose connections are manually inserted to open a quick-coupling valve to water any area selected by the operator.

2. The *section system,* or *block system,* where one control valve operates a section of several sprinkler heads. The valve controls for each section can be manually or automatically and sequentially operated by a timer control.

3. The remotely controlled *individually valved sprinkler heads,* where sprinklers in diverse areas having similar watering requirements can be run at the same time or where water supply permits running only one sprinkler at a time.

The type of land use, the irrigation needs of the property, the needs and desires of the owner, the economics of the installation, and the characteristics of the available water supply all work together to determine which of the above three systems or combination thereof should be used. The quick-coupling system has the lowest installation cost, but the labor required to place, move, and collect the insertable quick-coupling sprinklers makes the operational cost the highest. The section, or block, system is intermediate in installation costs. The individually valved sprinklers, remotely controlled, are the most costly for installation. A combination of any two systems, and sometimes a combination of all three systems, is often found to provide the best answer to the question of system selection.

A golf course is a typical example of a situation where all three basic design concepts could very well be utilized to satisfy all irrigation requirements. In most cases the fairways, greens, and tees would be automatically watered, but the roughs could have quick-coupling devices so that some distinctive vegetation could be watered as the special needs of that vegetation dictated, or perhaps the rough would need watering only during a dry year. For such infrequent use, it would not be economically sound to install a section system or the individually valved sprinkler heads.

10.2   SELECTING SPRINKLER HEADS

Once the type of system has been selected, the next step is to make a trial selection of sprinkler heads at spacings determined by the watering requirements of the vegetation, the soil-absorption characteristics, and the available supply flow and pressure.

Sprinkler heads are of two basic types, spray and rotary heads. Spray heads are either of a pop-up type or a fixed (non-pop-up) type, either surface-mounted or on a riser stem. Rotary heads are either a pop-up type or non-pop-up type permanently mounted on a riser or demountable as a quick-coupling rotating spray nozzle.

Spray heads operate at low pressure—15- to 35-psi (pounds per square inch) range. They cover small areas 20 to 40 ft in diameter and apply water at a high rate (1 to 2 in. per hr). They are most efficiently used for small turf areas and in areas of irregular shape.

Rotary heads operate at a higher pressure—30 to 90 psi. They cover larger areas, 80 to 200 ft in diameter, but they apply water at a low rate (0.10 to 0.50 in. per hr). They are referred to as *geared, cam,* or *impulse heads,* depending on the type of rotating mechanism used. Rotary sprinklers are most efficiently used on large open turf areas. All three types of heads can cover full or partial circles. The geared head can be two-speed, adjusted to move at a fast rate through overlap segments and at a slow rate in the nonoverlap segment of the watering circle.

Do not mix the spray heads and rotary types of sprinklers in the same section. In any section the application rate should be relatively the same for each head in the section; otherwise parts of the area covered will be overwatered or underwatered. If half-circle heads are used in the same section as full-circle heads, it is necessary to select half-circle heads with the same rate of application as the full-circle heads; otherwise zone the half-circle heads separately. Other part-circle heads must be selected having discharges proportionate to the area covered. This also applies to the selection of specialty heads such as bubblers, jets, and shrub heads. Select heads with application rates as nearly equal to the rest of the heads in the section as possible.

Within any given section the design should be such that the operating pressure between the first and last sprinkler head in the section will be within the manufacturer's recommended pressure limitations for satisfactory operation of the system.

In selecting sprinkler heads, remember that each of the various models of heads has an ideal operating pressure. Pressures that are too low give poor water distribution, and pressures that are too high tend to mist, with resulting wind drift and uneven coverage. In addition to the operating pressure, other considerations when selecting the type and size of sprinkler heads are the size and shape of the area, the number and type of obstructions, the volume of flow available, the maximum permissible rate of application for the type of soil, and any special kind of plants or vegetation.

10.3   ARRANGEMENT AND SPACING OF SPRINKLER HEADS

The type and size of sprinkler heads selected will dictate to a large extent the pattern and spacing of the heads.   Sprinkler heads are usually set in a geometrical pattern, either rectangular or triangular.   In most instances a triangular pattern seems to work out best.   In some cases both square and triangular patterns are used, a hybrid transitional pattern being worked out where the two patterns join.   Any pattern not having consistent spacing between sprinkler heads tends to result in uneven water coverage.

Each sprinkler head covers a circular spray area, the heaviest distribution of water being at the center nearest the sprinkler, gradually reducing to zero at the peripheral circumference of the spray area.   To obtain an even distribution of water, it is necessary to overlap the spray areas of adjacent sprinklers.   The pattern of distribution varies with the different types of sprinkler heads and with the different designs of the various manufacturers.   It is essential that the manufacturer's recommended spacing be followed to obtain an even distribution of water.   In lieu of the manufacturer's recommended spacing, the following spacing is suggested:

   60% of diameter of coverage where wind is 0–5 mph
   50% of diameter of coverage where wind is 5–10 mph
   40% of diameter of coverage where wind is over 10 mph

It is common practice to use the 60 percent of diameter in most designs, and this spacing is used between heads in a row and between rows in square patterns.   In triangular spacing, the distance between heads in a row is the same, but the rows are spaced at 86 percent of that distance.   See Fig. 10.1.

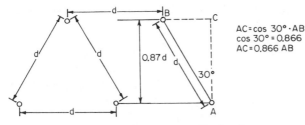

Fig. 10.1   Triangular spacing of sprinkler heads.

In no case should the spacing between heads and between rows be increased beyond the manufacturer's recommendations or the 60 percent of diameter.   If the area is not fully covered in the trial run, add an extra head to each row and prorate the overall row length equally between the increased number of heads; and if the number of rows does not fully cover the area, add an extra row and prorate the overall distance equally between the increased number of rows.   In each case the distance between sprinkler heads is reduced from the trial-run distance.   In some cases it may be necessary to make a new sprinkler-head selection.

10.4   DIVIDING THE SYSTEM INTO SECTIONS

After the sprinkler-head-pattern selection has been made, the next step is to divide the system into sections.   In doing this there are two situations to consider:

1. When the supply flow is fixed by the size of the pump, or by the service line and meter if on a city water main

2. When the supply flow is not limited because the pump size or, if on a municipal system, the service line and meter are yet to be selected

In the first situation, the system must be divided into sections (blocks), each having a gallon-per-minute (gpm) demand not exceeding that of the supply source.   If the available watering time permits it, the number of heads per section can be reduced, thus making more sections, but in no instance can the gallon-per-minute demand of any section be made greater than the available volume.

In the second situation, where the water supply is not limited by the capacity (gpm) of existing pumps or by the size of the existing service line and meter, the usual procedure in dividing the system into sections is to make the following determinations:

1. The application rate of sprinklers, in inches of precipitation per hour.

2. The watering demand of each situation during the driest season, in inches of precipitation per week

3. The maximum available time for watering

The application rate of sprinklers is given in the manufacturer's catalog either as gallons per minute or as inches of precipitation per hour when placed at the manufacturer's prescribed spacing. If the application rate is given in gallons per minute, the rate of precipitation can be found by using the following formula:

$$\text{Inches precipitation per hour} = \frac{96.26 \times \text{gpm of 1 sprinkler}}{\text{spacing in rows} \times \text{spacing between rows}}$$

The amount of precipitation required for most turf and shrubbery is approximately 1 in. per week in moderate climates and 1¾ in. per week in warm climates. Golf courses in moderate climates require a weekly precipitation of approximately 1 in. on fairways and up to 2 in. on greens. In order to better visualize these application rates, a 1-in. rain is equivalent to about 625 gal per 1,000 sq ft of turf or to a sprinkler covering 1,000 sq ft running full flow at the end of a 50-ft hose on city water pressure for 2 hr.

When the amount of precipitation in inches per week required by the turf or vegetation during the driest season is divided by the rate in inches per hour applied by the sprinklers, the answer will be the number of hours each sprinkler must run each week. Convert this to minutes by multiplying by 60, and divide by 7 to find the number of minutes each sprinkler must run each day. Usually there is a limitation on the hours during which watering can be done. By dividing the number of sprinkler minutes available each day by the number of minutes each sprinkler must run, the number of sections (blocks) can be found. If the answer comes out with a fractional part of a section, discard the fraction and use the whole number as the number of sections.

The number of heads per section can be found by dividing the total number of equivalent heads by the number of sections. The term *equivalent heads* means the number of heads expressed as units of any selected head; i.e., if a head applying 20 gpm is called a unit, then a head applying 10 gpm is called 0.5 unit and a head applying 5 gpm is called 0.25 unit. If the answer comes out with a fraction, discard the fraction and spread the leftover heads among any convenient sections as evenly as possible. Another way to make the sections as equal as possible is to total the gpm demand of all the heads in the system and divide by the number of sections to obtain the gpm demand per section. Then put together enough heads of whatever gpm demand to total the gpm demand for a section.   Remember that all heads in any one section should have the same rate of application (precipitation).

The purpose in keeping the gpm demand for all sections as nearly equal as possible is to make the gpm demand on the supply as constant as possible.   Select a pump that will provide the gallons per minute equal to that of the section having the greatest gallons-per-minute demand.

Example 10.1   Assume that the selection of sprinkler heads resulted in 50 full-circle heads at 10 gpm and 40 half-circle heads at 5 gpm.   All the heads are at triangular spacing 50 ft c-c in the rows, and rows at 43 ft apart.   Watering can be done between 1 A.M. and 7 A.M.   The size of the supply pump has not been established.   During the driest season the precipitation demand of the vegetation is 1.5 in. per week.

1. Find the rate of precipitation for the sprinkler heads.
   Each full-circle head:

$$\frac{96.26 \times 10 \text{ gpm}}{50 \text{ ft} \times 43 \text{ ft}} = \frac{96.26}{215} = 0.448 \text{ in. per hr (call it 0.50 in. per hr)}$$

   Each half-circle head:

$$\frac{96.26 \times 5 \text{ gpm}}{\frac{1}{2}(50 \text{ ft} \times 43 \text{ ft})} = \frac{96.26}{215} = 0.448 \text{ in. per hr (call it 0.50 in. per hr)}$$

2. The demand of the vegetation is 1.5 in. per week.   Divide this by the application rate of the sprinklers.   Then each sprinkler would have to run 3 hr per week (1.5 in. ÷ 0.50 in. = 3 hr).   3 hours = 180 min per week, or 26 min per day (180 min ÷ 7 days = 26 min per day).

3. The maximum available time for watering is 6 hr each night.   6 hr = 360 min.   Divide 360 min by 26 min to determine the number of sections.   360 ÷ 26 = 13.8 sections.   Therefore use 13 or 14 sections.   The 14 sections at 26 min each would run 364 min.   This is 4 min over each day, which is of no consequence.   In fact, most controllers cannot be set closer than 5-min intervals, that is, 25-min cycles rather than 26-min cycles.   Thirteen sections would allow about 20+ min of extra time in the 6 hr of available watering time.   This would be a good safety factor.

4. The demand load in gallons per minute should be about the same for all the sections.   Calculate the total gpm demand for the system and divide by the number of sections to obtain the gpm demand per section.

50 full-circle heads at 10 gpm = 500 gpm
40 half-circle heads at 5 gpm = 200 gpm
                        Total = 700 gpm

700 gpm ÷ 14 sections = 50 gpm per section.

Therefore use a pump with a capacity of 50 gpm and arrange the heads in each section to total 50 gpm, thus:

10 sections at   5 heads at 10 gpm per head
 4 sections at 10 heads at   5 gpm per head
¯¯¯¯¯¯¯¯¯¯¯¯¯¯¯¯
14 sections total

or

10 sections at 4 full-circle heads at 10 gpm = 40 gpm
                      2 half-circle heads at 5 gpm = 10 gpm
                                                 ¯¯¯¯¯¯¯¯¯
                                         Total = 50 gpm
  2 sections at   5 full-circle heads at 10 gpm = 50 gpm
  2 sections at 10 half-circle heads at   5 gpm = 50 gpm
¯¯¯¯¯¯¯¯¯¯¯¯¯¯¯¯
14 sections total

or any other combination that will work out to 50 gpm per section.

10.5   TOTAL PRESSURE LOSS FOR THE SYSTEM

When the sections (blocks) have been established, the piping alignment can be drawn on the plans and worked out so that the control valves will operate the sections individually in whatever sequence and timing are desired.   Once the piping layout is established, the pressure losses in the system must be determined in order to size the pipe.

As water flows through pipe, there is a loss of pressure due to the so-called friction with the walls of the pipe, fittings, and valves, plus any gain or loss in pressure due to any difference in elevation between the supply point and the discharge point.   Pressure is measured as pounds per square inch (psi) or as feet of head, meaning the height of a column of water in feet.   Pounds per square inch and feet of head can be converted from one to the other by the following conversion factors:

Feet of head $\times$ 0.4335 = pounds per square inch
Pounds per square inch $\times$ 2.307 = feet of head

The pressure required at the sprinkler head is specified by the manufacturer.   If the available pressure at the pump, or in the case of city water supply, at the main, is known, the allowable pressure loss in the piping will be the difference between the pressure at the supply and that required at the sprinkler head.

In the case of a city water supply there will be a pressure loss in going through the service line and meter.   Figure 10.2 shows pressure losses through water meters of various sizes.   Water meters are often installed one size smaller than the service line.   The size is usually cast or stamped on the meter case at the inlet or outlet connection.

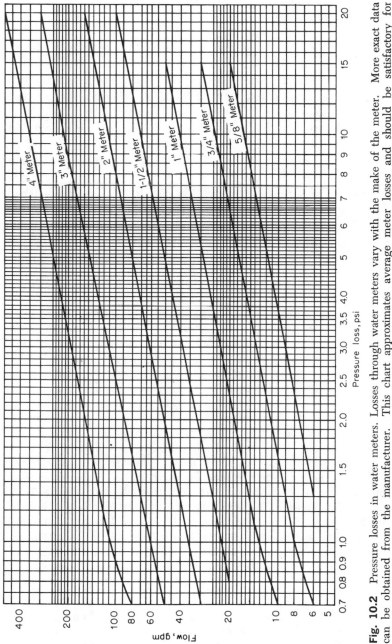
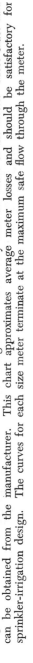

Fig. 10.2 Pressure losses in water meters. Losses through water meters vary with the make of the meter. More exact data can be obtained from the manufacturer. This chart approximates average meter losses and should be satisfactory for sprinkler-irrigation design. The curves for each size meter terminate at the maximum safe flow through the meter.

127

The gallons-per-minute (gpm) flow required by the sprinkler irrigation system should be limited to 75 percent of the maximum safe flow through the meter or to a flow that will not produce a pressure loss through the meter greater than 10 percent of the static pressure in the main, whichever is lower.

Figure 10.3 shows pressure losses per 100 ft of pipe length for various flows through type K copper pipe. Type K, a heavy-walled pipe, is the type commonly used in service lines to buildings. Type L is a lighter-walled pipe, generally used for the plumbing within a building. Type M has the lightest wall and is normally the type specified where copper is used for irrigation lines. Conversion factors are given for types L and M.

The pressure variation in any section should not be greater than 20 percent of the required pressure at the sprinkler. In addition to this, there should be an allowance of 10 percent of the section-piping pressure loss to cover estimated pressure losses through fittings. On the basis of these rules of thumb, the pressure losses for the whole system can be found.

> **Example 10.2** The property is served by a city water main at 60 psi static pressure. There is a 1½-in. copper service line from the main to the meter 70 ft long. The meter is a 1-in. meter, and the sprinkler heads will be at an elevation 6 ft higher than the water main. The irrigation system is set up with heads requiring 30 psi.
>
> Figure 10.2 shows maximum safe flow through 1-in. meter to be 50 gpm. Also note that pressure loss through the meter should not exceed 10 percent of the static pressure in the main; for example, 10 percent of 60 psi = 6 psi maximum allowable pressure loss through the meter. Check pressure losses under 1-in. meter in Fig. 10.2 and find 30 gpm produces a loss of 5.3 psi. A 35-gpm flow would produce a loss of 7.4 psi, which exceeds the allowable pressure loss of 6 psi (10 percent of 60 psi) and therefore cannot be used. The 30 gpm comes within the 75 percent of maximum safe flow through the meter (75% of 50 gpm = 37.5 gpm). The flow through the 1½-in. service line would be 30 gpm, and from Fig. 10.3 find pressure loss to be 4.2 psi per 100 ft. The loss through 70 ft will be 0.70 × 4.2 psi, or 2.94 psi. The maximum pressure loss in a section is limited to 20 percent of the pressure at the head, in this case 20 percent of 30 psi, or 6.00 psi, thus:

70 ft of 1½-in. service line at 30 gpm	= 2.94 psi
1-in. meter—loss at 30 gpm	= 5.30 psi
Section-piping pressure loss	= 6.00 psi
Fittings loss (10% of piping loss)	= 0.60 psi
Control valve at 30 gpm	= 4.60 psi
Pressure required at sprinkler	= 30.00 psi
Elevation change—6 ft higher (0.433 × 6 = 2.598) =	2.60 psi
Total loss for system	52.04 psi

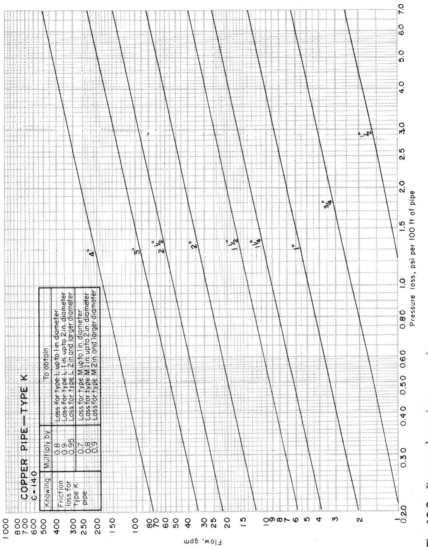

Fig. 10.3 Pressure losses in copper pipe.

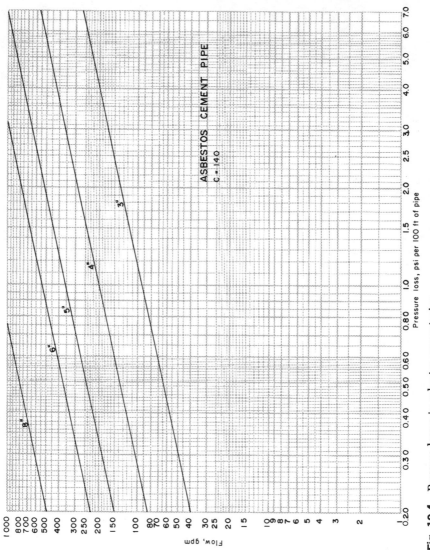

Fig. 10.4 Pressure losses in asbestos cement pipe.

130

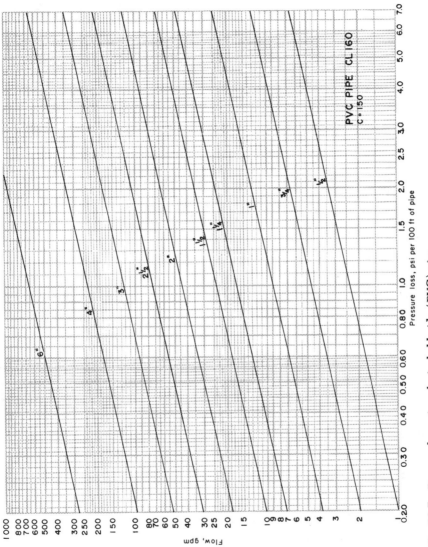

Fig. 10.5 Pressure losses in polyvinyl chloride (PVC) pipe.

131

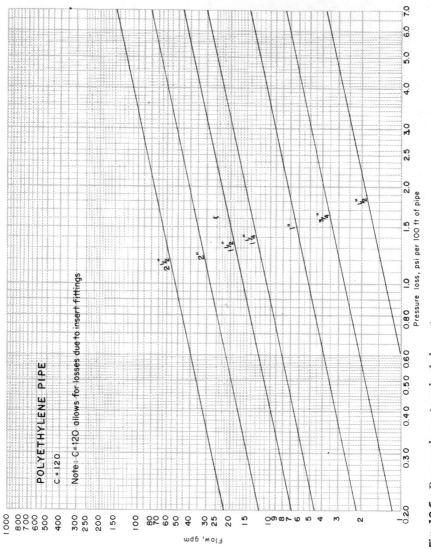

Fig. 10.6 Pressure losses in polyethylene pipes.

If it were a pump system, as in Example 10.1 in Sec. 10.4, the pressure loss for the total system would be as follows:

2-in. control valve at 50 gpm	= 1.70 psi
Section piping (20 % of 50 psi)	= 10.00 psi
Fittings loss (10 % of piping loss)	= 1.00 psi
Pressure required at sprinkler	= 50.00 psi
Elevation change—7 ft higher	= 3.03 psi
Total loss for system	= 65.73 psi

In addition to the above pressure losses, the pump must be sized to overcome any loss in the main between the pump discharge and the control valve. Assume this to be 200 ft of 2-in. polyvinyl chorilde (PVC). Then, from Fig. 10.5,

200 ft of 2-in. PVC at 1.30 psi per 100 ft = 2.60 psi

So the pump must be sized to handle 50 gpm at 68.33 psi (call it 50 gpm at 70 psi).

10.6 SIZING THE PIPE

In Sec. 10.4 the sprinkler irrigation system was divided into sections, each with a determined gpm demand. In Sec. 10.5, the total pressure loss for the whole system was determined, and in that computation there was an allowance of 20 percent of the pressure required at the sprinkler head as the allowable pressure loss in a section. This is the maximum allowable if the pressures between the first and last sprinklers in a section are to be within 20 percent of each other.

The total length of pipe (regardless of diameter) in a section can be scaled off or calculated. Divide the total allowable pressure loss for the section by this total length of pipe to obtain an allowable pressure loss per foot. Then, using Figs. 10.3, 10.4, 10.5, and/or 10.6 select pipe sizes that will not exceed this loss per foot, but in no case use pipes so small as to have velocities of over 5 fps. Experience indicates that velocities of over 5 fps often cause water-hammer damage to the system.

Table 10.1 shows a simplified list of capacities for polyethylene and polyvinyl chloride pipe commonly used in sprinkler irrigation systems. The capacities shown do not exceed velocities of 5 fps.

On most jobs the smallest size of pipe used is ¾ in. The pipe is usually installed with a machine, and the cost of the reducing fittings and of the labor necessary to switch to the ½-in. polyethylene in the machine (usually for a run of 20 ft or less) is more than the saving in pipe costs.

If more accurate pipe sizing and pressure losses are desired, use Figs. 10.3 to 10.6 and find more accurate figures.

TABLE 10.1

Flow, gpm	Pipe size, in.	Pipe material
0–8	¾	Polyethylene
9–13	1	Polyethylene
14–22	1¼	Polyethylene
23–30	1½	Polyethylene
31–50	2	Polyethylene
0–10	¾	Polyvinyl chloride
10–18	1	Polyvinyl chloride
19–28	1¼	Polyvinyl chloride
29–38	1½	Polyvinyl chloride
39–60	2	Polyvinyl chloride
60–87	2½	Polyvinyl chloride
88–130	3	Polyvinyl chloride
130–210	4	Polyvinyl chloride
210–310	5	Polyvinyl chloride
310–430	6	Polyvinyl chloride

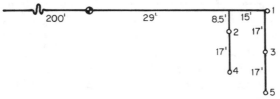

Fig. 10.7 Plan of a portion of sprinkler system.

Using Table 10.1, the pipe sizes in Fig. 10.7 are seen to be:

Point	Flow, gpm	Run, ft	Diameter, in.
Head 5	5	17	¾
Head 3	10	17	1
Head 1	15	15	1¼
Head 4	5	17	¾
Head 2	10	8.5	1
Control	25	29	1½

Compare with the following, based on Figs. 10.4 to 10.6:

Point	Flow, gpm	Run, ft	Dia., in.	Loss, psi/100 ft	Total loss, psi
Head 5	5	17	½	4.1	0.697
Head 3	10	17	¾	4.3	0.731
Head 1	15	15	1	2.6	0.390
Control	25	29	1¼	2.1	0.609
					2.427

Size the pipe in each section in a similar manner. Note that the method described in Sec. 10.5 for determining the total pressure losses for the whole system automatically incorporates a safety factor in the computations. For instance, the actual pressure losses for Example 10.1, in Sec. 10.4, are:

200 ft of 2-in. PVC at 1.30 psi per 100 ft	= 2.60 psi
2-in. control at 50 gpm	= 1.70 psi
Section piping	= 3.49 psi
Fittings losses (estimated 10 % of 3.49)	= 0.35 psi
Pressure required at sprinkler	= 50.00 psi
Elevation change—7 ft higher	= 3.03 psi
Total loss for system	= 61.17 psi

Comparing 61.17 psi with the overall pressure of 68.33 psi worked out in Sec. 10.5 shows a safety allowance of 7.16 psi. This is more than enough to allow for any pressure losses not specifically itemized in the pressure-loss calculations.

10.7 PRESSURE LOSSES IN LOOPS

Often, in larger work such as golf courses and parks, the main supply lines are looped as shown in Fig. 10.8. Pressure losses in loops are difficult to calculate accurately, particularly if there are several points of discharge from the loops. However, a fine degree of accuracy is not necessary in sprinkler-irrigation work as long as the method of calculation provides safe answers.

For simple loops where the pipes are all the same diameter and the flow around and out of the loop is uniform, figure one-half the length of the whole loop as carrying one-half the gpm demand.

Where loops become complicated with subloops, varied pipe sizes, and nonuniform discharges from several points of the loops and subloops,

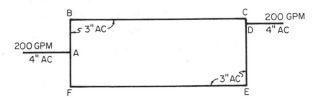

Fig. 10.8 Plan of a simple feeder loop.

the calculation of pipe losses is complicated, and it is suggested that a problem such as this be given to a sprinkler-irrigation design service or to an engineering computer service that has a program for solving such problems.

10.8   PUMP AND PUMP INTAKE

Many sprinkler irrigation systems are installed beyond the reach of municipal and metropolitan water mains. In those cases the water is taken from a lake, reservoir, pond, or stream. In small-volume pumps the intake chamber or suction screen is relatively easy to provide. Large-volume pumps will have a gulping suction that will carry stones, sand, and anything else near the intake into the system. These things will soon wear out the pump impellers and clog up the sprinkler nozzles. In such cases masonry or wood intake chambers must be built. Masonry is the preferable material. Usually, the bottom under the intake of the pump should be of concrete and at least two times the diameter of the pump intake below the intake. The flow to the intake should be direct and free. In all cases follow the pump manufacturer's instructions for setting, clearance, and submergence. Any constrictions, enlargements, or curves in the flow to the intake must be at least 5 diameters away from the intake and as subtle as possible. Any walls surrounding the pump intake must be at least 2 diameters of the intake away from the intake. Obviously, the intake must have enough submergence to avoid vortexing. This will vary with the shape of the reservoir and the size of the pump. The height of suction left on the pump is critical. This must be kept within the manufacturer's requirements—usually not exceeding 15 ft of head inclusive of intake friction and elevation losses.

The pump should have a *nonoverloading* motor. This means that the motor must be large enough to handle all pump-capacity capability.

All pond water should be screened. The box should be large enough so that the flow volume will go through the screen at a very low velocity—0.5 fps or less. The smaller the mesh of the screen, the larger its area should be. The size of the mesh depends on the clearness of the water, the type of pump, and the size of the nozzle openings on the sprinklers. Fine plastic or copper window screen is usually very satisfactory. A good arrangement is to lay the fine window screen over ¼-in.-mesh hardware cloth supported by cross-members 8 to 12 in. apart. In addition to the screened intake chamber, the pump suction line should also be screened, and in some cases a wye-type discharge screen is desirable.

10.9   APPURTENANCES

Most municipalities and many states require backflow prevention by an antisyphon device installed on the discharge side of the meter. In lieu of a backflow preventer, some municipalities will allow a double-check valve or a vacuum breaker installed 1 ft above the highest outlet.

Check with local authorities on their specific requirements. The purpose of this device is to prevent surface water from entering a low-point nozzle or open drain and being drawn back into the household-water-supply piping. It is wise to install backflow prevention in every system that is connected with any domestic- or drinking-water supply. The location of the backflow prevention must be given serious consideration at the very beginning of the layout study. As a last resort, the supply line can drop water into a reservoir from which it can be pumped into the irrigation system. Pressure loss through the backflow-prevention device must be allowed for when calculating pressure losses in the system.

In climates where freezing is a consideration, the lines must be so arranged that they can be completely drained. Polyethylene pipe has the advantage that it can be fully frozen without being damaged. However, it is better to drain all lines as completely as possible, and in addition to the main manual drains, automatic drains should be installed at low points or sags in the smaller lines.

A large system should have manual gate valves installed periodically on all main lines (in addition to the automatic valves) so that they can be closed off for repair work without shutting down the entire system.

It is good planning to also place quick couplers at periodic intervals along the mains on automatic systems to provide convenient hose connections. These will also serve as discharge points for blowing out the system at start-up. Ideally, a system should be completely washed out (blown out) after initial construction prior to the installation of the sprinkler nozzles in order to eliminate any foreign matter that may have collected in the lines during construction.

CHAPTER ELEVEN

Wood Construction

Wood is frequently used in landscape developments. It is one of the most beautiful and versatile materials known. It is a natural material that fits into almost any design and combines well with almost any other material.

Since wood is a natural material, it is impossible to avoid variation in strength caused by natural differences in moisture content and density and such natural defects as checks, splits, decay, knots, pitch pockets, and other irregularities. Some woods inherently withstand moisture and decay, while others are much more subject to this type of deterioration and cannot be used under conditions conducive to rot and decay. Preservatives such as paint, creosote, and penta are used to protect wood to lengthen its useful life.

11.1 WOOD AS A CONSTRUCTION MATERIAL

In the lumber trade the deciduous species are referred to as *hardwoods* and the coniferous species are referred to as *softwoods*. This classification incorrectly implies that the one group of wood is hard wood and the other is soft, but this is not true. Poplar and basswood are classified as hardwoods but are actually very soft. On the other hand, yellow pine is classified as a softwood, but is actually very hard.

Most trees have two distinguishing types of wood, the heartwood from the inner part of the trunk and the sapwood from the outer part of the trunk. The heartwood is generally darker in color, more dense, stronger, and more durable than the sapwood. The sapwood has larger, more open cells and will absorb preservatives better.

The various lumber manufacturers' associations have established standard systems of grading and classifying lumber. If lumber is dressed (surfaced) on one side, it is marked S1S; if dressed on two sides, it is labeled S2S; if dressed on one edge, it is labeled S1E; if dressed on two edges, S2E; and if dressed on both sides and both edges, S4S.

The National Forest Products Association has established a national design specification for stress-grade lumber and its fastenings. It divides structural lumber into three classifications, known as *dimension, beams and stringers,* and *posts and timbers.*

Dimension refers to lumber 2 in. to (but not including) 5 in. in nominal thickness and 2 in. or more in nominal width. This is often referred to as the joists-and-planks classification.

Beams and stringers refers to lumber 5 in. or more thick and 8 in. or more wide.

Posts and timbers refers to lumber of approximately square cross sections 5 × 5 in. and larger, graded primarily for use as posts or columns carrying longitudinal load but adapted for miscellaneous uses in which strength in bending is not especially important.

Each of the above three classifications is further graded as numbers 1, 2, and 3, number 1 being the most perfect. Other grade classifications such as *select structural, dense structural, appearance,* and *stud* are also used by some of the lumber manufacturers' associations. Each grade is prescribed as to allowable imperfections. In addition to these grading classifications, some lumber is machine-stress-rated and is classified by its allowable stress.

Specialized publications such as those of the various lumber manufacturers' associations, the Timber Engineering Co., the National Forest Products Association, and the U.S. government provide more specific information for those who need more detailed information. A very useful set of tables for joists and rafters is published by the Federal Housing Authority in "Minimum Standards for One and Two Unit Residential Construction."

Some species of wood are better adapted to outdoor use than others. The common species most suitable for outdoor use available to the landscape architect include redwood, cedar, larch, cypress, and Douglas fir.   A brief summary of their characteristics follows.

Redwood is available as heartwood and sapwood.   The heartwood is a durable redwood that will resist deterioration from weather, wetness, fungi, and insects.   The sapwood is more red-brown in color but is not as durable.   It is more open-celled and will absorb preservatives better than the heartwood.   When the primary consideration is a use in contact with the moist earth or other use that favors decay, a heartwood grade of redwood should be specified.

Cedar is available in several varieties, but the one most available is western cedar.   Cedar is completely nonresinous and very light in weight, with a sapwood of white or cream color and a heartwood of a light- to dark-reddish brown.   The heartwood of cedar requires no preservatives against decay; the sapwood requires treatment but is easily penetrated with all standard commercial preservatives.   When exposed to weather without protective coating, cedar will turn dark in a few years and then become lighter, stabilizing as a driftwood gray with a silvery sheen.   Cedar takes paints, stains, and varnishes very well.

Western larch is tough-fibered and fine-textured.   It is classed as a resinous wood but the amount of resin is very small.   It is one of the strongest softwoods known.   Most of the log is heartwood.   Generally, the sapwod is only ½ to ¾ in. thick.   The sapwood is straw-colored, and the heartwood is dark russet or reddish brown and uniformly bright and clear in color.   Larch is dimensionally stable and shrinks very little from green to seasoned wood.   Aluminum paint is recommended as a prime coat.   In contact with the soil, preservative treatment is recommended.   Larch can be successfully treated with standard preservatives under pressure.   The wood is in the upper bracket for durability under decay-inducing situations.   It is ideal for heavy construction, trestles, beams, posts, etc.

Southern cypress ranks as one of the most durable of American woods. The heartwood is extremely resistant to decay under adverse conditions. The sapwood is nearly white, and the heartwood ranges from a very light yellowish color through chocolate to almost black.   The coastal cypress has the darker-colored heartwood, and the inland trees the lighter-colored heartwood.   Cypress takes paint, stain, and varnish exceptionally well.   It is a strong, fairly lightweight wood, good for general outdoor construction where durability under adverse conditions is required.

Douglas fir is usually more available than the other woods mentioned. It is strong, straight-grained, and fairly dense.   The sapwood ring is white and very narrow.   The heartwood is orange-red.   The wood is classed as a resinous wood but the amount of resin is limited.   The sapwood can be treated with preservatives, but the heartwood does not easily absorb preservatives. The heartwood can be painted. Aluminum paint is recommended as a prime coat. This wood should not be used in decay inducing situations.

In wood-frame construction, the planks that directly support the floor are called *joists,* and the planks that support the roof are called *rafters.* Beams are generally considered as those structural members subjected to transverse loads, usually having nominal dimensions of 5 in. or more in thickness and 8 in. or more in width. In construction uses, the larger dimension is commonly used in the vertical position.

It is important to realize that all structural members in a structure are in a state of equilibrium. Equilibrium is a condition where all forces acting simultaneously produce no motion; i.e.,

1. The algebraic sum of all horizontal forces equals zero.
2. The algebraic sum of all vertical forces equals zero.
3. The algebraic sum of the moments of all forces acting about any point equals zero.

Besides being limited in their load-bearing capacity by their horizontal shear (strength in bending), beams are limited by their *deflection.* Deflection is important when plaster or vibration is a consideration. Deflection is limited to $\frac{1}{360}$ of the beam span in situations where the beam is supporting plastered walls. In most cases neither plaster nor vibration is a consideration in site work, and deflection can be $\frac{1}{200}$ of the span, and even greater.

After a beam has been selected on the basis of bending strength, it is usually further checked for horizontal shear and shear across the grain; but in site work these steps can be omitted, since seldom, if ever, do situations develop where such shears become a concern.

11.2 CALCULATION OF LIVE AND DEAD LOADS

The load on a beam consists of the *dead load,* which is composed of the supported weights of the construction such as decking materials, walls, columns, and the weight of the beam itself, plus the *live load,* due to human occupancy, furniture, snow, wind, etc. These weights are shown in Tables 11.1 to 11.3.

Live loads on roofs may include snow, water, ice, wind, and floor-type loads for roof decks. Snow is usually estimated at 0.5 to 0.7 psf per in. of depth. The snow and wind loads are usually combined, since any increase in wind load will reduce the snow load by blowing it off the roof. The tabulation of equivalent vertical loads on various slopes of roofs in Table 11.1 takes this into consideration.

Table 11.2 shows wind loads on vertical surfaces such as signs and

TABLE 11.1 Combined Wind and Snow Loads

Locality	Roof pitch				
	45°	30°	25°	20°	Flat
Northwestern and New England states	28*	25*	24*	35*	40*
Western and Central states	28	25	24	30	35
Southern and Pacific states	28	25	24	22	20

* Pounds per square foot of roof surface.

TABLE 11.2

Type of wind	Velocity, mph	Pressure on vertical surface, psf
Gentle breeze	10	0.5
Fresh breeze	20	1.5
Strong breeze	30	3.5
Gale	40	6.5
Strong gale	50	10.0
Whole gale	60	15.0
Hurricane	75–100	25–40

SOURCE: "Timber Design and Construction Handbook,"
McGraw-Hill Book Company, New York, 1956.

solid walls.   Wind loads for average structures should be considered as acting on the gross area of the vertical projection of the structure at not less than 15 psf for those portions less than 60 ft above the ground, and 20 psf for those portions of the structure more than 60 ft above the ground.   Greenhouses, lath houses, etc., in which there is less hazard

TABLE 11.3

Use	Load, psf
Dwellings	40
Auditoriums	
Fixed-seat	50
Movable-seat	100
Bleachers	100
Dance halls	100
Public rooms	100
Offices	50
Schools	
Classrooms	40
Corridors	100

to life are often designed for pressure as low as 10 psf. On open-framed structures such as lath houses, bridges, and towers, the pressure area should be 1½ times the net area exposed to the wind.

Live floor loads should be determined in accordance with local code requirements. The requirements in most instances are as given in Table 11.3.

Most of the uses shown in Table 11.3 are not those encountered in landscape architecture, but the list does serve as an excellent guide to the amount of live load that should be allowed for, under a variety of uses. For example, a pedestrian bridge or wood deck should be designed to support a live load of 100 psf plus its own deadweight for places where it is used by the public (parks, golf courses, etc.). On private property for family use, a live load of 40 psf should be sufficient.

11.3 DETERMINING BEAM SIZES

Construction design using structural timbers can be very involved, and anyone particularly interested can find a number of publications on the subject. In lieu of spending a great deal of time studying the principles of the mechanics involved, a little time spent learning how to use the tables and charts that have been worked out for the common situations of beam use will solve practically all the beam problems which most landscape architects encounter.

There are three kinds of beams that must be recognized; a simple beam, a cantilevered beam, and a continuous beam.

A *simple beam* is a beam that rests upon a support at each end.
A *cantilevered beam* is a beam that projects beyond a support.
A *continuous beam* is a beam that rests on three or more supports.

The *effective span* of a beam is the horizontal distance between supports, and in practice is generally considered as the distance between the faces of the supports.

The common situations of beam use occur so frequently that charts have been prepared to fit these situations, and it is only necessary to know the numbers to insert into the formulas to determine the size of beam required. The procedure is as follows:

1. Determine the amount and type of loading on the beam and select the case applicable from Table 11.4. Each case gives the pertinent formula or formulas to be used in finding *M*, the maximum bending moment.

2. Compute *M* in foot-pounds by using the applicable formula or formulas for the case determined. Convert this answer to inch-pounds by multiplying by 12.

3. Select the species and grade of wood to be used for the beam and find the extreme fiber stress f in Table 11.5.

4. Compute the required section modulus S by dividing M, the maximum bending moment in inch-pounds (from step 2 above), by f, the allowable fiber stress in pounds per square inch (from step 3 above).

5. Check Table 11.6 for all beams having this section modulus S_{x-x}. Beams selected should have a section modulus equal to or greater than the required section modulus. The beam selected should also have a width no less than one-third the depth of the beam in order to obviate lateral bending. This requirement is not essential if the beam is braced horizontally, i.e., by decking, etc.

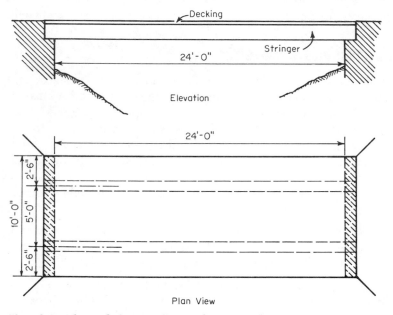

Fig. 11.1   Plan and elevation for a pedestrian bridge.

Example 11.1   Figure 11.1 shows a redwood pedestrian bridge spanning a creek. The stringer beams span 24 ft and rest on concrete abutments at each end. The walk is 10 ft wide and is intended to be used by pedestrians and light maintenance equipment. Use 100 psf live load in designing this bridge.

Over each lineal foot of the stringer the decking will be carrying a uniformly distributed live load of 100 psf plus its own weight. It is a cantilevered beam with the maximum bending moment over each stringer. Therefore, from Table 11.4, use case 24 with

$$M_2 = \frac{wa^2}{2}$$

Then the steps are as follows:

1. w is the load on each square foot of deck. This will be the 100 lb of live load plus an estimated 5 psf for the weight of the decking itself. The overhang a is 2.5 ft. Then

$$M_2 = \frac{105 \times 2.5 \times 2.5}{2} = 328.125 \text{ ft-lb}$$

2. $328.125 \times 12 = 3{,}937.5$ in.-lb
3. From Table 11.5, find extreme fiber stress in bending, f, for redwood plank to be 1,200 psi.
4. Determine section modulus S by dividing the maximum bending moment M by the allowable fiber stress f:

$$S = \frac{M}{f} = \frac{3{,}937.5}{1{,}200} = 3.28$$

In the flat position of this decking the governing S would be the S_{y-y}.
5. Therefore find plank with S_{y-y} equal to or greater than 3.28 cu in., in Table 11.6. Use 2×10 in. (S_{y-y} of 3.5 cu in.) for decking.
6. Size the stringers. Both stringers support equal weights of the load. Each foot of length of either stringer supports a deck 5 ft wide by 1 ft long at 105 psf (100 lb of live load plus 5 lb of decking) or 525 lb plus 1 lin ft (lineal foot) of beam that will be estimated at 40 lb, or a total of 565 lb per lin ft.

   Each stringer is a simple beam supporting a uniformly distributed load; hence use case 1 in Table 11.4.

$$M = \frac{wl^2}{8} = \frac{565 \times 24 \times 24}{8} = 40{,}680 \text{ ft-lb}$$

$40{,}680 \times 12 = 488{,}160$ in.-lb

From Table 11.5, find that No. 1 redwood stringers have an extreme fiber stress of 1,200 psi. Then

$$S = \frac{M}{f} = \frac{488{,}160}{1{,}200} = 406.8 \text{ cu in.}$$

Since these beams will be used on edge, find beam in Table 11.6 with a stress modulus S_{x-x} equal to or greater than 406.8 cu in.

$8 \times 20 = 475$ cu in.
$10 \times 18 = 485$ cu in.
$12 \times 16 = 460$ cu in.
$14 \times 14 = 410$ cu in.

Use whichever one is available at the least cost.

Note that the weight of the plank or beam is estimated. If, in solving the problem, it is found that the estimated size (weight) was grossly in error, use the revised figures for the weight of the plank or beam and rework the problem. Table 11.7 give weights of wood.

Table 11.4   Maximum Bending Moments for Beams

Maximum Bending Moments for Simple Beams

1. Uniformly distributed load:

$$M = \frac{wl^2}{8}$$

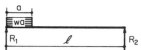

2. Load increasing uniformly to one end:

$$M = 0.1283Wl$$

3. Load increasing uniformly to the center:

$$M = \frac{Wl}{6}$$

4. Uniform load partially distributed:

$$M = R_1\left(a + \frac{R_1}{2w}\right)$$

$$R_1 = \frac{wb}{2l}(2c + b)$$

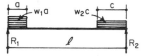

5. Uniform load partially distributed at one end:

$$M = \frac{(R_1)^2}{2w}$$

$$R_1 = \frac{wa}{2l}(2l - a)$$

6. Uniform load partially distributed at each end:

$$M = \begin{cases} \dfrac{(R_1)^2}{2w_1} & \text{when } R_1 < w_1a \\[2ex] \dfrac{(R_2)^2}{2w_2} & \text{when } R_2 < w_2c \end{cases}$$

$$R_1 = \frac{w_1a(2l - a) + w_2c^2}{2l}$$

$$R_2 = \frac{w_2c(2l - c) + w_1a^2}{2l}$$

7. Concentrated load at center:

$$M = \frac{Pl}{4}$$

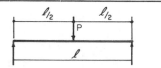

TABLE 11.4   Maximum Bending Moments for Beams *(Continued)*

8. Concentrated load at any point:

$$M = \frac{Pab}{l}$$

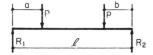

9. Two equal concentrated loads symmetrically placed:

$$M = Pa$$

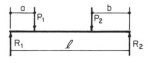

10. Two equal concentrated loads unsymmetrically placed:

$M_1 = R_1 a \qquad$ when $a > b$
$M_2 = R_2 b \qquad$ when $a < b$

$$R_1 = \frac{P}{l}(l - a + b)$$

$$R_2 = \frac{P}{l}(l - b + a)$$

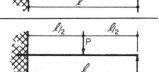

11. Two unequal concentrated loads unsymmetrically placed:

$M_1 = R_1 a \qquad$ when $R_1 < P_1$
$M_2 = R_2 b \qquad$ when $R_2 < P_2$

$$R_1 = \frac{P_1(l - a) + P_2 b}{l}$$

$$R_2 = \frac{P_1 a + P_2(l - b)}{l}$$

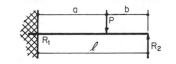

Maximum Bending Moments for Beams Fixed at One End, Supported at Other

12. Uniformly distributed load:

$$M = \frac{wl^2}{8}$$

13. Concentrated load at center:

$$M = \frac{3Pl}{16}$$

14. Concentrated load at any point:
$$M = R_2 b$$

$$R_2 = \frac{Pa^2}{2l^3}(b + 2l)$$

Maximum Bending Moments for Beams Fixed at Both Ends

15. Uniformly distributed load:

$$M = \frac{wl^2}{12}$$

TABLE 11.4   Maximum Bending Moments for Beams (*Continued*)

16. Concentrated load at center:

$$M = \frac{Pl}{8}$$

17. Concentrated load at any point:

$$M = \begin{cases} \dfrac{Pab^2}{l^2} & \text{when } a < b \\[2mm] \dfrac{Pa^2b}{l^2} & \text{when } a > b \end{cases}$$

Maximum Bending Moments for Cantilevered Beams

---

18. Beam fixed at one end, free but guided at the other—uniformly distributed load:

$$M = \frac{wl^2}{3}$$

19. Beam fixed at one end, free but guided at the other—concentrated load at guided end:

$$M = \frac{Pl}{2}$$

20. Uniformly distributed load:

$$M = \frac{wl^2}{2}$$

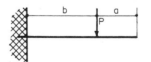

21. Load increasing uniformly to the fixed end:

$$M = \frac{Wl}{3}$$

22. Concentrated load at any point:

$$M = Pb$$

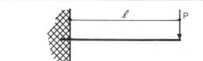

23. Concentrated load at free end:

$$M = Pl$$

TABLE 11.4 Maximum Bending Moments for Beams (Continued)

Maximum Bending Moments for Beams Overhanging One Support

24. Uniformly distributed load:

$$M_1 = \frac{w}{8l^2}(l + a)^2 (l - a)^2$$

$$M_2 = \frac{wa^2}{2} \quad \text{at } R_2$$

25. Uniformly distributed load on overhang:

$$M = \frac{wa^2}{2}$$

26. Concentrated load at end of overhang:

$$M = Pa$$

27. Uniformly distributed load between supports:

$$M = \frac{wl^2}{8}$$

28. Concentrated load at any point between supports:

$$M = \frac{Pab}{l}$$

Maximum Bending Moments for Continuous Beams

29. Two equal spans—uniform load on one span:

$$M = \frac{49}{512} wl^2$$

30. Two equal spans—concentrated load at center of one span:

$$M = \frac{13}{64} Pl$$

31. Two equal spans—concentrated load at any point:

$$M = \frac{Pab}{4l^3}[4l^2 - b(l + b)]$$

NOTE: Where two M's are given, either M could be the maximum, depending on the situation. In all cases R = reaction, M = moment, W = total weight (wl), w = weight per lineal foot, l = length between supports, P = concentrated load.

TABLE 11.5   Allowable Extreme Fiber Stress in Bending

Species	Classification	Grade	f, psi
Cedar, western	2–4 in. thick 6 in. and wider	Select Structural	1,250
		No. 1	1,050
		No. 2	875
		No. 3	525
	Beams and stringers	Select Structural	1,100
		No. 1	900
	Posts and timbers	Select Structural	1,050
		No. 1	850
	Decking	Selected Decking	1,400*
		Commercial Decking	1,200*
Douglas fir, larch, West Coast	2–4 in. thick 6 in. and wider	Dense Select Structural	2,100
		Select Structural	1,800
		Dense No. 1	1,800
		No. 1	1,500
		Dense No. 2	1,450
		No. 2	1,250
		No. 3	725
	Beams and stringers	Dense Select Structural	1,900
		Select Structural	1,600
		Dense No. 1	1,550
		No. 1	1,300
	Posts and timbers	Dense Select Structural	1,750
		Select Structural	1,500
		Dense No. 1	1,400
		No. 1	1,200
	Decking	Select Dex	2,000*
		Commercial Dex	1,650*
Douglas fir, inland	2–4 in. thick 6 in. and wider	Select Structural	1,700
		No. 1	1,450
		No. 2	1,200
		No. 3	700
	Beams and stringers	Select Structural	1,550
		No. 1	1,300
	Posts and timbers	Select Structural	1,400
		No. 1	1,150
	Decking	Selected Decking	1,900*
		Commercial Decking	1,600*

TABLE 11.5   Allowable Extreme Fiber Stress in Bending *(Continued)*

Species	Classification	Grade	f, psi
Hemlock, mountain, West Coast	2–4 in. thick 6 in. and wider	Select Structural No. 1 No. 2 No. 3	1,500 1,250 1,050 625
	Beams and stringers	Select Structural No. 1	1,350 1,100
	Posts and timbers	Select Structural No. 1	1,250 1,000
	Decking	Select Dex Commercial Dex	1,650* 1,400*
Hemlock, tamarack, eastern	2–4 in. thick 6 in. and wider	Select Structural No. 1 No. 2 No. 3	1,550 1,300 1,050 625
	Beams and stringers	Select Structural No. 1	1,400 1,150
	Posts and timbers	Select Structural No. 1	1,300 1,050
	Decking	Select Commercial	1,700* 1,450*
Pine, red, Canada	2–4 in. thick 6 in. and wider	Select Structural No. 1 No. 2 No. 3	1,200 1,000 825 500
	Beams and stringers	Select Structural No. 1 Structural	1,050 875
	Posts and timbers	Select Structural No. 1 Structural	1,000 800
	Wall and roof plank	Select Commercial	1,350 1,100
Pine, southern	2–4 in. thick 6 in. and wider	Dense Select Structural Select Structural	2,100 1,800

TABLE 11.5 Allowable Extreme Fiber Stress in Bending *(Continued)*

Species	Classification	Grade	*f*, psi
		No. 1 Dense	1,800
		No. 1	1,500
		No. 2 Dense	1,450
		No. 2 Medium Grain	1,250
		No. 2	1,050
		No. 3 Dense	850
		No. 3	725
	5 in. and thicker	Dense Structural 65	1,650
		No. 1 Dense SR	1,500
		No. 1 SR	1,300
		No. 2 Dense SR	1,300
		No. 2 SR	1,100
Pine, western, sugar, ponderosa, lodgepole	2–4 in. thick 6 in. and wider	Select Structural	1,200
		No. 1	1,050
		No. 2	850
		No. 3	500
	Beams and stringers	Select Structural	1,100
		No. 1	925
	Posts and timbers	Select Structural	1,000
		No. 1	825
	Decking	Selected Decking	1,350*
		Commercial Decking	1,150*
Redwood, California	2–4 in. thick 6 in. and wider	Selected Structural	1,750
		Select Structural Open Grain	1,400
		No. 1	1,500
		No. 1 Open Grain	1,150
		No. 2	1,200
		No. 2 Open Grain	950
		No. 3	700
		No. 3 Open Grain	550
	5 × 5 in. and larger	Clear Heart Structural	1,850
		Clear Structural	1,850
		Select Structural	1,400
		No. 1	1,200
		No. 2	975
		No. 3	550

TABLE 11.5   Allowable Extreme Fiber Stress in Bending *(Continued)*

Species	Classification	Grade	f, psi
Spruce, eastern	2–4 in. thick 6 in. and wider	Select Structural	1,300
		No. 1	1,100
		No. 2	900
		No. 3	525
	Beams and stringers	Select Structural	1,150
		No. 1	950
	Posts and timbers	Select Structural	1,100
		No. 1	875
	Decking	Select	1,450*
		Commercial	1,200*
Spruce, Sitka, Canadian coastal	2–4 in. thick 6 in. and wider	Select Structural	1,300
		No. 1	1,100
		No. 2	900
		No. 3	525
	Beams and stringers	Select Structural	1,150
		No. 1 Structural	950
	Posts and timbers	Select Structural	1,100
		No. 1 Structural	875
	Decking	Select	1,450*
		Commercial	1,200*

* Allowable unit stresses for repetitive-member use.   For individual-member use, 87 percent of value shown is applicable.

source: Adapted from "National Design Specification," National Forest Products Association, April 1973.

TABLE 11.6   Properties of Structural Lumber

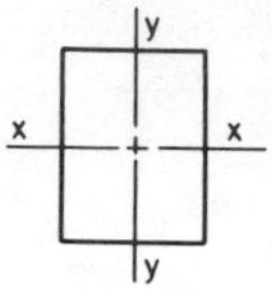

Nominal size, in.	American std. dressed size, in.	Area of section, sq in.	Lb* per lin ft	Section modulus, cu in.	
				S_{x-x}	S_{y-y}
1 × 4	¾ × 3½	2.63	0.7	1.5	0.3
1 × 6	¾ × 5½	4.13	1.1	3.8	0.5
1 × 8	¾ × 7¼	5.44	1.5	6.6	0.7
1 × 10	¾ × 9¼	6.94	1.9	10.7	0.9
1 × 12	¾ × 11¼	8.44	2.3	15.8	1.1
2 × 3	1½ × 2½	3.75	1.0	1.5	0.9
2 × 4	1½ × 3½	5.25	1.5	3.1	1.3
2 × 6	1½ × 5½	8.25	2.3	7.6	2.1
2 × 8	1½ × 7¼	10.88	3.0	13.1	2.7
2 × 10	1½ × 9¼	13.88	3.8	21.4	3.5
2 × 12	1½ × 11¼	16.88	4.7	31.6	4.2
2 × 14	1½ × 13¼	19.88	5.5	43.9	5.0
3 × 4	2½ × 3½	8.75	2.4	5.1	3.6
3 × 6	2½ × 5½	13.75	3.8	12.6	5.7
3 × 8	2½ × 7¼	18.13	5.0	21.9	7.6
3 × 10	2½ × 9¼	23.13	6.4	35.7	9.6
3 × 12	2½ × 11¼	28.13	8.4	52.7	11.7
3 × 14	2½ × 13¼	33.13	9.2	73.2	13.8
3 × 16	2½ × 15¼	38.13	10.6	96.9	15.9
4 × 4	3½ × 3½	12.2	3.4	7.1	7.1
4 × 6	3½ × 5½	19.2	5.3	17.7	11.2
4 × 8	3½ × 7¼	25.38	7.0	30.7	14.8
4 × 10	3½ × 9¼	32.38	8.9	49.9	18.9
4 × 12	3½ × 11¼	39.38	10.9	73.8	23.0
4 × 14	3½ × 13¼	46.38	12.9	102.4	27.1
4 × 16	3½ × 15¼	53.38	14.8	135.7	31.1
6 × 6	5½ × 5½	30.3	8.4	27.7	27.7
6 × 8	5½ × 7½	41.3	11.5	51.6	37.8
6 × 10	5½ × 9½	52.3	14.5	82.7	47.9
6 × 12	5½ × 11½	63.3	17.6	121.2	58
6 × 14	5½ × 13½	74.3	20.6	167.1	68.1
6 × 16	5½ × 15½	85.3	23.7	220.2	78.1
6 × 18	5½ × 17½	96.3	26.7	280.7	88.2

TABLE 11.6 Properties of Structural Lumber (Continued)

Nominal size, in.	American std. dressed size, in.	Area of section, sq in.	Lb* per lin ft	Section modulus, cu in.	
				S_{x-x}	S_{y-y}
8 × 8	7½ × 7½	56.3	15.6	70.3	70.3
8 × 10	7½ × 9½	71.3	19.8	112.8	89.1
8 × 12	7½ × 11½	86.3	24.0	165.3	107.8
8 × 14	7½ × 13½	101.3	28.1	228	127
8 × 16	7½ × 15½	116.3	32.3	300	145
8 × 18	7½ × 17½	131.3	36.5	383	164
8 × 20	7½ × 19½	146.3	40.6	475	183
10 × 10	9½ × 9½	90.3	25.0	143	143
10 × 12	9½ × 11½	109	30.3	209	173
10 × 14	9½ × 13½	128	35.6	289	203
10 × 16	9½ × 15½	147	40.9	380	233
10 × 18	9½ × 17½	166	46.2	485	263
10 × 20	9½ × 19½	185	51.5	602	293
10 × 24	9½ × 23½	223	62.0	874	353
12 × 12	11½ × 11½	132	36.7	253	253
12 × 14	11½ × 13½	155	43.1	349	298
12 × 16	11½ × 15½	178	49.5	460	342
12 × 18	11½ × 17½	201	55.9	587	386
12 × 20	11½ × 19½	224	62.3	729	430
12 × 22	11½ × 21½	247	68.7	886	474
12 × 24	11½ × 23½	270	75.0	1,058	518
14 × 14	13½ × 13½	182	50.6	410	410
14 × 16	13½ × 15½	209	58.1	541	471
14 × 18	13½ × 17½	236	65.6	689	532
14 × 20	13½ × 19½	263	73.1	856	592
14 × 24	13½ × 23½	317	88.1	1,243	714

* Based on 40 pcf.
SOURCE: Adapted from National Forest Products Association 1973 data.

TABLE 11.7   Wood-Weight Per Cubic Foot

Common name	Approx. weight	
	Green	Dry
Ash	48	41
Aspen	43	26
Basswood	42	26
Beech	54	45
Birch, yellow	57	44
Birch, paper	50	38
Cedar, red	37	33
Cedar, western	27	23
Cherry, black	45	35
Cypress, southern	51	32
Elm	55	36
Fir, Douglas	36	31
Fir, balsam	45	25
Gum, black	45	35
Hemlock, eastern	50	28
Hemlock, West Coast	41	29
Hickory	63	51
Larch, western	48	36
Maple, hard	55	42
Maple, soft	47	35
Oak	64	44
Pecan	62	45
Pine, northern white	36	25
Pine, southern shortleaf	52	36
Poplar, yellow	38	28
Redwood	50	28
Spruce	34	28
Sycamore	52	34
Tamarack	47	37
Walnut, black	58	38

SOURCE: "Timber Design and Construction Handbook," Timber Engineering Company, McGraw-Hill Book Company, New York, 1956.

Mathematics

A.1 BASIC ALGEBRA

Solutions to many site problems are found by the use of algebraic equations. Unfortunately, algebra is easily forgotten unless used rather frequently. A restatement of the rules of procedure in solving algebraic problems should readily recall the algebraic process and method of procedure to the landscape architect. Some of these are:

1. Parentheses and brackets are symbols of aggregation which are used to indicate that some operation is to be extended over the whole expression enclosed by the parentheses or brackets.

2. In a succession of indicated operations involving addition, subtraction, multiplication, division, powers, and roots, when no parentheses or brackets are used:

    a. All powers and roots are found first.

    b. All multiplications are performed next (in any order).

    c. All divisions are performed next, and these are done in order from left to right.

    d. Finally, additions and subtractions are performed (and these may be taken in any order).

Algebraic equations involving one unknown are referred to as *linear equations,* or *equations of the first degree.* Equations involving two unknowns are referred to as *quadratic equations,* or *equations of the second degree.* Algebraic equations involving more than two unknowns will seldom, if ever, be encountered in solving site-work problems and will not be considered in this brief review of basic algebra.

Algebraic equations involving one or more unknowns have been solved algebraically to provide formulas for finding the values of the unknowns:

1. Linear equations are equations of the first degree and have but one root (one unknown).

EXAMPLE: $ax + b = 0$ is a linear equation.   It has only one root:

$$x = \frac{-b}{a}$$

2. Quadratic equations are equations of the second degree and have two roots (two unknowns).

EXAMPLE: $x^2 + 2ax + b = 0$ is a quadratic equation.   It has two roots:

$$x = -a + \sqrt{a^2 - b}$$
$$x = -a - \sqrt{a^2 - b}$$

An algebraic equation is a statement of equality.   That which is on the left of the equal sign is equal to that on the right of the equal sign.   Since these are equal:

1. Both sides of an equation may be multiplied or divided by the same number without disturbing the equality of the statement.

EXAMPLE: $ax = -b$ $\dfrac{\cancel{a}x}{\cancel{a}} = \dfrac{-b}{a}$ $x = \dfrac{-b}{a}$

Divide by c: $\dfrac{ax}{c} = \dfrac{-b}{c}$ $ax = \dfrac{-b\cancel{c}}{\cancel{c}}$ $ax = -b$

Multiply by c: $c(ax) = c(-b)$ $ax = \dfrac{\cancel{c}(-b)}{\cancel{c}}$ $ax = -b$

2. The same number may be added or subtracted from both sides of an equation without disturbing the equality of the statement.

EXAMPLE: $ax + b = 0$ $x = \dfrac{-b}{a}$

and $ax + b - b = 0 - b$ $ax = -b$ $x = \dfrac{-b}{a}$

In a statement where one fraction equals another fraction, the equation is sometimes referred to as a *proportional statement.*   In such an equation the product of the means equals the product of the extremes.

EXAMPLE: $\dfrac{a}{b} = \dfrac{c}{x}$

In this equation, a and x are called the *extremes* and b and c are called the *means*, and $ax = bc$.

This equation can be read: $a \div b = c \div x$ or a is to b as c is to x. For those who have not been associated with algebra for some time, this relationship can probably be made more understandable by using numbers.

Let $a = 1$, $b = 4$, and $c = 5$.

In the equation $\dfrac{a}{b} = \dfrac{c}{x}$, solve for x.

Substituting the numbers for their letters:

$$\frac{1}{4} = \frac{5}{x} \qquad 1x = 4 \times 5 \qquad x = 20$$

or 1 is to 4 as 5 is to 20.

A.2 LOGARITHMS

Before the development of calculators, the work of multiplying and dividing large numbers was time-consuming and tedious. At that time logarithms were in extensive use since the process of multiplying two numbers was simply adding their logarithms, and dividing was a matter of subtracting their logarithms. Today's calculators are accurate and instantaneous; so multiplying and dividing large numbers are no longer time-consuming or tedious. Logarithms are seldom, if ever, needed in the numerical work that a landscape architect will undertake. However, many landscape architects have a confused impression of logarithms from high school mathematics, and in order to clear up this confusion, a brief explanation of logarithms follows.

First of all, do not confuse logarithms with trigonometric functions! Trigonometric functions are explained in Sec. A.3. There are also logarithms of trigonometric functions.

In a sense, logarithms and exponents are equivalents. In general, handle logarithms by the same mathematical rules as those established for exponents. The difference is that the logarithm is labeled "log" and is that power of a selected base number which would produce the number that the log represents. Any number can be used as a base for a system of logarithms. Two bases are in general use. These are the *common*, or Briggs, system and the *natural*, or Naperian, system. In the natural system the base is a certain irrational number, $e = 2.71828\ \ldots$. In the common system the base is 10. The natural system is adapted to analytical work, whereas the common system is adapted to numerical work. The latter is the system with which we are concerned in this section.

If we state the equivalents of the various powers of 10:

$$10^0 = 1 \qquad\qquad\qquad 10^{-1} = 0.1$$
$$10^1 = 10 \qquad\qquad\quad\ 10^{-2} = 0.01$$
$$10^2 = 100 \qquad\qquad\ \ 10^{-3} = 0.001$$
$$10^3 = 1{,}000 \qquad\qquad 10^{-4} = 0.0001$$

then it follows that:

log 1	= 0	log 0.1	= −1
log 10	= 1	log 0.01	= −2
log 100	= 2	log 0.001	= −3
log 1,000	= 3	log 0.0001	= −4

and that numbers between 1 and 10 will have a log between 0 and 1 which will obviously be some decimal number. Numbers between 10 and 100 will have a log between 1 and 2 which obviously will be a 1 plus a decimal. Numbers between 100 and 1,000 will have a log between 2 and 3 which will be a 2 plus a decimal, and numbers less than 1 will have as a log a negative number greater by one numerically than the number of zeros immediately following the decimal point.

The decimal part of the logarithm is called the *mantissa*, and the integer part is called the *characteristic*. Tables give the mantissa part of the logarithm, and the characteristic is supplied according to the following rules:

1. When the number is greater than 1, the characteristic of its log is positive and is numerically one less than the number of figures preceding the decimal point.

2. When the number is less than 1, the characteristic is negative and is numerically one greater than the number of zeros immediately following the decimal point.

EXAMPLE: Multiply 1,259 by 125 using logs.

Find the log of 125.
The characteristic is 2 (from rule 1 above).
The mantissa is 096910 (from table of logs).
The log of 125 is 2.096910.

Find the log of 1,259.
The characteristic is 3 (from rule 1 above).
The mantissa is 100026 (from table of logs).
The log of 1,259 is 3.100026.
Multiply 125 × 1,259.

log 125	= 2.096910
log 1,259	= 3.100026
	5.196936

Look up the mantissa in a table of logs.
Mantissa 196936 = 157375.
The characteristic 5 means there are six places to the left of the decimal, thus:

125 × 1,259 = 157,375.000

A.3   TRIGONOMETRIC FUNCTIONS

Right-Triangle Formulas

Trigonometric functions are nothing more than the proportionate ratios of the sides of a right triangle.   For any angle there are six ratios (functions) that are of fundamental importance, and for every angle there exists but one value for each trigonometric ratio.

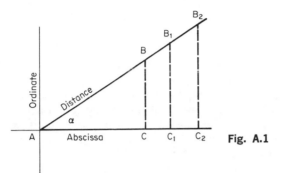

Fig. A.1

These six common trigonometric functions or ratios for any given angle α (Fig. A.1) are:

$$\sin \alpha = \text{sine } \alpha \qquad = \frac{\text{ordinate}}{\text{distance}} = \frac{BC}{AB} = \frac{\text{side opposite}}{\text{hypothenuse}}$$

$$\cos \alpha = \text{cosine } \alpha \qquad = \frac{\text{abscissa}}{\text{distance}} = \frac{AC}{AB} = \frac{\text{side adjacent}}{\text{hypothenuse}}$$

$$\tan \alpha = \text{tangent } \alpha \qquad = \frac{\text{ordinate}}{\text{abscissa}} = \frac{BC}{AC} = \frac{\text{side opposite}}{\text{side adjacent}}$$

$$\cot \alpha = \text{cotangent } \alpha = \frac{\text{abscissa}}{\text{ordinate}} = \frac{AC}{BC} = \frac{\text{side adjacent}}{\text{side opposite}}$$

$$\sec \alpha = \text{secant } \alpha \qquad = \frac{\text{distance}}{\text{abscissa}} = \frac{AB}{AC} = \frac{\text{hypothenuse}}{\text{side adjacent}}$$

$$\csc \alpha = \text{cosecant } \alpha \qquad = \frac{\text{distance}}{\text{ordinate}} = \frac{AB}{BC} = \frac{\text{hypothenuse}}{\text{side opposite}}$$

Note that these functions are simply the ratio relationship between the lengths of any selected two of the three sides of a right triangle.   The size of the triangle does not matter since, for any angle α,

$$\frac{BC}{AB} = \frac{B_1C_1}{AB_1} = \frac{B_2C_2}{AB_2} = \cdots$$

and the same holds true for the abscissa.

Modern calculators have so simplified dividing by five- or eight-place numbers that the inverse ratios (cot, sec, csc) are no longer used to any great extent, and landscape architects need concern themselves with only three of these functions, *sine, cosine,* and *tangent.*

Two other ratio relationships are sometimes convenient for the landscape architect to use.   Referring to Fig. A.2, these are:

$$\text{vers } \alpha \ = \text{versed sine } \alpha = \frac{c - b}{c} = \frac{d}{c}$$

$$\text{exsec } \alpha = \text{exsecant } \alpha = \frac{e}{c}$$

Tables of trigonometric functions are published as logarithmic trigonometric functions and as natural trigonometric functions.   Be sure to use the right tables.   Modern calculators make it so easy to use the natural functions that it is recommended that these and only these be used.

Trigonometric tables are published in any number of decimal places up to about 10.   Some are carried to the nearest minute; others are carried to the nearest second.   The advantage of the tables carried to seconds is that they eliminate any interpolation.   Interpolation can become quite a chore when using 8- or 10-place tables.

The advantage of the 8- or 10-place tables is in the greater degree of accuracy.   The degree of accuracy that can be depended upon in a computation is limited by the accuracy of the trigonometric tables used.   The greater the number of decimal places in the table, the more accurately can the angles generally be determined.   In a given table the accuracy is greater for angles where the function is changing rapidly.   For this reason try *not* to determine angles from the cosine when the angle is near 0°, nor from the sine when the angle is near 90°.

In solving a problem it is useless to carry out the computations to a greater degree of accuracy than that of the provided data.   The degree of accuracy required for landscape architects can probably be satisfied by four- or five-place tables.   However, traverse closures should probably best be done using six- or seven-place tables to eliminate concern over accumulated error.   The frus-

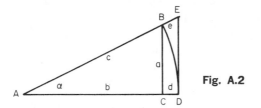

Fig. A.2

tration of trying to determine where to place the inaccuracies wastes more time than the extra time required to use the larger trigonometry tables.

It is always advisable to check your work as you go along.   This can be done graphically by constructing a careful layout to see if the figure closes.   Mistakes can often be found by making a check computation using a different formula.   Always check your work at each step.   It is easier to correct a single step than to have to go back over many steps.

Oblique-Triangle Formulas

When working with oblique triangles, the essential trigonometric formulas are:

1. $\text{Sin } \angle A = \dfrac{2 \sqrt{s(s-a)(s-b)(s-c)}}{bc}$

2. $\text{Area } \triangle ABC = \sqrt{s(s-a)(s-b)(s-c)}$ where $s = \frac{1}{2}(a+b+c)$.

3. $\dfrac{a}{\sin \angle A} = \dfrac{b}{\sin \angle B} = \dfrac{c}{\sin \angle C}$

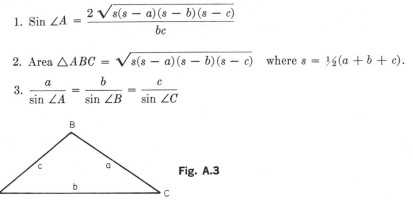

Fig. A.3

A.4   CIRCULAR MEASURE

The common and well-known measure of angles is *degrees:* a full circle, 360°; a half-circle, 180°; a quarter-circle, the so-called right angle, 90°; one-eighth circle, 45°; etc. The degree is further divided into 60 parts, each called a *minute,* and each minute is further divided into 60 parts, each called a *second.* Sometimes, as when using trigonometry tables going only to the nearest minute, it is easier to use decimals of a minute rather than going to seconds.

Somewhat less common and less understood is radian measure. It is a very convenient and useful measure and should be understood. The unit of angular measure in radian measure is an angle that intercepts an arc on the circumference of the circle equal in length to the radius of the circle. Since the circumference of a circle equals 2π radius, the total circle will contain 2π radians, or 6.2831853 radians (abbreviated rad). One radian will thus be equal to $\dfrac{360°}{6.2831853}$, or 57.2957795°, usually rounded off as 57.30°.

A.5 SQUARES, CUBES, SQUARE ROOTS, AND CUBE ROOTS

n	n^2	n^3	$\sqrt{n}$	$\sqrt{10n}$	$\sqrt[3]{n}$	$\sqrt[3]{10n}$	$\sqrt[3]{100n}$
1	1	1	1.000 000	3.162 278	1.000 000	2.154 435	4.641 589
2	4	8	1.414 214	4.472 136	1.259 921	2.714 418	5.848 035
3	9	27	1.732 051	5.477 226	1.442 250	3.107 233	6.694 330
4	16	64	2.000 000	6.324 555	1.587 401	3.419 952	7.368 063
5	25	125	2.236 068	7.071 068	1.709 976	3.684 031	7.937 005
6	36	216	2.449 490	7.745 967	1.817 121	3.914 868	8.434 327
7	49	343	2.645 751	8.366 600	1.912 931	4.121 285	8.879 040
8	64	512	2.828 427	8.944 272	2.000 000	4.308 869	9.283 178
9	81	729	3.000 000	9.486 833	2.080 084	4.481 405	9.654 894
10	100	1 000	3.162 278	10.000 00	2.154 435	4.641 589	10.000 00
11	121	1 331	3.316 625	10.488 09	2.223 980	4.791 420	10.322 80
12	144	1 728	3.464 102	10.954 45	2.289 428	4.932 424	10.626 59
13	169	2 197	3.605 551	11.401 75	2.351 335	5.065 797	10.913 93
14	196	2 744	3.741 657	11.832 16	2.410 142	5.192 494	11.186 89
15	225	3 375	3.872 983	12.247 45	2.466 212	5.313 293	11.447 14
16	256	4 096	4.000 000	12.649 11	2.519 842	5.428 835	11.696 07
17	289	4 913	4.123 106	13.038 40	2.571 282	5.539 658	11.934 83
18	324	5 832	4.242 641	13.416 41	2.620 741	5.646 216	12.164 40
19	361	6 859	4.358 899	13.784 05	2.668 402	5.748 897	12.385 62
20	400	8 000	4.472 136	14.142 14	2.714 418	5.848 035	12.599 21
21	441	9 261	4.582 576	14.491 38	2.758 924	5.943 922	12.805 79
22	484	10 648	4.690 416	14.832 40	2.802 039	6.036 811	13.005 91
23	529	12 167	4.795 832	15.165 75	2.843 867	6.126 926	13.200 06
24	576	13 824	4.898 979	15.491 93	2.884 499	6.214 465	13.388 66
25	625	15 625	5.000 000	15.811 39	2.924 018	6.299 605	13.572 09
26	676	17 576	5.099 020	16.124 52	2.962 496	6.382 504	13.750 69
27	729	19 683	5.196 152	16.431 68	3.000 000	6.463 304	13.924 77
28	784	21 952	5.291 503	16.733 20	3.036 589	6.542 133	14.094 60
29	841	24 389	5.385 165	17.029 39	3.072 317	6.619 106	14.260 43
30	900	27 000	5.477 226	17.320 51	3.107 233	6.694 330	14.422 50
31	961	29 791	5.567 764	17.606 82	3.141 381	6.767 899	14.581 00
32	1 024	32 768	5.656 854	17.888 54	3.174 802	6.839 904	14.736 13
33	1 089	35 937	5.744 563	18.165 90	3.207 534	6.910 423	14.888 06
34	1 156	39 304	5.830 952	18.439 09	3.239 612	6.979 532	15.036 95
35	1 225	42 875	5.916 080	18.708 29	3.271 066	7.047 299	15.182 94
36	1 296	46 656	6.000 000	18.973 67	3.301 927	7.113 787	15.326 19
37	1 369	50 653	6.082 763	19.235 38	3.332 222	7.179 054	15.466 80
38	1 444	54 872	6.164 414	19.493 59	3.361 975	7.243 156	15.604 91
39	1 521	59 319	6.244 998	19.748 42	3.391 211	7.306 144	15.740 61
40	1 600	64 000	6.324 555	20.000 00	3.419 952	7.368 063	15.874 01
41	1 681	68 921	6.403 124	20.248 46	3.448 217	7.428 959	16.005 21
42	1 764	74 088	6.480 741	20.493 90	3.476 027	7.488 872	16.134 29
43	1 849	79 507	6.557 439	20.736 44	3.503 398	7.547 842	16.261 33
44	1 936	85 184	6.633 250	20.976 18	3.530 348	7.605 905	16.386 43
45	2 025	91 125	6.708 204	21.213 20	3.556 893	7.663 094	16.509 64
46	2 116	97 336	6.782 330	21.447 61	3.583 048	7.719 443	16.631 03
47	2 209	103 823	6.855 655	21.679 48	3.608 826	7.774 980	16.750 69
48	2 304	110 592	6.928 203	21.908 90	3.634 241	7.829 735	16.868 65
49	2 401	117 649	7.000 000	22.135 94	3.659 306	7.883 735	16.984 99
50	2 500	125 000	7.071 068	22.360 68	3.684 031	7.937 005	17.099 76
51	2 601	132 651	7.141 428	22.583 18	3.708 430	7.989 570	17.213 01
52	2 704	140 608	7.211 103	22.803 51	3.732 511	8.041 452	17.324 78
53	2 809	148 877	7.280 110	23.021 73	3.756 286	8.092 672	17.435 13
54	2 916	157 464	7.348 469	23.237 90	3.779 763	8.143 253	17.544 11
55	3 025	166 375	7.416 198	23.452 08	3.802 952	8.193 213	17.651 74
56	3 136	175 616	7.483 315	23.664 32	3.825 862	8.242 571	17.758 08
57	3 249	185 193	7.549 834	23.874 67	3.848 501	8.291 344	17.863 16
58	3 364	195 112	7.615 773	24.083 19	3.870 877	8.339 551	17.967 02
59	3 481	205 379	7.681 146	24.289 92	3.892 996	8.387 207	18.069 69
60	3 600	216 000	7.745 967	24.494 90	3.914 868	8.434 327	18.171 21
61	3 721	226 981	7.810 250	24.698 18	3.936 497	8.480 926	18.271 60
62	3 844	238 328	7.874 008	24.899 80	3.957 892	8.527 019	18.370 91
63	3 969	250 047	7.937 254	25.099 80	3.979 057	8.572 619	18.469 15
64	4 096	262 144	8.000 000	25.298 22	4.000 000	8.617 739	18.566 36

n	n^2	n^3	$\sqrt{n}$	$\sqrt{10n}$	$\sqrt[3]{n}$	$\sqrt[3]{10n}$	$\sqrt[3]{100n}$
65	4 225	274 625	8.062 258	25.495 10	4.020 726	8.662 391	18.662 56
66	4 356	287 496	8.124 038	25.690 47	4.041 240	8.706 588	18.757 77
67	4 489	300 763	8.185 353	25.884 36	4.061 548	8.750 340	18.852 04
68	4 624	314 432	8.246 211	26.076 81	4.081 655	8.793 659	18.945 36
69	4 761	328 509	8.306 624	26.267 85	4.101 566	8.836 556	19.037 78
70	4 900	343 000	8.366 600	26.457 51	4.121 285	8.879 040	19.129 31
71	5 041	357 911	8.426 150	26.645 83	4.140 818	8.921 121	19.219 97
72	5 184	373 248	8.485 281	26.832 82	4.160 168	8.962 809	19.309 79
73	5 329	389 017	8.544 004	27.018 51	4.179 339	9.004 113	19.398 77
74	5 476	405 224	8.602 325	27.202 94	4.198 336	9.045 042	19.486 95
75	5 625	421 875	8.660 254	27.386 13	4.217 163	9.085 603	19.574 34
76	5 776	438 976	8.717 798	27.568 10	4.235 824	9.125 805	19.660 95
77	5 929	456 533	8.774 964	27.748 87	4.254 321	9.165 656	19.746 81
78	6 084	474 552	8.831 761	27.928 48	4.272 659	9.205 164	19.831 92
79	6 241	493 039	8.888 194	28.106 94	4.290 840	9.244 335	19.916 32
80	6 400	512 000	8.944 272	28.284 27	4.308 869	9.283 178	20.000 00
81	6 561	531 441	9.000 000	28.460 50	4.326 749	9.321 698	20.082 99
82	6 724	551 368	9.055 385	28.635 64	4.344 481	9.359 902	20.165 30
83	6 889	571 787	9.110 434	28.809 72	4.362 071	9.397 796	20.246 94
84	7 056	592 704	9.165 151	28.982 75	4.379 519	9.435 388	20.327 93
85	7 225	614 125	9.219 544	29.154 76	4.396 830	9.472 682	20.408 28
86	7 396	636 056	9.273 618	29.325 76	4.414 005	9.509 685	20.488 00
87	7 569	658 503	9.327 379	29.495 76	4.431 048	9.546 403	20.567 10
88	7 744	681 472	9.380 832	29.664 79	4.447 960	9.582 840	20.645 60
89	7 921	704 969	9.433 981	29.832 87	4.464 745	9.619 002	20.723 51
90	8 100	729 000	9.486 833	30.000 00	4.481 405	9.654 894	20.800 84
91	8 281	753 571	9.539 392	30.166 21	4.497 941	9.690 521	20.877 59
92	8 464	778 688	9.591 663	30.331 50	4.514 357	9.725 888	20.953 79
93	8 649	804 357	9.643 651	30.495 90	4.530 655	9.761 000	21.029 44
94	8 836	830 584	9.695 360	30.659 42	4.546 836	9.795 861	21.104 54
95	9 025	857 375	9.746 794	30.822 07	4.562 903	9.830 476	21.179 12
96	9 216	884 736	9.797 959	30.983 87	4.578 857	9.864 848	21.253 17
97	9 409	912 673	9.848 858	31.144 82	4.594 701	9.898 983	21.326 71
98	9 604	941 192	9.899 495	31.304 95	4.610 436	9.932 884	21.399 75
99	9 801	970 299	9.949 874	31.464 27	4.626 065	9.966 555	21.472 29
100	10 000	1 000 000	10.000 00	31.622 78	4.641 589	10.000 00	21.544 35
101	10 201	1 030 301	10.049 88	31.780 50	4.657 010	10.033 22	21.615 92
102	10 404	1 061 208	10.099 50	31.937 44	4.672 329	10.066 23	21.687 03
103	10 609	1 092 727	10.148 89	32.093 61	4.687 548	10.099 02	21.757 67
104	10 816	1 124 864	10.198 04	32.249 03	4.702 669	10.131 59	21.827 86
105	11 025	1 157 625	10.246 95	32.403 70	4.717 694	10.163 96	21.897 60
106	11 236	1 191 016	10.295 63	32.557 64	4.732 623	10.196 13	21.966 89
107	11 449	1 225 043	10.344 08	32.710 85	4.747 459	10.228 09	22.035 75
108	11 664	1 259 712	10.392 30	32.863 35	4.762 203	10.259 86	22.104 19
109	11 881	1 295 029	10.440 31	33.015 15	4.776 856	10.291 42	22.172 20
110	12 100	1 331 000	10.488 09	33.166 25	4.791 420	10.322 80	22.239 80
111	12 321	1 367 631	10.535 65	33.316 66	4.805 896	10.353 99	22.306 99
112	12 544	1 404 928	10.583 01	33.466 40	4.820 285	10.384 99	22.373 78
113	12 769	1 442 897	10.630 15	33.615 47	4.834 588	10.415 80	22.440 17
114	12 996	1 481 544	10.677 08	33.763 89	4.848 808	10.446 44	22.506 17
115	13 225	1 520 875	10.723 81	33.911 65	4.862 944	10.476 90	22.571 79
116	13 456	1 560 896	10.770 33	34.058 77	4.876 999	10.507 18	22.637 02
117	13 689	1 601 613	10.816 65	34.205 26	4.890 973	10.537 28	22.701 89
118	13 924	1 643 032	10.862 78	34.351 13	4.904 868	10.567 22	22.766 38
119	14 161	1 685 159	10.908 71	34.496 38	4.918 685	10.596 99	22.830 51
120	14 400	1 728 000	10.954 45	34.641 02	4.932 424	10.626 59	22.894 28
121	14 641	1 771 561	11.000 00	34.785 05	4.946 087	10.656 02	22.957 70
122	14 884	1 815 848	11.045 36	34.928 50	4.959 676	10.685 30	23.020 78
123	15 129	1 860 867	11.090 54	35.071 36	4.973 190	10.714 41	23.083 50
124	15 376	1 906 624	11.135 53	35.213 63	4.986 631	10.743 37	23.145 89
125	15 625	1 953 125	11.180 34	35.355 34	5.000 000	10.772 17	23.207 94
126	15 876	2 000 376	11.224 97	35.496 48	5.013 298	10.800 82	23.269 67
127	16 129	2 048 383	11.269 43	35.637 06	5.026 526	10.829 32	23.331 07
128	16 384	2 097 152	11.313 71	35.777 09	5.039 684	10.857 67	23.392 14
129	16 641	2 146 689	11.357 82	35.916 57	5.052 774	10.885 87	23.452 90

A.5   SQUARES, CUBES, SQUARE ROOTS, AND CUBE ROOTS *(Continued)*

n	n^2	n^3	$\sqrt{n}$	$\sqrt{10n}$	$\sqrt[3]{n}$	$\sqrt[3]{10n}$	$\sqrt[3]{100n}$
130	16 900	2 197 000	11.401 75	36.055 51	5.065 797	10.913 93	23.513 35
131	17 161	2 248 091	11.445 52	36.193 92	5.078 753	10.941 84	23.573 48
132	17 424	2 299 968	11.489 13	36.331 80	5.091 643	10.969 61	23.633 32
133	17 689	2 352 637	11.532 56	36.469 17	5.104 469	10.997 24	23.692 85
134	17 956	2 406 104	11.575 84	36.606 01	5.117 230	11.024 74	23.752 08
135	18 225	2 460 375	11.618 95	36.742 35	5.129 928	11.052 09	23.811 02
136	18 496	2 515 456	11.661 90	36.878 18	5.142 563	11.079 32	23.869 66
137	18 769	2 571 353	11.704 70	37.013 51	5.155 137	11.106 41	23.928 03
138	19 044	2 628 072	11.747 34	37.148 35	5.167 649	11.133 36	23.986 10
139	19 321	2 685 619	11.789 83	37.282 70	5.180 101	11.160 19	24.043 90
140	19 600	2 744 000	11.832 16	37.416 57	5.192 494	11.186 89	24.101 42
141	19 881	2 803 221	11.874 34	37.549 97	5.204 828	11.213 46	24.158 67
142	20 164	2 863 288	11.916 38	37.682 89	5.217 103	11.239 91	24.215 65
143	20 449	2 924 207	11.958 26	37.815 34	5.229 322	11.266 23	24.272 36
144	20 736	2 985 984	12.000 00	37.947 33	5.241 483	11.292 43	24.328 81
145	21 025	3 048 625	12.041 59	38.078 87	5.253 588	11.318 51	24.384 99
146	21 316	3 112 136	12.083 05	38.209 95	5.265 637	11.344 47	24.440 92
147	21 609	3 176 523	12.124 36	38.340 58	5.277 632	11.370 31	24.496 60
148	21 904	3 241 792	12.165 53	38.470 77	5.289 572	11.396 04	24.552 02
149	22 201	3 307 949	12.206 56	38.600 52	5.301 459	11.421 65	24.607 19
150	22 500	3 375 000	12.247 45	38.729 83	5.313 293	11.447 14	24.662 12
151	22 801	3 442 951	12.288 21	38.858 72	5.325 074	11.472 52	24.716 80
152	23 104	3 511 808	12.328 83	38.987 18	5.336 803	11.497 79	24.771 25
153	23 409	3 581 577	12.369 32	39.115 21	5.348 481	11.522 95	24.825 45
154	23 716	3 652 264	12.409 67	39.242 83	5.360 108	11.548 00	24.879 42
155	24 025	3 723 875	12.449 90	39.370 04	5.371 685	11.572 95	24.933 15
156	24 336	3 796 416	12.490 00	39.496 84	5.383 213	11.597 78	24.986 66
157	24 649	3 869 893	12.529 96	39.623 23	5.394 691	11.622 51	25.039 94
158	24 964	3 944 312	12.569 81	39.749 21	5.406 120	11.647 13	25.092 99
159	25 281	4 019 679	12.609 52	39.874 80	5.417 502	11.671 65	25.145 81
160	25 600	4 096 000	12.649 11	40.000 00	5.428 835	11.696 07	25.198 42
161	25 921	4 173 281	12.688 58	40.124 81	5.440 122	11.720 39	25.250 81
162	26 244	4 251 528	12.727 92	40.249 22	5.451 362	11.744 60	25.302 98
163	26 569	4 330 747	12.767 15	40.373 26	5.462 556	11.768 72	25.354 94
164	26 896	4 410 944	12.806 25	40.496 91	5.473 704	11.792 74	25.406 68
165	27 225	4 492 125	12.845 23	40.620 19	5.484 807	11.816 66	25.458 22
166	27 556	4 574 296	12.884 10	40.743 10	5.495 865	11.840 48	25.509 54
167	27 889	4 657 463	12.922 85	40.865 63	5.506 878	11.864 21	25.560 67
168	28 224	4 741 632	12.961 48	40.987 80	5.517 848	11.887 84	25.611 58
169	28 561	4 826 809	13.000 00	41.109 61	5.528 775	11.911 38	25.662 30
170	28 900	4 913 000	13.038 40	41.231 06	5.539 658	11.934 83	25.712 82
171	29 241	5 000 211	13.076 70	41.352 15	5.550 499	11.958 19	25.763 13
172	29 584	5 088 448	13.114 88	41.472 88	5.561 298	11.981 45	25.813 26
173	29 929	5 177 717	13.152 95	41.593 27	5.572 055	12.004 63	25.863 19
174	30 276	5 268 024	13.190 91	41.713 31	5.582 770	12.027 71	25.912 92
175	30 625	5 359 375	13.228 76	41.833 00	5.593 445	12.050 71	25.962 47
176	30 976	5 451 776	13.266 50	41.952 35	5.604 079	12.073 62	26.011 83
177	31 329	5 545 233	13.304 13	42.071 37	5.614 672	12.096 45	26.061 00
178	31 684	5 639 752	13.341 66	42.190 05	5.625 226	12.119 18	26.109 99
179	32 041	5 735 339	13.379 09	42.308 39	5.635 741	12.141 84	26.158 79
180	32 400	5 832 000	13.416 41	42.426 41	5.646 216	12.164 40	26.207 41
181	32 761	5 929 741	13.453 62	42.544 09	5.656 653	12.186 89	26.255 86
182	33 124	6 028 568	13.490 74	42.661 46	5.667 051	12.209 29	26.304 12
183	33 489	6 128 487	13.527 75	42.778 50	5.677 411	12.231 61	26.352 21
184	33 856	6 229 504	13.564 66	42.895 22	5.687 734	12.253 85	26.400 12
185	34 225	6 331 625	13.601 47	43.011 63	5.698 019	12.276 01	26.447 86
186	34 596	6 434 856	13.638 18	43.127 72	5.708 267	12.298 09	26.495 43
187	34 969	6 539 203	13.674 79	43.243 50	5.718 479	12.320 09	26.542 83
188	35 344	6 644 672	13.711 31	43.358 97	5.728 654	12.342 01	26.590 06
189	35 721	6 751 269	13.747 73	43.474 13	5.738 794	12.363 86	26.637 12
190	36 100	6 859 000	13.784 05	43.588 99	5.748 897	12.385 62	26.684 02
191	36 481	6 967 871	13.820 27	43.703 55	5.758 965	12.407 31	26.730 75
192	36 864	7 077 888	13.856 41	43.817 80	5.768 998	12.428 93	26.777 32
193	37 249	7 189 057	13.892 44	43.931 77	5.778 997	12.450 47	26.823 73
194	37 636	7 301 384	13.928 39	44.045 43	5.788 960	12.471 94	26.869 97

n	n^2	n^3	$\sqrt{n}$	$\sqrt{10n}$	$\sqrt[3]{n}$	$\sqrt[3]{10n}$	$\sqrt[3]{100n}$
195	38 025	7 414 875	13.964 24	44.158 80	5.798 890	12.493 33	26.916 06
196	38 416	7 529 536	14.000 00	44.271 89	5.808 786	12.514 65	26.961 99
197	38 809	7 645 373	14.035 67	44.384 68	5.818 648	12.535 90	27.007 77
198	39 204	7 762 392	14.071 25	44.497 19	5.828 477	12.557 07	27.053 39
199	39 601	7 880 599	14.106 74	44.609 42	5.838 272	12.578 18	27.098 86
200	40 000	8 000 000	14.142 14	44.721 36	5.848 035	12.599 21	27.144 18
201	40 401	8 120 601	14.177 45	44.833 02	5.857 766	12.620 17	27.189 34
202	40 804	8 242 408	14.212 67	44.944 41	5.867 464	12.641 07	27.234 36
203	41 209	8 365 427	14.247 81	45.055 52	5.877 131	12.661 89	27.279 22
204	41 616	8 489 664	14.282 86	45.166 36	5.886 765	12.682 65	27.323 94
205	42 025	8 615 125	14.317 82	45.276 93	5.896 369	12.703 34	27.368 52
206	42 436	8 741 816	14.352 70	45.387 22	5.905 941	12.723 96	27.412 95
207	42 849	8 869 743	14.387 49	45.497 25	5.915 482	12.744 52	27.457 23
208	43 264	8 990 912	14.422 21	45.607 02	5.924 992	12.765 01	27.501 38
209	43 681	9 129 329	14.456 83	45.716 52	5.934 472	12.785 43	27.545 38
210	44 100	9 261 000	14.491 38	45.825 76	5.943 922	12.805 79	27.589 24
211	44 521	9 393 931	14.525 84	45.934 74	5.953 342	12.826 09	27.632 96
212	44 944	9 528 128	14.560 22	46.043 46	5.962 732	12.846 32	27.676 55
213	45 369	9 663 597	14.594 52	46.151 92	5.972 093	12.866 48	27.720 00
214	45 796	9 800 344	14.628 74	46.260 13	5.981 424	12.886 59	27.763 31
215	46 225	9 938 375	14.662 88	46.368 09	5.990 726	12.906 63	27.806 49
216	46 656	10 077 696	14.696 94	46.475 80	6.000 000	12.926 61	27.849 53
217	47 089	10 218 313	14.730 92	46.583 26	6.009 245	12.946 53	27.892 44
218	47 524	10 360 232	14.764 82	46.690 47	6.018 462	12.966 38	27.935 22
219	47 961	10 503 459	14.798 65	46.797 44	6.027 650	12.986 18	27.977 87
220	48 400	10 648 000	14.832 40	46.904 16	6.036 811	13.005 91	28.020 39
221	48 841	10 793 861	14.866 07	47.010 64	6.045 944	13.025 59	28.062 78
222	49 284	10 941 048	14.899 66	47.116 88	6.055 049	13.045 21	28.105 05
223	49 729	11 089 567	14.933 18	47.222 88	6.064 127	13.064 77	28.147 18
224	50 176	11 239 424	14.966 63	47.328 64	6.073 178	13.084 27	28.189 19
225	50 625	11 390 625	15.000 00	47.434 16	6.082 202	13.103 71	28.231 08
226	51 076	11 543 176	15.033 30	47.539 46	6.091 199	13.123 09	28.272 84
227	51 529	11 697 083	15.066 52	47.644 52	6.100 170	13.142 42	28.314 48
228	51 984	11 852 352	15.099 67	47.749 35	6.109 115	13.161 69	28.356 00
229	52 441	12 008 989	15.132 75	47.853 94	6.118 033	13.180 90	28.397 39
230	52 900	12 167 000	15.165 75	47.958 32	6.126 926	13.200 06	28.438 67
231	53 361	12 326 391	15.198 68	48.062 46	6.135 792	13.219 16	28.479 83
232	53 824	12 487 168	15.231 55	48.166 38	6.144 634	13.238 21	28.520 86
233	54 289	12 649 337	15.264 34	48.270 07	6.153 449	13.257 21	28.561 78
234	54 756	12 812 904	15.297 06	48.373 55	6.162 240	13.276 14	28.602 59
235	55 225	12 977 875	15.329 71	48.476 80	6.171 006	13.295 03	28.643 27
236	55 696	13 144 256	15.362 29	48.579 83	6.179 747	13.313 86	28.683 84
237	56 169	13 312 053	15.394 80	48.682 65	6.188 463	13.332 64	28.724 30
238	56 644	13 481 272	15.427 25	48.785 24	6.197 154	13.351 36	28.764 64
239	57 121	13 651 919	15.459 62	48.887 63	6.205 822	13.370 04	28.804 87
240	57 600	13 824 000	15.491 93	48.989 79	6.214 465	13.388 66	28.844 99
241	58 081	13 997 521	15.524 17	49.091 75	6.223 084	13.407 23	28.885 00
242	58 564	14 172 488	15.556 35	49.193 50	6.231 680	13.425 75	28.924 89
243	59 049	14 348 907	15.588 46	49.295 03	6.240 251	13.444 21	28.964 68
244	59 536	14 526 784	15.620 50	49.396 36	6.248 800	13.462 63	29.004 36
245	60 025	14 706 125	15.652 48	49.497 47	6.257 325	13.481 00	29.043 93
246	60 516	14 886 936	15.684 39	49.598 39	6.265 827	13.499 31	29.083 39
247	61 009	15 069 223	15.716 23	49.699 09	6.274 305	13.517 58	29.122 75
248	61 504	15 252 992	15.748 02	49.799 60	6.282 761	13.535 80	29.161 99
249	62 001	15 438 249	15.779 73	49.899 90	6.291 195	13.553 97	29.201 14
250	62 500	15 625 000	15.811 39	50.000 00	6.299 605	13.572 09	29.240 18
251	63 001	15 813 251	15.842 98	50.099 90	6.307 994	13.590 16	29.279 11
252	63 504	16 003 008	15.874 51	50.199 60	6.316 360	13.608 18	29.317 94
253	64 009	16 194 277	15.905 97	50.299 11	6.324 704	13.626 16	29.356 67
254	64 516	16 387 064	15.937 38	50.398 41	6.333 026	13.644 09	29.395 30
255	65 025	16 581 375	15.968 72	50.497 52	6.341 326	13.661 97	29.433 83
256	65 536	16 777 216	16.000 00	50.596 44	6.349 604	13.679 81	29.472 25
257	66 049	16 974 593	16.031 22	50.695 17	6.357 861	13.697 60	29.510 58
258	66 564	17 173 512	16.062 38	50.793 70	6.366 097	13.715 34	29.548 80
259	67 081	17 373 979	16.093 48	50.892 04	6.374 311	13.733 04	29.586 93

A.5   SQUARES, CUBES, SQUARE ROOTS, AND CUBE ROOTS *(Continued)*

n	n^2	n^3	$\sqrt{n}$	$\sqrt{10n}$	$\sqrt[3]{n}$	$\sqrt[3]{10n}$	$\sqrt[3]{100n}$
260	67 600	17 576 000	16.124 52	50.990 20	6.382 504	13.750 69	29.624 96
261	68 121	17 779 581	16.155 49	51.088 16	6.390 677	13.768 30	29.662 89
262	68 644	17 984 728	16.186 41	51.185 94	6.398 828	13.785 86	29.700 73
263	69 169	18 191 447	16.217 27	51.283 53	6.406 959	13.803 37	29.738 47
264	69 696	18 399 744	16.248 08	51.380 93	6.415 069	13.820 85	29.776 11
265	70 225	18 609 625	16.278 82	51.478 15	6.423 158	13.838 28	29.813 66
266	70 756	18 821 096	16.309 51	51.575 19	6.431 228	13.855 66	29.851 11
267	71 289	19 034 163	16.340 13	51.672 04	6.439 277	13.873 00	29.888 47
268	71 824	19 248 832	16.370 71	51.768 72	6.447 306	13.890 30	29.925 74
269	72 361	19 465 109	16.401 22	51.865 21	6.455 315	13.907 55	29.962 92
270	72 900	19 683 000	16.431 68	51.961 52	6.463 304	13.924 77	30.000 00
271	73 441	19 902 511	16.462 08	52.057 66	6.471 274	13.941 94	30.036 99
272	73 984	20 123 648	16.492 42	52.153 62	6.479 224	13.959 06	30.073 89
273	74 529	20 346 417	16.522 71	52.249 40	6.487 154	13.976 15	30.110 70
274	75 076	20 570 824	16.552 95	52.345 01	6.495 065	13.993 19	30.147 42
275	75 625	20 796 875	16.583 12	52.440 44	6.502 957	14.010 20	30.184 05
276	76 176	21 024 576	16.613 25	52.535 70	6.510 830	14.027 16	30.220 60
277	76 729	21 253 933	16.643 32	52.630 79	6.518 684	14.044 08	30.257 05
278	77 284	21 484 952	16.673 33	52.725 71	6.526 519	14.060 96	30.293 42
279	77 841	21 717 639	16.703 29	52.820 45	6.534 335	14.077 80	30.329 70
280	78 400	21 952 000	16.733 20	52.915 03	6.542 133	14.094 60	30.365 89
281	78 961	22 188 041	16.763 05	53.009 43	6.549 912	14.111 36	30.402 00
282	79 524	22 425 768	16.792 86	53.103 67	6.557 672	14.128 08	30.438 02
283	80 089	22 665 187	16.822 60	53.197 74	6.565 414	14.144 76	30.473 95
284	80 656	22 906 304	16.852 30	53.291 65	6.573 138	14.161 40	30.509 81
285	81 225	23 149 125	16.881 94	53.385 39	6.580 844	14.178 00	30.545 57
286	81 796	23 393 656	16.911 53	53.478 97	6.588 532	14.194 56	30.581 26
287	82 369	23 639 903	16.941 07	53.572 38	6.596 202	14.211 09	30.616 86
288	82 944	23 887 872	16.970 56	53.665 63	6.603 854	14.227 57	30.652 38
289	83 521	24 137 569	17.000 00	53.758 72	6.611 489	14.244 02	30.687 81
290	84 100	24 389 000	17.029 39	53.851 65	6.619 106	14.260 43	30.723 17
291	84 681	24 642 171	17.058 72	53.944 42	6.626 705	14.276 80	30.758 44
292	85 264	24 897 088	17.088 01	54.037 02	6.634 287	14.293 14	30.793 63
293	85 849	25 153 757	17.117 24	54.129 47	6.641 852	14.309 44	30.828 75
294	86 436	25 412 184	17.146 43	54.221 77	6.649 400	14.325 70	30.863 78
295	87 025	25 672 375	17.175 56	54.313 90	6.656 930	14.341 92	30.898 73
296	87 616	25 934 336	17.204 65	54.405 88	6.664 444	14.358 11	30.933 61
297	88 209	26 198 073	17.233 69	54.497 71	6.671 940	14.374 26	30.968 40
298	88 804	26 463 592	17.262 68	54.589 38	6.679 420	14.390 37	31.003 12
299	89 401	26 730 899	17.291 62	54.680 89	6.686 883	14.406 45	31.037 76
300	90 000	27 000 000	17.320 51	54.772 26	6.694 330	14.422 50	31.072 33
301	90 601	27 270 901	17.349 35	54.863 47	6.701 759	14.438 50	31.106 81
302	91 204	27 543 608	17.378 15	54.954 53	6.709 173	14.454 47	31.141 22
303	91 809	27 818 127	17.406 90	55.045 44	6.716 570	14.470 41	31.175 56
304	92 416	28 094 464	17.435 60	55.136 20	6.723 951	14.486 31	31.209 82
305	93 025	28 372 625	17.464 25	55.226 81	6.731 315	14.502 18	31.244 00
306	93 636	28 652 616	17.492 86	55.317 27	6.738 664	14.518 01	31.278 11
307	94 249	28 934 443	17.521 42	55.407 58	6.745 997	14.533 81	31.312 14
308	94 864	29 218 112	17.549 93	55.497 75	6.753 313	14.549 57	31.346 10
309	95 481	29 503 629	17.578 40	55.587 77	6.760 614	14.565 30	31.379 99
310	96 100	29 791 000	17.606 82	55.677 64	6.767 899	14.581 00	31.413 81
311	96 721	30 080 231	17.635 19	55.767 37	6.775 169	14.596 66	31.447 55
312	97 344	30 371 328	17.663 52	55.856 96	6.782 423	14.612 29	31.481 22
313	97 969	30 664 297	17.691 81	55.946 40	6.789 661	14.627 88	31.514 82
314	98 596	30 959 144	17.720 05	56.035 70	6.796 884	14.643 44	31.548 34
315	99 225	31 255 875	17.748 24	56.124 86	6.804 092	14.658 97	31.581 80
316	99 856	31 554 496	17.776 39	56.213 88	6.811 285	14.674 47	31.615 18
317	100 489	31 855 013	17.804 49	56.302 75	6.818 462	14.689 93	31.648 50
318	101 124	32 157 432	17.832 55	56.391 49	6.825 624	14.705 36	31.681 74
319	101 761	32 461 759	17.860 57	56.480 08	6.832 771	14.720 76	31.714 92
320	102 400	32 768 000	17.888 54	56.568 54	6.839 904	14.736 13	31.748 02
321	103 041	33 076 161	17.916 47	56.656 86	6.847 021	14.751 46	31.781 06
322	103 684	33 386 248	17.944 36	56.745 04	6.854 124	14.766 76	31.814 03
323	104 329	33 698 267	17.972 20	56.833 09	6.861 212	14.782 03	31.846 93
324	104 976	34 012 224	18.000 00	56.921 00	6.868 285	14.797 27	31.879 76

n	n^2	n^3	$\sqrt{n}$	$\sqrt{10n}$	$\sqrt[3]{n}$	$\sqrt[3]{10n}$	$\sqrt[3]{100n}$
325	105 625	34 328 125	18.027 76	57.008 77	6.875 344	14.812 48	31.912 52
326	106 276	34 645 976	18.055 47	57.096 41	6.882 389	14.827 66	31.945 22
327	106 929	34 965 783	18.083 14	57.183 91	6.889 419	14.842 80	31.977 85
328	107 584	35 287 552	18.110 77	57.271 28	6.896 434	14.857 92	32.010 41
329	108 241	35 611 289	18.138 36	57.358 52	6.903 436	14.873 00	32.042 91
330	108 900	35 937 000	18.165 90	57.445 63	6.910 423	14.888 06	32.075 34
331	109 561	36 264 691	18.193 41	57.532 60	6.917 396	14.903 08	32.107 71
332	110 224	36 594 368	18.220 87	57.619 44	6.924 356	14.918 07	32.140 01
333	110 889	36 926 037	18.248 29	57.706 15	6.931 301	14.933 03	32.172 25
334	111 556	37 259 704	18.275 67	57.792 73	6.938 232	14.947 97	32.204 42
335	112 225	37 595 375	18.303 01	57.879 18	6.945 150	14.962 87	32.236 53
336	112 896	37 933 056	18.330 30	57.965 51	6.952 053	14.977 74	32.268 57
337	113 569	38 272 753	18.357 56	58.051 70	6.958 -943	14.992 59	32.300 55
338	114 244	38 614 472	18.384 78	58.137 77	6.965 820	15.007 40	32.332 47
339	114 921	38 958 219	18.411 95	58.223 71	6.972 683	15.022 19	32.364 33
340	115 600	39 304 000	18.439 09	58.309 52	6.979 532	15.036 95	32.396 12
341	116 281	39 651 821	18.466 19	58.395 21	6.986 368	15.051 67	32.427 85
342	116 964	40 001 688	18.493 24	58.480 77	6.993 191	15.066 37	32.459 52
343	117 649	40 353 607	18.520 26	58.566 20	7.000 000	15.081 04	32.491 12
344	118 336	40 707 584	18.547 24	58.651 51	7.006 796	15.095 68	32.522 67
345	119 025	41 063 625	18.574 18	58.736 70	7.013 579	15.110 30	32.554 15
346	119 716	41 421 736	18.601 08	58.821 76	7.020 349	15.124 88	32.585 57
347	120 409	41 781 923	18.627 94	58.906 71	7.027 106	15.139 44	32.616 94
348	121 104	42 144 192	18.654 76	58.991 52	7.033 850	15.153 97	32.648 24
349	121 801	42 508 549	18.681 54	59.076 22	7.040 581	15.168 47	32.679 48
350	122 500	42 875 000	18.708 29	59.160 80	7.047 299	15.182 94	32.710 66
351	123 201	43 243 551	18.734 99	59.245 25	7.054 004	15.197 39	32.741 79
352	123 904	43 614 208	18.761 66	59.329 59	7.060 697	15.211 81	32.772 85
353	124 609	43 986 977	18.788 29	59.413 80	7.067 377	15.226 20	32.803 86
354	125 316	44 361 864	18.814 89	59.497 90	7.074 044	15.240 57	32.834 80
355	126 025	44 738 875	18.841 44	59.581 88	7.080 699	15.254 90	32.865 69
356	126 736	45 118 016	18.867 96	59.665 74	7.087 341	15.269 21	32.896 52
357	127 449	45 499 293	18.894 44	59.749 48	7.093 971	15.283 50	32.927 30
358	128 164	45 882 712	18.920 89	59.833 10	7.100 588	15.297 75	32.958 01
359	128 881	46 268 279	18.947 30	59.916 61	7.107 194	15.311 98	32.988 67
360	129 600	46 656 000	18.973 67	60.000 00	7.113 787	15.326 19	33.019 27
361	130 321	47 045 881	19.000 00	60.083 28	7.120 367	15.340 37	33.049 82
362	131 044	47 437 928	19.026 30	60.166 44	7.126 936	15.354 52	33.080 31
363	131 769	47 832 147	19.052 56	60.249 48	7.133 492	15.368 64	33.110 74
364	132 496	48 228 544	19.078 78	60.332 41	7.140 037	15.382 74	33.141 12
365	133 225	48 627 125	19.104 97	60.415 23	7.146 569	15.396 82	33.171 44
366	133 956	49 027 896	19.131 13	60.497 93	7.153 090	15.410 87	33.201 70
367	134 689	49 430 863	19.157 24	60.580 52	7.159 599	15.424 89	33.231 91
368	135 424	49 836 032	19.183 33	60.663 00	7.166 096	15.438 89	33.262 07
369	136 161	50 243 409	19.209 37	60.745 37	7.172 581	15.452 86	33.292 17
370	136 900	50 653 000	19.235 38	60.827 63	7.179 054	15.466 80	33.322 22
371	137 641	51 064 811	19.261 36	60.909 77	7.185 516	15.480 73	33.352 21
372	138 384	51 478 848	19.287 30	60.991 80	7.191 966	15.494 62	33.382 15
373	139 129	51 895 117	19.313 21	61.073 73	7.198 405	15.508 49	33.412 04
374	139 876	52 313 624	19.339 08	61.155 54	7.204 832	15.522 34	33.441 87
375	140 625	52 734 375	19.364 92	61.237 24	7.211 248	15.536 16	33.471 65
376	141 376	53 157 376	19.390 72	61.318 84	7.217 652	15.549 96	33.501 37
377	142 129	53 582 633	19.416 49	61.400 33	7.224 045	15.563 73	33.531 05
378	142 884	54 010 152	19.442 22	61.481 70	7.230 427	15.577 48	33.560 67
379	143 641	54 439 939	19.467 92	61.562 98	7.236 797	15.591 21	33.590 24
380	144 400	54 872 000	19.493 59	61.644 14	7.243 156	15.604 91	33.619 75
381	145 161	55 306 341	19.519 22	61.725 20	7.249 505	15.618 58	33.649 22
382	145 924	55 742 968	19.544 82	61.806 15	7.255 842	15.632 24	33.678 63
383	146 689	56 181 887	19.570 39	61.886 99	7.262 167	15.645 87	33.708 00
384	147 456	56 623 104	19.595 92	61.967 73	7.268 482	15.659 47	33.737 31
385	148 225	57 066 625	19.621 42	62.048 37	7.274 786	15.673 05	33.766 57
386	148 996	57 512 456	19.646 88	62.128 90	7.281 079	15.686 61	33.795 78
387	149 769	57 960 603	19.672 32	62.209 32	7.287 362	15.700 14	33.824 94
388	150 544	58 411 072	19.697 72	62.289 65	7.293 633	15.713 66	33.854 05
389	151 321	58 863 869	19.723 08	62.369 86	7.299 894	15.727 14	33.883 10

A.5 SQUARES, CUBES, SQUARE ROOTS, AND CUBE ROOTS *(Continued)*

n	n^2	n^3	$\sqrt{n}$	$\sqrt{10n}$	$\sqrt[3]{n}$	$\sqrt[3]{10n}$	$\sqrt[3]{100n}$
390	152 100	59 319 000	19.748 42	62.449 98	7.306 144	15.740 61	33.912 11
391	152 881	59 776 471	19.773 72	62.529 99	7.312 383	15.754 05	33.941 07
392	153 664	60 236 288	19.798 99	62.609 90	7.318 611	15.767 47	33.969 99
393	154 449	60 698 457	19.824 23	62.689 71	7.324 829	15.780 87	33.998 85
394	155 236	61 162 984	19.849 43	62.769 42	7.331 037	15.794 24	34.027 66
395	156 025	61 629 875	19.874 61	62.849 03	7.337 234	15.807 59	34.056 42
396	156 816	62 099 136	19.899 75	62.928 53	7.343 420	15.820 92	34.085 14
397	157 609	62 570 773	19.924 86	63.007 94	7.349 597	15.834 23	34.113 81
398	158 404	63 044 792	19.949 94	63.087 24	7.355 762	15.847 51	34.142 42
399	159 201	63 521 199	19.974 98	63.166 45	7.361 918	15.860 77	34.171 00
400	160 000	64 000 000	20.000 00	63.245 55	7.368 063	15.874 01	34.199 52
401	160 801	64 481 201	20.024 98	63.324 56	7.374 198	15.887 23	34.227 99
402	161 604	64 964 808	20.049 94	63.403 47	7.380 323	15.900 42	34.256 42
403	162 409	65 450 827	20.074 86	63.482 28	7.386 437	15.913 60	34.284 80
404	163 216	65 939 264	20.099 75	63.560 99	7.392 542	15.926 75	34.313 14
405	164 025	66 430 125	20.124 61	63.639 61	7.398 636	15.939 88	34.341 43
406	164 836	66 923 416	20.149 44	63.718 13	7.404 721	15.952 99	34.369 67
407	165 649	67 419 143	20.174 24	63.796 55	7.410 795	15.966 07	34.397 86
408	166 464	67 917 312	20.199 01	63.874 88	7.416 860	15.979 14	34.426 01
409	167 281	68 417 929	20.223 75	63.953 11	7.422 914	15.992 18	34.454 12
410	168 100	68 921 000	20.248 46	64.031 24	7.428 959	16.005 21	34.482 17
411	168 921	69 426 531	20.273 13	64.109 28	7.434 994	16.018 21	34.510 18
412	169 744	69 934 528	20.297 78	64.187 23	7.441 019	16.031 19	34.538 15
413	170 569	70 444 997	20.322 40	64.265 08	7.447 034	16.044 15	34.566 07
414	171 396	70 957 944	20.346 99	64.342 83	7.453 040	16.057 09	34.593 95
415	172 225	71 473 375	20.371 55	64.420 49	7.459 036	16.070 01	34.621 78
416	173 056	71 991 296	20.396 08	64.498 06	7.465 022	16.082 90	34.649 56
417	173 889	72 511 713	20.420 58	64.575 54	7.470 999	16.095 78	34.677 31
418	174 724	73 034 632	20.445 05	64.652 92	7.476 966	16.108 64	34.705 00
419	175 561	73 560 059	20.469 49	64.730 21	7.482 924	16.121 47	34.732 66
420	176 400	74 088 000	20.493 90	64.807 41	7.488 872	16.134 29	34.760 27
421	177 241	74 618 461	20.518 28	64.884 51	7.494 811	16.147 08	34.787 83
422	178 084	75 151 448	20.542 64	64.961 53	7.500 741	16.159 86	34.815 35
423	178 929	75 686 967	20.566 96	65.038 45	7.506 661	16.172 61	34.842 83
424	179 776	76 225 024	20.591 26	65.115 28	7.512 572	16.185 34	34.870 27
425	180 625	76 765 625	20.615 53	65.192 02	7.518 473	16.198 06	34.897 66
426	181 476	77 308 776	20.639 77	65.268 68	7.524 365	16.210 75	34.925 01
427	182 329	77 854 483	20.663 98	65.345 24	7.530 248	16.223 43	34.952 32
428	183 184	78 402 752	20.688 16	65.421 71	7.536 122	16.236 08	34.979 58
429	184 041	78 953 589	20.712 32	65.498 09	7.541 987	16.248 72	35.006 80
430	184 900	79 507 000	20.736 44	65.574 39	7.547 842	16.261 33	35.033 98
431	185 761	80 062 991	20.760 54	65.650 59	7.553 689	16.273 93	35.061 12
432	186 624	80 621 568	20.784 61	65.726 71	7.559 526	16.286 51	35.088 21
433	187 489	81 182 737	20.808 65	65.802 74	7.565 355	16.299 06	35.115 27
434	188 356	81 746 504	20.832 67	65.878 68	7.571 174	16.311 60	35.142 28
435	189 225	82 312 875	20.856 65	65.954 53	7.576 985	16.324 12	35.169 25
436	190 096	82 881 856	20.880 61	66.030 30	7.582 787	16.336 62	35.196 18
437	190 969	83 453 453	20.904 54	66.105 98	7.588 579	16.349 10	35.223 07
438	191 844	84 027 672	20.928 45	66.181 57	7.594 363	16.361 56	35.249 91
439	192 721	84 604 519	20.952 33	66.257 08	7.600 139	16.374 00	35.276 72
440	193 600	85 184 000	20.976 18	66.332 50	7.605 905	16.386 43	35.303 48
441	194 481	85 766 121	21.000 00	66.407 83	7.611 663	16.398 83	35.330 21
442	195 364	86 350 888	21.023 80	66.483 08	7.617 412	16.411 22	35.356 89
443	196 249	86 938 307	21.047 57	66.558 25	7.623 152	16.423 58	35.383 54
444	197 136	87 528 384	21.071 31	66.633 32	7.628 884	16.435 93	35.410 14
445	198 025	88 121 125	21.095 02	66.708 32	7.634 607	16.448 26	35.436 71
446	198 916	88 716 536	21.118 71	66.783 23	7.640 321	16.460 57	35.463 23
447	199 809	89 314 623	21.142 37	66.858 06	7.646 027	16.472 87	35.489 71
448	200 704	89 915 392	21.166 01	66.932 80	7.651 725	16.485 14	35.516 16
449	201 601	90 518 849	21.189 62	67.007 46	7.657 414	16.497 40	35.542 57
450	202 500	91 125 000	21.213 20	67.082 04	7.663 094	16.509 64	35.568 93
451	203 401	91 733 851	21.236 76	67.156 53	7.668 766	16.521 86	35.595 26
452	204 304	92 345 408	21.260 29	67.230 95	7.674 430	16.534 06	35.621 55
453	205 209	92 959 677	21.283 80	67.305 27	7.680 086	16.546 24	35.647 80
454	206 116	93 576 664	21.307 28	67.379 52	7.685 733	16.558 41	35.674 01

n	n^2	n^3	$\sqrt{n}$	$\sqrt{10n}$	$\sqrt[3]{n}$	$\sqrt[3]{10n}$	$\sqrt[3]{100n}$
455	207 025	94 196 375	21.330 73	67.453 69	7.691 372	16.570 56	35.700 18
456	207 936	94 818 816	21.354 16	67.527 77	7.697 002	16.582 69	35.726 32
457	208 849	95 443 993	21.377 56	67.601 78	7.702 625	16.594 80	35.752 42
458	209 764	96 071 912	21.400 93	67.675 70	7.708 239	16.606 90	35.778 48
459	210 681	96 702 579	21.424 29	67.749 54	7.713 845	16.618 97	35.804 50
460	211 600	97 336 000	21.447 61	67.823 30	7.719 443	16.631 03	35.830 48
461	212 521	97 972 181	21.470 91	67.896 98	7.725 032	16.643 08	35.856 42
462	213 444	98 611 128	21.494 19	67.970 58	7.730 614	16.655 10	35.882 33
463	214 369	99 252 847	21.517 43	68.044 10	7.736 188	16.667 11	35.908 20
464	215 296	99 897 344	21.540 66	68.117 55	7.741 753	16.679 10	35.934 04
465	216 225	100 544 625	21.563 86	68.190 91	7.747 311	16.691 08	35.959 83
466	217 156	101 194 696	21.587 03	68.264 19	7.752 861	16.703 03	35.985 59
467	218 089	101 847 563	21.610 18	68.337 40	7.758 402	16.714 97	36.011 31
468	219 024	102 503 232	21.633 31	68.410 53	7.763 936	16.726 89	36.037 00
469	219 961	103 161 709	21.656 41	68.483 57	7.769 462	16.738 80	36.062 65
470	220 900	103 823 000	21.679 48	68.556 55	7.774 980	16.750 69	36.088 26
471	221 841	104 487 111	21.702 53	68.629 44	7.780 490	16.762 56	36.113 84
472	222 784	105 154 048	21.725 56	68.702 26	7.785 993	16.774 41	36.139 38
473	223 729	105 823 817	21.748 56	68.775 00	7.791 488	16.786 25	36.164 88
474	224 676	106 496 424	21.771 54	68.847 66	7.796 975	16.798 07	36.190 35
475	225 625	107 171 875	21.794 49	68.920 24	7.802 454	16.809 88	36.215 78
476	226 576	107 850 176	21.817 42	68.992 75	7.807 925	16.821 67	36.241 18
477	227 529	108 531 333	21.840 33	69.065 19	7.813 389	16.833 44	36.266 54
478	228 484	109 215 352	21.863 21	69.137 54	7.818 846	16.845 19	36.291 87
479	229 441	109 902 239	21.886 07	69.209 83	7.824 294	16.856 93	36.317 16
480	230 400	110 592 000	21.908 90	69.282 03	7.829 735	16.868 65	36.342 41
481	231 361	111 284 641	21.931 71	69.354 16	7.835 169	16.880 36	36.367 63
482	232 324	111 980 168	21.954 50	69.426 22	7.840 595	16.892 05	36.392 82
483	233 289	112 678 587	21.977 26	69.498 20	7.846 013	16.903 72	36.417 97
484	234 256	113 379 904	22.000 00	69.570 11	7.851 424	16.915 38	36.443 08
485	235 225	114 084 125	22.022 72	69.641 94	7.856 828	16.927 02	36.468 17
486	236 196	114 791 256	22.045 41	69.713 70	7.862 224	16.938 65	36.493 21
487	237 169	115 501 303	22.068 08	69.785 39	7.867 613	16.950 26	36.518 22
488	238 144	116 214 272	22.090 72	69.857 00	7.872 994	16.961 85	36.543 20
489	239 121	116 930 169	22.113 34	69.928 53	7.878 368	16.973 43	36.568 15
490	240 100	117 649 000	22.135 94	70.000 00	7.883 735	16.984 99	36.593 06
491	241 081	118 370 771	22.158 52	70.071 39	7.889 095	16.996 54	36.617 93
492	242 064	119 095 488	22.181 07	70.142 71	7.894 447	17.008 07	36.642 78
493	243 049	119 823 157	22.203 60	70.213 96	7.899 792	17.019 59	36.667 58
494	244 036	120 553 784	22.226 11	70.285 13	7.905 129	17.031 08	36.692 36
495	245 025	121 287 375	22.248 60	70.356 24	7.910 460	17.042 57	36.717 10
496	246 016	122 023 936	22.271 06	70.427 27	7.915 783	17.054 04	36.741 81
497	247 009	122 763 473	22.293 50	70.498 23	7.921 099	17.065 49	36.766 49
498	248 004	123 505 992	22.315 91	70.569 12	7.926 408	17.076 93	36.791 13
499	249 001	124 251 499	22.338 31	70.639 93	7.931 710	17.088 35	36.815 74
500	250 000	125 000 000	22.360 68	70.710 68	7.937 005	17.099 76	36.840 31
501	251 001	125 751 501	22.383 03	70.781 35	7.942 293	17.111 15	36.864 86
502	252 004	126 506 008	22.405 36	70.851 96	7.947 574	17.122 53	36.889 37
503	253 009	127 263 527	22.427 66	70.922 49	7.952 848	17.133 89	36.913 85
504	254 016	128 024 064	22.449 94	70.992 96	7.958 114	17.145 24	36.938 30
505	255 025	128 787 625	22.472 21	71.063 35	7.963 374	17.156 57	36.962 71
506	256 036	129 554 216	22.494 44	71.133 68	7.968 627	17.167 89	36.987 09
507	257 049	130 323 843	22.516 66	71.203 93	7.973 873	17.179 19	37.011 44
508	258 064	131 096 512	22.538 86	71.274 12	7.979 112	17.190 48	37.035 76
509	259 081	131 872 229	22.561 03	71.344 24	7.984 344	17.201 75	37.060 04
510	260 100	132 651 000	22.583 18	71.414 28	7.989 570	17.213 01	37.084 30
511	261 121	133 432 831	22.605 31	71.484 26	7.994 788	17.224 25	37.108 52
512	262 144	134 217 728	22.627 42	71.554 18	8.000 000	17.235 48	37.132 71
513	263 169	135 005 697	22.649 50	71.624 02	8.005 205	17.246 69	37.156 87
514	264 196	135 796 744	22.671 57	71.693 79	8.010 403	17.257 89	37.181 00
515	265 225	136 590 875	22.693 61	71.763 50	8.015 595	17.269 08	37.205 09
516	266 256	137 388 096	22.715 63	71.833 14	8.020 779	17.280 25	37.229 16
517	267 289	138 188 413	22.737 63	71.902 71	8.025 957	17.291 40	37.253 19
518	268 324	138 991 832	22.759 61	71.972 22	8.031 129	17.302 54	37.277 20
519	269 361	139 798 359	22.781 57	72.041 65	8.036 293	17.313 67	37.301 17

A.5 SQUARES, CUBES, SQUARE ROOTS, AND CUBE ROOTS *(Continued)*

n	n^2	n^3	$\sqrt{n}$	$\sqrt{10n}$	$\sqrt[3]{n}$	$\sqrt[3]{10n}$	$\sqrt[3]{100n}$
520	270 400	140 608 000	22.803 51	72.111 03	8.041 452	17.324 78	37.325 11
521	271 441	141 420 761	22.825 42	72.180 33	8.046 603	17.335 88	37.349 02
522	272 484	142 236 648	22.847 32	72.249 57	8.051 748	17.346 96	37.372 90
523	273 529	143 055 667	22.869 19	72.318 74	8.056 886	17.358 04	37.396 75
524	274 576	143 877 824	22.891 05	72.387 84	8.062 018	17.369 09	37.420 57
525	275 625	144 703 125	22.912 88	72.456 88	8.067 143	17.380 13	37.444 36
526	276 676	145 531 576	22.934 69	72.525 86	8.072 262	17.391 16	37.468 12
527	277 729	146 363 183	22.956 48	72.594 77	8.077 374	17.402 18	37.491 85
528	278 784	147 197 952	22.978 25	72.663 61	8.082 480	17.413 18	37.515 55
529	279 841	148 035 889	23.000 00	72.732 39	8.087 579	17.424 16	37.539 22
530	280 900	148 877 000	23.021 73	72.801 10	8.092 672	17.435 13	37.562 86
531	281 961	149 721 291	23.043 44	72.869 75	8.097 759	17.446 09	37.586 47
532	283 024	150 568 768	23.065 13	72.938 33	8.102 839	17.457 04	37.610 05
533	284 089	151 419 437	23.086 79	73.006 85	8.107 913	17.467 97	37.633 60
534	285 156	152 273 304	23.108 44	73.075 30	8.112 980	17.478 89	37.657 12
535	286 225	153 130 375	23.130 07	73.143 69	8.118 041	17.489 79	37.680 61
536	287 296	153 990 656	23.151 67	73.212 02	8.123 096	17.500 68	37.704 07
537	288 369	154 854 153	23.173 26	73.280 28	8.128 145	17.511 56	37.727 51
538	289 444	155 720 872	23.194 83	73.348 48	8.133 187	17.522 42	37.750 91
539	290 521	156 590 819	23.216 37	73.416 62	8.138 223	17.533 27	37.774 29
540	291 600	157 464 000	23.237 90	73.484 69	8.143 253	17.544 11	37.797 63
541	292 681	158 340 421	23.259 41	73.552 70	8.148 276	17.554 93	37.820 95
542	293 764	159 220 088	23.280 89	73.620 65	8.153 294	17.565 74	37.844 24
543	294 849	160 103 007	23.302 36	73.688 53	8.158 305	17.576 54	37.867 50
544	295 936	160 989 184	23.323 81	73.756 36	8.163 310	17.587 32	37.890 73
545	297 025	161 878 625	23.345 24	73.824 12	8.168 309	17.598 09	37.913 93
546	298 116	162 771 336	23.366 64	73.891 81	8.173 302	17.608 85	37.937 11
547	299 209	163 667 323	23.388 03	73.959 45	8.178 289	17.619 59	37.960 25
548	300 304	164 566 592	23.409 40	74.027 02	8.183 269	17.630 32	37.983 37
549	301 401	165 469 149	23.430 75	74.094 53	8.188 244	17.641 04	38.006 46
550	302 500	166 375 000	23.452 08	74.161 98	8.193 213	17.651 74	38.029 52
551	303 601	167 284 151	23.473 39	74.229 37	8.198 175	17.662 43	38.052 56
552	304 704	168 196 608	23.494 68	74.296 70	8.203 132	17.673 11	38.075 57
553	305 809	169 112 377	23.515 95	74.363 97	8.208 082	17.683 78	38.098 54
554	306 916	170 031 464	23.537 20	74.431 18	8.213 027	17.694 43	38.121 49
555	308 025	170 953 875	23.558 44	74.498 32	8.217 966	17.705 07	38.144 42
556	309 136	171 879 616	23.579 65	74.565 41	8.222 899	17.715 70	38.167 31
557	310 249	172 808 693	23.600 85	74.632 43	8.227 825	17.726 31	38.190 18
558	311 364	173 741 112	23.622 02	74.699 40	8.232 746	17.736 91	38.213 02
559	312 481	174 676 879	23.643 18	74.766 30	8.237 661	17.747 50	38.235 84
560	313 600	175 616 000	23.664 32	74.833 15	8.242 571	17.758 08	38.258 62
561	314 721	176 558 481	23.685 44	74.899 93	8.247 474	17.768 64	38.281 38
562	315 844	177 504 328	23.706 54	74.966 66	8.252 372	17.779 20	38.304 12
563	316 969	178 453 547	23.727 62	75.033 33	8.257 263	17.789 73	38.326 82
564	318 096	179 406 144	23.748 68	75.099 93	8.262 149	17.800 26	38.349 50
565	319 225	180 362 125	23.769 73	75.166 48	8.267 029	17.810 77	38.372 15
566	320 356	181 321 496	23.790 75	75.232 97	8.271 904	17.821 28	38.394 78
567	321 489	182 284 263	23.811 76	75.299 40	8.276 773	17.831 77	38.417 37
568	322 624	183 250 432	23.832 75	75.365 77	8.281 635	17.842 24	38.439 95
569	323 761	184 220 009	23.853 72	75.432 09	8.286 493	17.852 71	38.462 49
570	324 900	185 193 000	23.874 67	75.498 34	8.291 344	17.863 16	38.485 01
571	326 041	186 169 411	23.895 61	75.564 54	8.296 190	17.873 60	38.507 50
572	327 184	187 149 248	23.916 52	75.630 68	8.301 031	17.884 03	38.529 97
573	328 329	188 132 517	23.937 42	75.696 76	8.305 865	17.894 44	38.552 41
574	329 476	189 119 224	23.958 30	75.762 79	8.310 694	17.904 85	38.574 82
575	330 625	190 109 375	23.979 16	75.828 75	8.315 517	17.915 24	38.597 21
576	331 776	191 102 976	24.000 00	75.894 66	8.320 335	17.925 62	38.619 58
577	332 929	192 100 033	24.020 82	75.960 52	8.325 148	17.935 99	38.641 91
578	334 084	193 100 552	24.041 63	76.026 31	8.329 954	17.946 34	38.664 22
579	335 241	194 104 539	24.062 42	76.092 05	8.334 755	17.956 69	38.686 51
580	336 400	195 112 000	24.083 19	76.157 73	8.339 551	17.967 02	38.708 77
581	337 561	196 122 941	24.103 94	76.223 36	8.344 341	17.977 34	38.731 00
582	338 724	197 137 368	24.124 68	76.288 92	8.349 126	17.987 65	38.753 21
583	339 889	198 155 287	24.145 39	76.354 44	8.353 905	17.997 94	38.775 39
584	341 056	199 176 704	24.166 09	76.419 89	8.358 678	18.008 23	38.797 55

n	n^2	n^3	$\sqrt{n}$	$\sqrt{10n}$	$\sqrt[3]{n}$	$\sqrt[3]{10n}$	$\sqrt[3]{100n}$
585	342 225	200 201 625	24.186 77	76.485 29	8.363 447	18.018 50	38.819 68
586	343 396	201 230 056	24.207 44	76.550 64	8.368 209	18.028 76	38.841 79
587	344 569	202 262 003	24.228 08	76.615 93	8.372 967	18.039 01	38.863 87
588	345 744	203 297 472	24.248 71	76.681 16	8.377 719	18.049 25	38.885 93
589	346 921	204 336 469	24.269 32	76.746 34	8.382 465	18.059 47	38.907 96
590	348 100	205 379 000	24.289 92	76.811 46	8.387 207	18.069 69	38.929 96
591	349 281	206 425 071	24.310 49	76.876 52	8.391 942	18.079 89	38.951 95
592	350 464	207 474 688	24.331 05	76.941 54	8.396 673	18.090 08	38.973 90
593	351 649	208 527 857	24.351 59	77.006 49	8.401 398	18.100 26	38.995 84
594	352 836	209 584 584	24.372 12	.77.071 40	8.406 118	18.110 43	39.017 74
595	354 025	210 644 875	24.392 62	77.136 24	8.410 833	18.120 59	39.039 63
596	355 216	211 708 736	24.413 11	77.201 04	8.415 542	18.130 74	39.061 49
597	356 409	212 776 173	24.433 58	77.265 78	8.420 246	18.140 87	39.083 32
598	357 604	213 847 192	24.454 04	77.330 46	8.424 945	18.150 99	39.105 13
599	358 801	214 921 799	24.474 48	77.395 09	8.429 638	18.161 11	39.126 92
600	360 000	216 000 000	24.494 90	77.459 67	8.434 327	18.171 21	39.148 68
601	361 201	217 081 801	24.515 30	77.524 19	8.439 010	18.181 30	39.170 41
602	362 404	218 167 208	24.535 69	77.588 66	8.443 688	18.191 37	39.192 13
603	363 609	219 256 227	24.556 06	77.653 07	8.448 361	18.201 44	39.213 82
604	364 816	220 348 864	24.576 41	77.717 44	8.453 028	18.211 50	39.235 48
605	366 025	221 445 125	24.596 75	77.781 75	8.457 691	18.221 54	39.257 12
606	367 236	222 545 016	24.617 07	77.846 00	8.462 348	18.231 58	39.278 74
607	368 449	223 648 543	24.637 37	77.910 20	8.467 000	18.241 60	39.300 33
608	369 664	224 755 712	24.657 66	77.974 35	8.471 647	18.251 61	39.321 90
609	370 881	225 866 529	24.677 93	78.038 45	8.476 289	18.261 61	39.343 45
610	372 100	226 981 000	24.698 18	78.102 50	8.480 926	18.271 60	39.364 97
611	373 321	228 099 131	24.718 41	78.166 49	8.485 558	18.281 58	39.386 47
612	374 544	229 220 928	24.738 63	78.230 43	8.490 185	18.291 55	39.407 95
613	375 769	230 346 397	24.758 84	78.294 32	8.494 807	18.301 51	39.429 40
614	376 996	231 475 544	24.779 02	78.358 15	8.499 423	18.311 45	39.450 83
615	378 225	232 608 375	24.799 19	78.421 94	8.504 035	18.321 39	39.472 23
616	379 456	233 744 896	24.819 35	78.485 67	8.508 642	18.331 31	39.493 62
617	380 689	234 885 113	24.839 48	78.549 35	8.513 243	18.341 23	39.514 98
618	381 924	236 029 032	24.859 61	78.612 98	8.517 840	18.351 13	39.536 31
619	383 161	237 176 659	24.879 71	78.676 55	8.522 432	18.361 02	39.557 63
620	384 400	238 328 000	24.899 80	78.740 08	8.527 019	18.370 91	39.578 92
621	385 641	239 483 061	24.919 87	78.803 55	8.531 601	18.380 78	39.600 18
622	386 884	240 641 848	24.939 93	78.866 98	8.536 178	18.390 64	39.621 43
623	388 129	241 804 367	24.959 97	78.930 35	8.540 750	18.400 49	39.642 65
624	389 376	242 970 624	24.979 99	78.993 67	8.545 317	18.410 33	39.663 85
625	390 625	244 140 625	25.000 00	79.056 94	8.549 880	18.420 16	39.685 03
626	391 876	245 314 376	25.019 99	79.120 16	8.554 437	18.429 98	39.706 18
627	393 129	246 491 883	25.039 97	79.183 33	8.558 990	18.439 78	39.727 31
628	394 384	247 673 152	25.059 93	79.246 45	8.563 538	18.449 58	39.748 42
629	395 641	248 858 189	25.079 87	79.309 52	8.568 081	18.459 37	39.769 51
630	396 900	250 047 000	25.099 80	79.372 54	8.572 619	18.469 15	39.790 57
631	398 161	251 239 591	25.119 71	79.435 51	8.577 152	18.478 91	39.811 61
632	399 424	252 435 968	25.139 61	79.498 43	8.581 681	18.488 67	39.832 63
633	400 689	253 636 137	25.159 49	79.561 30	8.586 205	18 498 42	39.853 63
634	401 956	254 840 104	25.179 36	79.624 12	8.590 724	18.508 15	39.874 61
635	403 225	256 047 875	25.199 21	79.686 89	8.595 238	18.517 88	39.895 56
636	404 496	257 259 456	25.219 04	79.749 61	8.599 748	18.527 59	39.916 49
637	405 769	258 474 853	25.238 86	79.812 28	8.604 252	18.537 30	39.937 40
638	407 044	259 694 072	25.258 66	79.874 90	8.608 753	18.547 00	39.958 29
639	408 321	260 917 119	25.278 45	79.937 48	8.613 248	18.556 68	39.979 16
640	409 600	262 144 000	25.298 22	80.000 00	8.617 739	18.566 36	40.000 00
641	410 881	263 374 721	25.317 98	80.062 48	8.622 225	18.576 02	40.020 82
642	412 164	264 609 288	25.337 72	80.124 90	8.626 706	18.585 68	40.041 62
643	413 449	265 847 707	25.357 44	80.187 28	8.631 183	18.595 32	40.062 40
644	414 736	267 089 984	25.377 16	80.249 61	8.635 655	18.604 95	40.083 16
645	416 025	268 336 125	25.396 85	80.311 89	8.640 123	18.614 58	40.103 90
646	417 316	269 586 136	25.416 53	80.374 13	8.644 585	18.624 19	40.124 61
647	418 609	270 840 023	25.436 19	80.436 31	8.649 044	18.633 80	40.145 30
648	419 904	272 097 792	25.455 84	80.498 45	8.653 497	18.643 40	40.165 98
649	421 201	273 359 449	25.475 48	80.560 54	8.657 947	18.652 98	40.186 63

A.5 SQUARES, CUBES, SQUARE ROOTS, AND CUBE ROOTS *(Continued)*

n	n^2	n^3	$\sqrt{n}$	$\sqrt{10n}$	$\sqrt[3]{n}$	$\sqrt[3]{10n}$	$\sqrt[3]{100n}$
650	422 500	274 625 000	25.495 10	80.622 58	8.662 391	18.662 56	40.207 26
651	423 801	275 894 451	25.514 70	80.684 57	8.666 831	18.672 12	40.227 87
652	425 104	277 167 808	25.534 29	80.746 52	8.671 266	18.681 68	40.248 45
653	426 409	278 445 077	25.553 86	80.808 42	8.675 697	18.691 22	40.269 02
654	427 716	279 726 264	25.573 42	80.870 27	8.680 124	18.700 76	40.289 57
655	429 025	281 011 375	25.592 97	80.932 07	8.684 546	18.710 29	40.310 09
656	430 336	282 300 416	25.612 50	80.993 83	8.688 963	18.719 80	40.330 59
657	431 649	283 593 393	25.632 01	81.055 54	8.693 376	18.729 31	40.351 08
658	432 964	284 890 312	25.651 51	81.117 20	8.697 784	18.738 81	40.371 54
659	434 281	286 191 179	25.671 00	81.178 81	8.702 188	18.748 30	40.391 98
660	435 600	287 496 000	25.690 47	81.240 38	8.706 588	18.757 77	40.412 40
661	436 921	288 804 781	25.709 92	81.301 91	8.710 983	18.767 24	40.432 80
662	438 244	290 117 528	25.729 36	81.363 38	8.715 373	18.776 70	40.453 18
663	439 569	291 434 247	25.748 79	81.424 81	8.719 760	18.786 15	40.473 54
664	440 896	292 754 944	25.768 20	81.486 20	8.724 141	18.795 59	40.493 88
665	442 225	294 079 625	25.787 59	81.547 53	8.728 519	18.805 02	40.514 20
666	443 556	295 408 296	25.806 98	81.608 82	8.732 892	18.814 44	40.534 49
667	444 889	296 740 963	25.826 34	81.670 07	8.737 260	18.823 86	40.554 77
668	446 224	298 077 632	25.845 70	81.731 27	8.741 625	18.833 26	40.575 03
669	447 561	299 418 309	25.865 03	81.792 42	8.745 985	18.842 65	40.595 26
670	448 900	300 763 000	25.884 36	81.853 53	8.750 340	18.852 04	40.615 48
671	450 241	302 111 711	25.903 67	81.914 59	8.754 691	18.861 41	40.635 68
672	451 584	303 464 448	25.922 96	81.975 61	8.759 038	18.870 78	40.655 85
673	452 929	304 821 217	25.942 24	82.036 58	8.763 381	18.880 13	40.676 01
674	454 276	306 182 024	25.961 51	82.097 50	8.767 719	18.889 48	40.696 15
675	455 625	307 546 875	25.980 76	82.158 38	8.772 053	18.898 82	40.716 26
676	456 976	308 915 776	26.000 00	82.219 22	8.776 383	18.908 14	40.736 36
677	458 329	310 288 733	26.019 22	82.280 01	8.780 708	18.917 46	40.756 44
678	459 684	311 665 752	26.038 43	82.340 76	8.785 030	18.926 77	40.776 50
679	461 041	313 046 839	26.057 63	82.401 46	8.789 347	18.936 07	40.796 53
680	462 400	314 432 000	26.076 81	82.462 11	8.793 659	18.945 36	40.816 55
681	463 761	315 821 241	26.095 98	82.522 72	8.797 968	18.954 65	40.836 55
682	465 124	317 214 568	26.115 13	82.583 29	8.802 272	18.963 92	40.856 53
683	466 489	318 611 987	26.134 27	82.643 81	8.806 572	18.973 18	40.876 49
684	467 856	320 013 504	26.153 39	82.704 29	8.810 868	18.982 44	40.896 43
685	469 225	321 419 125	26.172 50	82.764 73	8.815 160	18.991 69	40.916 35
686	470 596	322 828 856	26.191 60	82.825 12	8.819 447	19.000 92	40.936 25
687	471 969	324 242 703	26.210 68	82.885 46	8.823 731	19.010 15	40.956 13
688	473 344	325 660 672	26.229 75	82.945 77	8.828 010	19.019 37	40.975 99
689	474 721	327 082 769	26.248 81	83.006 02	8.832 285	19.028 58	40.995 84
690	476 100	328 509 000	26.267 85	83.066 24	8.836 556	19.037 78	41.015 66
691	477 481	329 939 371	26.286 88	83.126 41	8.840 823	19.046 98	41.035 46
692	478 864	331 373 888	26.305 89	83.186 54	8.845 085	19.056 16	41.055 25
693	480 249	332 812 557	26.324 89	83.246 62	8.849 344	19.065 33	41.075 02
694	481 636	334 255 384	26.343 88	83.306 66	8.853 599	19.074 50	41.094 76
695	483 025	335 702 375	26.362 85	83.366 66	8.857 849	19.083 66	41.114 49
696	484 416	337 153 536	26.381 81	83.426 61	8.862 095	19.092 81	41.134 20
697	485 809	338 608 873	26.400 76	83.486 53	8.866 338	19.101 95	41.153 89
698	487 204	340 068 392	26.419 69	83.546 39	8.870 576	19.111 08	41.173 57
699	488 601	341 532 099	26.438 61	83.606 22	8.874 810	19.120 20	41.193 22
700	490 000	343 000 000	26.457 51	83.666 00	8.879 040	19.129 31	41.212 85
701	491 401	344 472 101	26.476 40	83.725 74	8.883 266	19.138 42	41.232 47
702	492 804	345 948 408	26.495 28	83.785 44	8.887 488	19.147 51	41.252 07
703	494 209	347 428 927	26.514 15	83.845 10	8.891 706	19.156 60	41.271 64
704	495 616	348 913 664	26.533 00	83.904 71	8.895 920	19.165 68	41.291 20
705	497 025	350 402 625	26.551 84	83.964 28	8.900 130	19.174 75	41.310 75
706	498 436	351 895 816	26.570 66	84.023 81	8.904 337	19.183 81	41.330 27
707	499 849	353 393 243	26.589 47	84.083 29	8.908 539	19.192 86	41.349 77
708	501 264	354 894 912	26.608 27	84.142 74	8.912 737	19.201 91	41.369 26
709	502 681	356 400 829	26.627 05	84.202 14	8.916 931	19.210 95	41.388 73
710	504 100	357 911 000	26.645 83	84.261 50	8.921 121	19.219 97	41.408 18
711	505 521	359 425 431	26.664 58	84.320 82	8.925 308	19.228 99	41.427 61
712	506 944	360 944 128	26.683 33	84.380 09	8.929 490	19.238 00	41.447 02
713	508 369	362 467 097	26.702 06	84.439 33	8.933 669	19.247 01	41.466 42
714	509 796	363 994 344	26.720 78	84.498 52	8.937 843	19.256 00	41.485 79

n	n²	n³	√n	√10n	∛n	∛10n	∛100n
715	511 225	365 525 875	26.739 48	84.557 67	8.942 014	19.264 99	41.505 15
716	512 656	367 061 696	26.758 18	84.616 78	8.946 181	19.273 96	41.524 49
717	514 089	368 601 813	26.776 86	84.675 85	8.950 344	19.282 93	41.543 82
718	515 524	370 146 232	26.795 52	84.734 88	8.954 503	19.291 89	41.563 12
719	516 961	371 694 959	26.814 18	84.793 87	8.958 658	19.300 84	41.582 41
720	518 400	373 248 000	26.832 82	84.852 81	8.962 809	19.309 79	41.601 68
721	519 841	374 805 361	26.851 44	84.911 72	8.966 957	19.318 72	41.620 93
722	521 284	376 367 048	26.870 06	84.970 58	8.971 101	19.327 65	41.640 16
723	522 729	377 933 067	26.888 66	85.029 41	8.975 241	19.336 57	41.659 38
724	524 176	379 503 424	26.907 25	85.088 19	8.979 377	19.345 48	41.678 57
725	525 625	381 078 125	26.925 82	85.146 93	8.983 509	19.354 38	41.697 75
726	527 076	382 657 176	26.944 39	85.205 63	8.987 637	19.363 28	41.716 92
727	528 529	384 240 583	26.962 94	85.264 29	8.991 762	19.372 16	41.736 06
728	529 984	385 828 352	26.981 48	85.322 92	8.995 883	19.381 04	41.755 19
729	531 441	387 420 489	27.000 00	85.381 50	9.000 000	19.389 91	41.774 30
730	532 900	389 017 000	27.018 51	85.440 04	9.004 113	19.398 77	41.793 39
731	534 361	390 617 891	27.037 01	85.498 54	9.008 223	19.407 63	41.812 47
732	535 824	392 223 168	27.055 50	85.557 00	9.012 329	19.416 47	41.831 52
733	537 289	393 832 837	27.073 97	85.615 42	9.016 431	19.425 31	41.850 56
734	538 756	395 446 904	27.092 43	85.673 80	9.020 529	19.434 14	41.869 59
735	540 225	397 065 375	27.110 88	85.732 14	9.024 624	19.442 96	41.888 59
736	541 696	398 688 256	27.129 32	85.790 44	9.028 715	19.451 78	41.907 58
737	543 169	400 315 553	27.147 74	85.848 70	9.032 802	19.460 58	41.926 55
738	544 644	401 947 272	27.166 16	85.906 93	9.036 886	19.469 38	41.945 51
739	546 121	403 583 419	27.184 55	85.965 11	9.040 966	19.478 17	41.964 44
740	547 600	405 224 000	27.202 94	86.023 25	9.045 042	19.486 95	41.983 30
741	549 081	406 869 021	27.221 32	86.081 36	9.049 114	19.495 73	42.002 27
742	550 564	408 518 488	27.239 68	86.139 42	9.053 183	19.504 49	42.021 15
743	552 049	410 172 407	27.258 03	86.197 45	9.057 248	19.513 25	42.040 02
744	553 536	411 830 784	27.276 36	86.255 43	9.061 310	19.522 00	42.058 87
745	555 025	413 493 625	27.294 69	86.313 38	9.065 368	19.530 74	42.077 71
746	556 516	415 160 936	27.313 00	86.371 29	9.069 422	19.539 48	42.096 53
747	558 009	416 832 723	27.331 30	86.429 16	9.073 473	19.548 20	42.115 33
748	559 504	418 508 992	27.349 59	86.486 99	9.077 520	19.556 92	42.134 11
749	561 001	420 189 749	27.367 86	86.544 79	9.081 563	19.565 63	42.152 88
750	562 500	421 875 000	27.386 13	86.602 54	9.085 603	19.574 34	42.171 63
751	564 001	423 564 751	27.404 38	86.660 26	9.089 639	19.583 03	42.190 37
752	565 504	425 259 008	27.422 62	86.717 93	9.093 672	19.591 72	42.209 09
753	567 009	426 957 777	27.440 85	86.775 57	9.097 701	19.600 40	42.227 79
754	568 516	428 661 064	27.459 06	86.833 17	9.101 727	19.609 08	42.246 47
755	570 025	430 368 875	27.477 26	86.890 74	9.105 748	19.617 74	42.265 14
756	571 536	432 081 216	27.495 45	86.948 26	9.109 767	19.626 40	42.283 79
757	573 049	433 798 093	27.513 63	87.005 75	9.113 782	19.635 05	42.302 43
758	574 564	435 519 512	27.531 80	87.063 20	9.117 793	19.643 69	42.321 05
759	576 081	437 245 479	27.549 95	87.120 61	9.121 801	19.652 32	42.339 65
760	577 600	438 976 000	27.568 10	87.177 98	9.125 805	19.660 95	42.358 24
761	579 121	440 711 081	27.586 23	87.235 31	9.129 806	19.669 57	42.376 81
762	580 644	442 450 728	27.604 35	87.292 61	9.133 803	19.678 18	42.395 36
763	582 169	444 194 947	27.622 45	87.349 87	9.137 797	19.686 79	42.413 90
764	583 696	445 943 744	27.640 55	87.407 09	9.141 787	19.695 38	42.432 42
765	585 225	447 697 125	27.658 63	87.464 28	9.145 774	19.703 97	42.450 92
766	586 756	449 455 096	27.676 71	87.521 43	9.149 758	19.712 56	42.469 41
767	588 289	451 217 663	27.694 76	87.578 54	9.153 738	19.721 13	42.487 89
768	589 824	452 984 832	27.712 81	87.635 61	9.157 714	19.729 70	42.506 34
769	591 361	454 756 609	27.730 85	87.692 65	9.161 687	19.738 26	42.524 78
770	592 900	456 533 000	27.748 87	87.749 64	9.165 656	19.746 81	42.543 21
771	594 441	458 314 011	27.766 89	87.806 61	9.169 623	19.755 35	42.561 62
772	595 984	460 099 648	27.784 89	87.863 53	9.173 585	19.763 89	42.580 01
773	597 529	461 889 917	27.802 88	87.920 42	9.177 544	19.772 42	42.598 39
774	599 076	463 684 824	27.820 86	87.977 27	9.181 500	19.780 94	42.616 75
775	600 625	465 484 375	27.838 82	88.034 08	9.185 453	19.789 46	42.635 09
776	602 176	467 288 576	27.856 78	88.090 86	9.189 402	19.797 97	42.653 42
777	603 729	469 097 433	27.874 72	88.147 60	9.193 347	19.806 47	42.671 74
778	605 284	470 910 952	27.892 65	88.204 31	9.197 290	19.814 96	42.690 04
779	606 841	472 729 139	27.910 57	88.260 98	9.201 229	19.823 45	42.708 32

A.5   SQUARES, CUBES, SQUARE ROOTS, AND CUBE ROOTS *(Continued)*

n	n^2	n^3	$\sqrt{n}$	$\sqrt{10n}$	$\sqrt[3]{n}$	$\sqrt[3]{10n}$	$\sqrt[3]{100n}$
780	608 400	474 552 000	27.928 48	88.317 61	9.205 164	19.831 92	42.726 59
781	609 961	476 379 541	27.946 38	88.374 20	9.209 096	19.840 40	42.744 84
782	611 524	478 211 768	27.964 26	88.430 76	9.213 025	19.848 86	42.763 07
783	613 089	480 048 687	27.982 14	88.487 29	9.216 950	19.857 32	42.781 29
784	614 656	481 890 304	28.000 00	88.543 77	9.220 873	19.865 77	42.799 50
785	616 225	483 736 625	28.017 85	88.600 23	9.224 791	19.874 21	42.817 69
786	617 796	485 587 656	28.035 69	88.656 64	9.228 707	19.882 65	42.835 86
787	619 369	487 443 403	28.053 52	88.713 02	9.232 619	19.891 07	42.854 02
788	620 944	489 303 872	28.071 34	88.769 36	9.236 528	19.899 50	42.872 16
789	622 521	491 169 069	28.089 14	88.825 67	9.240 433	19.907 91	42.890 29
790	624 100	493 039 000	28.106 94	88.881 94	9.244 335	19.916 32	42.908 40
791	625 681	494 913 671	28.124 72	88.938 18	9.248 234	19.924 72	42.926 50
792	627 264	496 793 088	28.142 49	88.994 38	9.252 130	19.933 11	42.944 58
793	628 849	498 677 257	28.160 26	89.050 55	9.256 022	19.941 50	42.962 65
794	630 436	500 566 184	28.178 01	89.106 68	9.259 911	19.949 87	42.980 70
795	632 025	502 459 875	28.195 74	89.162 77	9.263 797	19.958 25	42.998 74
796	633 616	504 358 336	28.213 47	89.218 83	9.267 680	19.966 61	43.016 76
797	635 209	506 261 573	28.231 19	89.274 86	9.271 559	19.974 97	43.034 77
798	636 804	508 169 592	28.248 89	89.330 85	9.275 435	19.983 32	43.052 76
799	638 401	510 082 399	28.266 59	89.386 80	9.279 308	19.991 66	43.070 73
800	640 000	512 000 000	28.284 27	89.442 72	9.283 178	20.000 00	43.088 69
801	641 601	513 922 401	28.301 94	89.498 60	9.287 044	20.008 33	43.106 64
802	643 204	515 849 608	28.319 60	89.554 45	9.290 907	20.016 65	43.124 57
803	644 809	517 781 627	28.337 25	89.610 27	9.294 767	20.024 97	43.142 49
804	646 416	519 718 464	28.354 89	89.666 05	9.298 624	20.033 28	43.160 39
805	648 025	521 660 125	28.372 52	89.721 79	9.302 477	20.041 58	43.178 28
806	649 636	523 606 616	28.390 14	89.777 50	9.306 328	20.049 88	43.196 15
807	651 249	525 557 943	28.407 75	89.833 18	9.310 175	20.058 16	43.214 00
808	652 864	527 514 112	28.425 34	89.888 82	9.314 019	20.066 45	43.231 85
809	654 481	529 475 129	28.442 93	89.944 43	9.317 860	20.074 72	43.249 67
810	656 100	531 441 000	28.460 50	90.000 00	9.321 698	20.082 99	43.267 49
811	657 721	533 411 731	28.478 06	90.055 54	9.325 532	20.091 25	43.285 29
812	659 344	535 387 328	28.495 61	90.111 04	9.329 363	20.099 50	43.303 07
813	660 969	537 367 797	28.513 15	90.166 51	9.333 192	20.107 75	43.320 84
814	662 596	539 353 144	28.530 69	90.221 95	9.337 017	20.115 99	43.338 59
815	664 225	541 343 375	28.548 20	90.277 35	9.340 839	20.124 23	43.356 33
816	665 856	543 338 496	28.565 71	90.332 72	9.344 657	20.132 45	43.374 06
817	667 489	545 338 513	28.583 21	90.388 05	9.348 473	20.140 67	43.391 77
818	669 124	547 343 432	28.600 70	90.443 35	9.352 286	20.148 89	43.409 47
819	670 761	549 353 259	28.618 18	90.498 62	9.356 095	20.157 10	43.427 15
820	672 400	551 368 000	28.635 64	90.553 85	9.359 902	20.165 30	43.444 81
821	674 041	553 387 661	28.653 10	90.609 05	9.363 705	20.173 49	43.462 47
822	675 684	555 412 248	28.670 54	90.664 22	9.367 505	20.181 68	43.480 11
823	677 329	557 441 767	28.687 98	90.719 35	9.371 302	20.189 86	43.497 73
824	678 976	559 476 224	28.705 40	90.774 45	9.375 096	20.198 03	43.515 34
825	680 625	561 515 625	28.722 81	90.829 51	9.378 887	20.206 20	43.532 94
826	682 276	563 559 976	28.740 22	90.884 54	9.382 675	20.214 36	43.550 52
827	683 929	565 609 283	28.757 61	90.939 54	9.386 460	20.222 52	43.568 09
828	685 584	567 663 552	28.774 99	90.994 51	9.390 242	20.230 66	43.585 64
829	687 241	569 722 789	28.792 36	91.049 44	9.394 021	20.238 80	43.603 18
830	688 900	571 787 000	28.809 72	91.104 34	9.397 796	20.246 94	43.620 71
831	690 561	573 856 191	28.827 07	91.159 20	9.401 569	20.255 07	43.638 22
832	692 224	575 930 368	28.844 41	91.214 03	9.405 339	20.263 19	43.655 72
833	693 889	578 009 537	28.861 74	91.268 83	9.409 105	20.271 30	43.673 20
834	695 556	580 093 704	28.879 06	91.323 60	9.412 869	20.279 41	43.690 67
835	697 225	582 182 875	28.896 37	91.378 33	9.416 630	20.287 51	43.708 12
836	698 896	584 277 056	28.913 66	91.433 04	9.420 387	20.295 61	43.725 56
837	700 569	586 376 253	28.930 95	91.487 70	9.424 142	20.303 70	43.742 99
838	702 244	588 480 472	28.948 23	91.542 34	9.427 894	20.311 78	43.760 41
839	703 921	590 589 719	28.965 50	91.596 94	9.431 642	20.319 86	43.777 81
840	705 600	592 704 000	28.982 75	91.651 51	9.435 388	20.327 93	43.795 19
841	707 281	594 823 321	29.000 00	91.706 05	9.439 131	20.335 99	43.812 56
842	708 964	596 947 688	29.017 24	91.760 56	9.442 870	20.344 05	43.829 92
843	710 649	599 077 107	29.034 46	91.815 03	9.446 607	20.352 10	43.847 27
844	712 336	601 211 584	29.051 68	91.869 47	9.450 341	20.360 14	43.864 60

n	n^2	n^3	$\sqrt{n}$	$\sqrt{10n}$	$\sqrt[3]{n}$	$\sqrt[3]{10n}$	$\sqrt[3]{100n}$
845	714 025	603 351 125	29.068 88	91.923 88	9.454 072	20.368 18	43.881 91
846	715 716	605 495 736	29.086 08	91.978 26'	9.457 800	20.376 21	43.899 22
847	717 409	607 645 423	29.103 26	92.032 60	9.461 525	20.384 24	43.916 51
848	719 104	609 800 192	29.120 44	92.086 92	9.465 247	20.392 26	43.933 78
849	720 801	611 960 049	29.137 60	92.141 20	9.468 966	20.400 27	43.951 05
850	722 500	614 125 000	29.154 76	92.195 44	9.472 682	20.408 28	43.968 30
851	724 201	616 295 051	29.171 90	92.249 66	9.476 396	20.416 28	43.985 53
852	725 904	618 470 208	29.189 04	92.303 85	9.480 106	20.424 27	44.002 75
853	727 609	620 650 477	29.206 16	92.358 00	9.483 814	20.432 26	44.019 96
854	729 316	622 835 864	29.223 28	92.412 12	9.487 518	20.440 24	44.037 16
855	731 025	625 026 375	29.240 38	92.466 21	9.491 220	20.448 21	44.054 34
856	732 736	627 222 016	29.257 48	92.520 27	9.494 919	20.456 18	44.071 51
857	734 449	629 422 793	29.274 56	92.574 29	9.498 615	20.464 15	44.088 66
858	736 164	631 628 712	29.291 64	92.628 29	9.502 308	20.472 10	44.105 81
859	737 881	633 839 779	29.308 70	92.682 25	9.505 998	20.480 05	44.122 93
860	739 600	636 056 000	29.325 76	92.736 18	9.509 685	20.488 00	44.140 05
861	741 321	638 277 381	29.342 80	92.790 09	9.513 370	20.495 93	44.157 15
862	743 044	640 503 928	29.359 84	92.843 96	9.517 052	20.503 87	44.174 24
863	744 769	642 735 647	29.376 86	92.897 79	9.520 730	20.511 79	44.191 32
864	746 496	644 972 544	29.393 88	92.951 60	9.524 406	20.519 71	44.208 38
865	748 225	647 214 625	29.410 88	93.005 38	9.528 079	20.527 62	44.225 43
866	749 956	649 461 896	29.427 88	93.059 12	9.531 750	20.535 53	44.242 46
867	751 689	651 714 363	29.444 86	93.112 83	9.535 417	20.543 43	44.259 49
868	753 424	653 972 032	29.461 84	93.166 52	9.539 082	20.551 33	44.276 50
869	755 161	656 234 909	29.478 81	93.220 17	9.542 744	20.559 22	44.293 49
870	756 900	658 503 000	29.495 76	93.273 79	9.546 403	20.567 10	44.310 48
871	758 641	660 776 311	29.512 71	93.327 38	9.550 059	20.574 98	44.327 45
872	760 384	663 054 848	29.529 65	93.380 94	9.553 712	20.582 85	44.344 40
873	762 129	665 338 617	29.546 57	93.434 47	9.557 363	20.590 71	44.361 35
874	763 876	667 627 624	29.563 49	93.487 97	9.561 011	20.598 57	44.378 28
875	765 625	669 921 875	29.580 40	93.541 43	9.564 656	20.606 43	44.395 20
876	767 376	672 221 376	29.597 30	93.594 87	9.568 298	20.614 27	44.412 11
877	769 129	674 526 133	29.614 19	93.648 28	9.571 938	20.622 11	44.429 00
878	770 884	676 836 152	29.631 06	93.701 65	9.575 574	20.629 95	44.445 88
879	772 641	679 151 439	29.647 93	93.755 00	9.579 208	20.637 78	44.462 75
880	774 400	681 472 000	29.664 79	93.808 32	9.582 840	20.645 60	44.479 60
881	776 161	683 797 841	29.681 64	93.861 60	9.586 468	20.653 42	44.496 44
882	777 924	686 128 968	29.698 48	93.914 86	9.590 094	20.661 23	44.513 27
883	779 689	688 465 387	29.715 32	93.968 08	9.593 717	20.669 04	44.530 09
884	781 456	690 807 104	29.732 14	94.021 27	9.597 337	20.676 84	44.546 89
885	783 225	693 154 125	29.748 95	94.074 44	9.600 955	20.684 63	44.563 68
886	784 996	695 506 456	29.765 75	94.127 57	9.604 570	20.692 42	44.580 46
887	786 769	697 864 103	29.782 55	94.180 68	9.608 182	20.700 20	44.597 23
888	788 544	700 227 072	29.799 33	94.233 75	9.611 791	20.707 98	44.613 98
889	790 321	702 595 369	29.816 10	94.286 80	9.615 398	20.715 75	44.630 72
890	792 100	704 969 000	29.832 87	94.339 81	9.619 002	20.723 51	44.647 45
891	793 881	707 347 971	29.849 62	94.392 80	9.622 603	20.731 27	44.664 17
892	795 664	709 732 288	29.866 37	94.445 75	9.626 202	20.739 02	44.680 87
893	797 449	712 121 957	29.883 11	94.498 68	9.629 797	20.746 77	44.697 56
894	799 236	714 516 984	29.899 83	94.551 57	9.633 391	20.754 51	44.714 24
895	801 025	716 917 375	29.916 55	94.604 44	9.636 981	20.762 25	44.730 90
896	802 816	719 323 136	29.933 26	94.657 28	9.640 569	20.769 98	44.747 56
897	804 609	721 734 273	29.949 96	94.710 08	9.644 154	20.777 70	44.764 20
898	806 404	724 150 792	29.966 65	94.762 86	9.647 737	20.785 42	44.780 83
899	808 201	726 572 699	29.983 33	94.815 61	9.651 317	20.793 13	44.797 44
900	810 000	729 000 000	30.000 00	94.868 33	9.654 894	20.800 84	44.814 05
901	811 801	731 432 701	30.016 66	94.921 02	9.658 468	20.808 54	44.830 64
902	813 604	733 870 808	30.033 31	94.973 68	9.662 040	20.816 23	44.847 22
903	815 409	736 314 327	30.049 96	95.026 31	9.665 610	20.823 92	44.863 79
904	817 216	738 763 264	30.066 59	95.078 91	9.669 176	20.831 61	44.880 34
905	819 025	741 217 625	30.083 22	95.131 49	9.672 740	20.839 29	44.896 88
906	820 836	743 677 416	30.099 83	95.184 03	9.676 302	20.846 96	44.913 41
907	822 649	746 142 643	30.116 44	95.236 55	9.679 860	20.854 63	44.929 93
908	824 464	748 613 312	30.133 04	95.289 03	9.683 417	20.862 29	44.946 44
909	826 281	751 089 429	30.149 63	95.341 49	9.686 970	20.869 94	44.962 93

A.5   SQUARES, CUBES, SQUARE ROOTS, AND CUBE ROOTS *(Continued)*

n	n^2	n^3	$\sqrt{n}$	$\sqrt{10n}$	$\sqrt[3]{n}$	$\sqrt[3]{10n}$	$\sqrt[3]{100n}$
910	828 100	753 571 000	30.166 21	95.393 92	9.690 521	20.877 59	44.979 41
911	829 921	756 058 031	30.182 78	95.446 32	9.694 069	20.885 24	44.995 88
912	831 744	758 550 528	30.199 34	95.498 69	9.697 615	20.892 88	45.012 34
913	833 569	761 048 497	30.215 89	95.551 03	9.701 158	20.900 51	45.028 79
914	835 396	763 551 944	30.232 43	95.603 35	9.704 699	20.908 14	45.045 22
915	837 225	766 060 875	30.248 97	95.655 63	9.708 237	20.915 76	45.061 64
916	839 056	768 575 296	30.265 49	95.707 89	9.711 772	20.923 38	45.078 05
917	840 889	771 095 213	30.282 01	95.760 12	9.715 305	20.930 99	45.094 45
918	842 724	773 620 632	30.298 51	95.812 32	9.718 835	20.938 60	45.110 84
919	844 561	776 151 559	30.315 01	95.864 49	9.722 363	20.946 20	45.127 21
920	846 400	778 688 000	30.331 50	95.916 63	9.725 888	20.953 79	45.143 57
921	848 241	781 229 961	30.347 98	95.968 74	9.729 411	20.961 38	45.159 92
922	850 084	783 777 448	30.364 45	96.020 83	9.732 931	20.968 96	45.176 26
923	851 929	786 330 467	30.380 92	96.072 89	9.736 448	20.976 54	45.192 59
924	853 776	788 889 024	30.397 37	96.124 92	9.739 963	20.984 11	45.208 91
925	855 625	791 453 125	30.413 81	96.176 92	9.743 476	20.991 68	45.225 21
926	857 476	794 022 776	30.430 25	96.228 89	9.746 986	20.999 24	45.241 50
927	859 329	796 597 983	30.446 67	96.280 84	9.750 493	21.006 80	45.257 78
928	861 184	799 178 752	30.463 09	96.332 76	9.753 998	21.014 35	45.274 05
929	863 041	801 765 089	30.479 50	96.384 65	9.757 500	21.021 90	45.290 30
930	864 900	804 357 000	30.495 90	96.436 51	9.761 000	21.029 44	45.306 55
931	866 761	806 954 491	30.512 29	96.488 34	9.764 497	21.036 97	45.322 78
932	868 624	809 557 568	30.528 68	96.540 15	9.767 992	21.044 50	45.339 00
933	870 489	812 166 237	30.545 05	96.591 93	9.771 485	21.052 03	45.355 21
934	872 356	814 780 504	30.561 41	96.643 68	9.774 974	21.059 54	45.371 41
935	874 225	817 400 375	30.577 77	96.695 40	9.778 462	21.067 06	45.387 60
936	876 096	820 025 856	30.594 12	96.747 09	9.781 946	21.074 56	45.403 77
937	877 969	822 656 953	30.610 46	96.798 76	9.785 429	21.082 07	45.419 94
938	879 844	825 293 672	30.626 79	96.850 40	9.788 909	21.089 56	45.436 09
939	881 721	827 936 019	30.643 11	96.902 01	9.792 386	21.097 06	45.452 23
940	883 600	830 584 000	30.659 42	96.953 60	9.795 861	21.104 54	45.468 36
941	885 481	833 237 621	30.675 72	97.005 15	9.799 334	21.112 02	45.484 48
942	887 364	835 896 888	30.692 02	97.056 68	9.802 804	21.119 50	45.500 58
943	889 249	838 561 807	30.708 31	97.108 19	9.806 271	21.126 97	45.516 68
944	891 136	841 232 384	30.724 58	97.159 66	9.809 736	21.134 44	45.532 76
945	893 025	843 908 625	30.740 85	97.211 11	9.813 199	21.141 90	45.548 83
946	894 916	846 590 536	30.757 11	97.262 53	9.816 659	21.149 35	45.564 90
947	896 809	849 278 123	30.773 37	97.313 93	9.820 117	21.156 80	45.580 95
948	898 704	851 971 392	30.789 61	97.365 29	9.823 572	21.164 24	45.596 98
949	900 601	854 670 349	30.805 84	97.416 63	9.827 025	21.171 68	45.613 01
950	902 500	857 375 000	30.822 07	97.467 94	9.830 476	21.179 12	45.629 03
951	904 401	860 085 351	30.838 29	97.519 23	9.833 924	21.186 55	45.645 03
952	906 304	862 801 408	30.854 50	97.570 49	9.837 369	21.193 97	45.661 02
953	908 209	865 523 177	30.870 70	97.621 72	9.840 813	21.201 39	45.677 01
954	910 116	868 250 664	30.886 89	97.672 92	9.844 254	21.208 80	45.692 98
955	912 025	870 983 875	30.903 07	97.724 10	9.847 692	21.216 21	45.708 94
956	913 936	873 722 816	30.919 25	97.775 25	9.851 128	21.223 61	45.724 89
957	915 849	876 467 493	30.935 42	97.826 38	9.854 562	21.231 01	45.740 82
958	917 764	879 217 912	30.951 58	97.877 47	9.857 993	21.238 40	45.756 75
959	919 681	881 974 079	30.967 73	97.928 55	9.861 422	21.245 79	45.772 67
960	921 600	884 736 000	30.983 87	97.979 59	9.864 848	21.253 17	45.788 57
961	923 521	887 503 681	31.000 00	98.030 61	9.868 272	21.260 55	45.804 46
962	925 444	890 277 128	31.016 12	98.081 60	9.871 694	21.267 92	45.820 35
963	927 369	893 056 347	31.032 24	98.132 56	9.875 113	21.275 29	45.836 22
964	929 296	895 841 344	31.048 35	98.183 50	9.878 530	21.282 65	45.852 08
965	931 225	898 632 125	31.064 45	98.234 41	9.881 945	21.290 01	45.867 93
966	933 156	901 428 696	31.080 54	98.285 30	9.885 357	21.297 36	45.883 76
967	935 089	904 231 063	31.096 62	98.336 16	9.888 767	21.304 70	45.899 59
968	937 024	907 039 232	31.112 70	98.386 99	9.892 175	21.312 04	45.915 41
969	938 961	909 853 209	31.128 76	98.437 80	9.895 580	21.319 38	45.931 21
970	940 900	912 673 000	31.144 82	98.488 58	9.898 983	21.326 71	45.947 01
971	942 841	915 498 611	31.160 87	98.539 33	9.902 384	21.334 04	45.962 79
972	944 784	918 330 048	31.176 91	98.590 06	9.905 782	21.341 36	45.978 57
973	946 729	921 167 317	31.192 95	98.640 76	9.909 178	21.348 68	45.994 33
974	948 676	924 010 424	31.208 97	98.691 44	9.912 571	21.355 99	46.010 08

n	n^2	n^3	$\sqrt{n}$	$\sqrt{10n}$	$\sqrt[3]{n}$	$\sqrt[3]{10n}$	$\sqrt[3]{100n}$
975	950 625	926 859 375	31.224 99	98.742 09	9.915 962	21.363 29	46.025 82
976	952 576	929 714 176	31.241 00	98.792 71	9.919 351	21.370 59	46.041 55
977	954 529	932 574 833	31.257 00	98.843 31	9.922 738	21.377 89	46.057 27
978	956 484	935 441 352	31.272 99	98.893 88	9.926 122	21.385 18	46.072 98
979	958 441	938 313 739	31.288 98	98.944 43	9.929 504	21.392 47	46.088 68
980	960 400	941 192 000	31.304 95	98.994 95	9.932 884	21.399 75	46.104 36
981	962 361	944 076 141	31.320 92	99.045 44	9.936 261	21.407 03	46.120 04
982	964 324	946 966 168	31.336 88	99.095 91	9.939 636	21.414 30	46.135 71
983	966 289	949 862 087	31.352 83	99.146 36	9.943 009	21.421 56	46.151 36
984	968 256	952 763 904	31.368 77	99.196 77	9.946 380	21.428 83	46.167 00
985	970 225	955 671 625	31.384 71	99.247 17	9.949 748	21.436 08	46.182 64
986	972 196	958 585 256	31.400 64	99.297 53	9.953 114	21.443 33	46.198 26
987	974 169	961 504 803	31.416 56	99.347 87	9.956 478	21.450 58	46.213 87
988	976 144	964 430 272	31.432 47	99.398 19	9.959 839	21.457 82	46.229 48
989	978 121	967 361 669	31.448 37	99.448 48	9.963 198	21.465 06	46.245 07
990	980 100	970 299 000	31.464 27	99.498 74	9.966 555	21.472 29	46.260 65
991	982 081	973 242 271	31.480 15	99.548 98	9.969 910	21.479 52	46.276 22
992	984 064	976 191 488	31.496 03	99.599 20	9.973 262	21.486 74	46.291 78
993	986 049	979 146 657	31.511 90	99.649 39	9.976 612	21.493 96	46.307 33
994	988 036	982 107 784	31.527 77	99.699 55	9.979 960	21.501 17	46.322 87
995	990 025	985 074 875	31.543 62	99.749 69	9.983 305	21.508 38	46.338 40
996	992 016	988 047 936	31.559 47	99.799 80	9.986 649	21.515 58	46.353 92
997	994 009	991 026 973	31.575 31	99.849 89	9.989 990	21.522 78	46.369 43
998	996 004	994 011 992	31.591 14	99.899 95	9.993 329	21.529 97	46.384 92
999	998 001	997 002 999	31.606 96	99.949 99	9.996 666	21.537 16	46.400 41

SOURCE: R. S. Burington, "Handbook of Mathematical Tables and Formulas," 5th ed., pp. 391–410, McGraw-Hill Book Company, New York, 1973. Copyright © 1973 by McGraw-Hill, Inc. Used with permission of the publisher.

A.6 MISCELLANEOUS AREA AND VOLUME FORMULAS

Areas of Plane Geometric Figures

1. Area of a triangle = ½ base × altitude (altitude measured perpendicular to the side selected as the base)

2. Area of an irregular quadrilateral = sum of areas of two triangles formed by either diagonal

3. Area of a parallelogram = length of any side × altitude (as measured perdicular to the selected side)

4. Area of a regular polygon = ½ sum of all sides × radius of inscribed circle

5. Area of a circle = $\pi \times r^2$

6. Area of a sector of a circle = $\alpha°/360° \times \pi r^2$ or arc length $\times r/2$

7. Area of a segment of a circle = area of sector less area of triangle, or $\dfrac{r^2}{2}\left(\dfrac{\pi\alpha°}{180°} - \sin\alpha\right)$

8. Area of an ellipse = $0.7854 \times$ long axis $\times$ short axis

9. Area of a parabola = base $\times$ 2/3 altitude

10. Area of pavement at each curb return = $0.2146r^2$

Volumes of Geometrical Solids

11. Volume of a cylinder, cube, or prism = area of base $\times$ altitude (as measured perpendicularly from base to center of top area if bases are not parallel)

12. Volume of a cone or pyramid = area of base $\times$ ⅓ altitude

13. Volume of a sphere = $4/3\ \pi r^3$ or $0.5236D^3$

14. Volume of a sector of a sphere = $2/3\pi r^2 b$

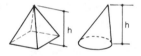

15. Volume of a segment of a sphere = volume of sector of sphere less volume of cone, or $\frac{1}{3}\pi b^2 \times (3r - b)$

16. Volume of an ellipsoid = $\pi abc/6$

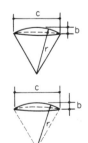

Surface Areas of Geometrical Solids

17. Surface area of a cylinder $= 2\pi r^2 + \pi D \times$ altitude (includes top and bottom)

18. Surface area of a pyramid $=$ sum of areas of all sides, or perimeter of base $\times$ ½ altitude

19. Surface area of a cone $=$ perimeter of base $\times$ ½ altitude

20. Surface area of a sphere $= 4\pi r^2$

21. Surface area of a sector of a sphere $= \frac{1}{2}\pi r(4b + c)$ (includes surface area of cone plus surface area of sphere)

22. Surface area of a segment of a sphere $= 2\pi rb$ (does not include area of circular base)

A.7 MISCELLANEOUS TRIGONOMETRIC FORMULAS

Right Triangles

1. $\sin \alpha = \dfrac{y}{r}$

2. $\cos \alpha = \dfrac{x}{r}$

3. $\tan \alpha = \dfrac{y}{x}$

4. $\csc \alpha = \dfrac{r}{y}$

5. $\sec \alpha = \dfrac{r}{x}$

6. $\cot \alpha = \dfrac{x}{y}$

7. $\csc \alpha = \dfrac{1}{\sin \alpha}$

8. $\sec \alpha = \dfrac{1}{\cos \alpha}$

9. $\cot \alpha = \dfrac{1}{\tan \alpha} = \dfrac{\cos \alpha}{\sin \alpha}$

10. $\tan \alpha = \dfrac{\sin \alpha}{\cos \alpha}$

11. $\text{vers } \alpha = \dfrac{CD}{r} = 1 - \cos \alpha$

12. $\text{exsec } \alpha = \dfrac{EB}{x} = \sec \alpha - 1$

13. $r = \dfrac{y}{\sin \alpha} = \dfrac{x}{\cos \alpha}$

14. $x = r \cdot \cos \alpha = y \cdot \cot \alpha$

15. $y = r \cdot \sin \alpha = x \cdot \tan \alpha$

16. $EB = x \cdot \text{exsec } \alpha$

17. $CD = r \cdot \text{vers } \alpha$

Oblique Triangles

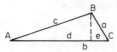

$$s = \frac{a + b + c}{2}$$

	Given	Sought	Formula
18.	A,B,a	b,c	$b = \dfrac{a}{\sin A} \cdot \sin B \qquad c = \dfrac{a}{\sin A} \cdot \sin(A + B)$
19.	A,B,b	a,c	$a = b\,\dfrac{\sin A}{\sin B} \qquad c = b\,\dfrac{\sin(A + B)}{\sin B}$
20.	A,B,c	a,b	$a = c\,\dfrac{\sin A}{\sin(A + B)} \qquad b = c\,\dfrac{\sin B}{\sin(A + B)}$
21.	a,b,c	A	$\sin \dfrac{A}{2} = \sqrt{\dfrac{(s - b)(s - c)}{bc}}$
22.			$\cos \dfrac{A}{2} = \sqrt{\dfrac{s(s - a)}{bc}}$
23.			$\tan \dfrac{A}{2} = \sqrt{\dfrac{(s - b)(s - c)}{s(s - a)}}$
24.			$\sin A = \dfrac{2\sqrt{s(s - a)(s - b)(s - c)}}{bc}$
25.	a,b,c	d,e	$d = \dfrac{b^2 + c^2 - a^2}{2b} \qquad e = \dfrac{a^2 + b^2 - c^2}{2b}$
26.		Area	$\text{Area} = \sqrt{s(s - a)(s - b)(s - c)}$
27.	A,B,C,a	Area	$\text{Area} = \dfrac{a^2 \cdot \sin B \cdot \sin C}{2 \sin A}$
28.	C,a,b	Area	$\text{Area} = \dfrac{ab \cdot \sin C}{2}$

A.8 TABLE OF ARC LENGTHS—
RADIUS EQUALS 1 FT

Sec.	Length	Min.	Length	Deg.	Length	Deg.	Length
1	0.0000048	1	0.0002909	1	0.0174533	61	1.0646508
2	0.0000097	2	0.0005818	2	0.0349066	62	1.0821041
3	0.0000145	3	0.0008727	3	0.0523599	63	1.0995574
4	0.0000194	4	0.0011636	4	0.0698132	64	1.1170107
5	0.0000242	5	0.0014544	5	0.0872665	65	1.1344640
6	0.0000291	6	0.0017453	6	0.1047198	66	1.1519173
7	0.0000339	7	0.0020362	7	0.1221730	67	1.1693706
8	0.0000388	8	0.0023271	8	0.1396263	68	1.1868239
9	0.0000436	9	0.0026180	9	0.1570796	69	1.2042772
10	0.0000485	10	0.0029089	10	0.1745329	70	1.2217305
11	0.0000533	11	0.0031998	11	0.1919862	71	1.2391838
12	0.0000582	12	0.0034907	12	0.2094395	72	1.2566371
13	0.0000630	13	0.0037815	13	0.2268928	73	1.2740904
14	0.0000679	14	0.0040724	14	0.2443461	74	1.2915436
15	0.0000727	15	0.0043633	15	0.2617994	75	1.3089969
16	0.0000776	16	0.0046542	16	0.2792527	76	1.3264502
17	0.0000824	17	0.0049451	17	0.2967060	77	1.3439035
18	0.0000873	18	0.0052360	18	0.3141593	78	1.3613568
19	0.0000921	19	0.0055269	19	0.3316126	79	1.3788101
20	0.0000970	20	0.0058178	20	0.3490659	80	1.3962634
21	0.0001018	21	0.0061087	21	0.3665191	81	1.4137167
22	0.0001067	22	0.0063995	22	0.3839724	82	1.4311700
23	0.0001115	23	0.0066904	23	0.4014257	83	1.4486233
24	0.0001164	24	0.0069813	24	0.4188790	84	1.4660766
25	0.0001212	25	0.0072722	25	0.4363323	85	1.4835299
26	0.0001261	26	0.0075631	26	0.4537856	86	1.5009832
27	0.0001309	27	0.0078540	27	0.4712389	87	1.5184364
28	0.0001357	28	0.0081449	28	0.4886922	88	1.5358897
29	0.0001406	29	0.0084358	29	0.5061455	89	1.5533430
30	0.0001454	30	0.0087266	30	0.5235988	90	1.5707963
31	0.0001503	31	0.0090175	31	0.5410521	91	1.5882496
32	0.0001551	32	0.0093084	32	0.5585054	92	1.6057029
33	0.0001600	33	0.0095993	33	0.5759587	93	1.6231562
34	0.0001648	34	0.0098902	34	0.5934119	94	1.6406095
35	0.0001697	35	0.0101811	35	0.6108652	95	1.6580628
36	0.0001745	36	0.0104720	36	0.6283185	96	1.6755161
37	0.0001794	37	0.0107629	37	0.6457718	97	1.6929694
38	0.0001842	38	0.0110538	38	0.6632251	98	1.7104227
39	0.0001891	39	0.0113446	39	0.6806784	99	1.7278760
40	0.0001939	40	0.0116355	40	0.6981317	100	1.7453293
41	0.0001988	41	0.0119264	41	0.7155850	101	1.7627825

A.8   TABLE OF ARC LENGTHS—RADIUS EQUALS 1 FT *(Continued)*

Sec.	Length	Min.	Length	Deg.	Length	Deg.	Length
42	0.0002036	42	0.0122173	42	0.7330383	102	1.7802358
43	0.0002085	43	0.0125082	43	0.7504916	103	1.7976891
44	0.0002133	44	0.0127991	44	0.7679449	104	1.8151424
45	0.0002182	45	0.0130900	45	0.7853982	105	1.8325957
46	0.0002230	46	0.0133809	46	0.8028515	106	1.8500490
47	0.0002279	47	0.0136717	47	0.8203047	107	1.8675023
48	0.0002327	48	0.0139626	48	0.8377580	108	1.8849556
49	0.0002376	49	0.0142535	49	0.8552113	109	1.9024089
50	0.0002424	50	0.0145444	50	0.8726646	110	1.9198622
51	0.0002473	51	0.0148353	51	0.8901179	111	1.9373155
52	0.0002521	52	0.0151262	52	0.9075712	112	1.9547688
53	0.0002570	53	0.0154171	53	0.9250245	113	1.9722221
54	0.0002618	54	0.0157080	54	0.9424778	114	1.9896753
55	0.0002666	55	0.0159989	55	0.9599311	115	2.0071286
56	0.0002715	56	0.0162897	56	0.9773844	116	2.0245819
57	0.0002763	57	0.0165806	57	0.9948377	117	2.0420352
58	0.0002812	58	0.0168715	58	1.0122910	118	2.0594885
59	0.0002860	59	0.0171624	59	1.0297443	119	2.0769418
60	0.0002909	60	0.0174533	60	1.0471976	120	2.0943951

Mathematical Devices

B.1 ARCHITECT'S AND ENGINEER'S DIMENSIONING SYSTEM

In March of 1972, the Congress of the United States filed a bill that recommended that the official policy of the U.S. government shall be:

1. To facilitate and encourage use of the Metric System in all sectors of the economy as the predominant but not exclusive language of measurement in this country.

2. To encourage rapid development of new or revised engineering standards based on the Metric System.

3. To cooperate with foreign governments, public and private corporations, to encourage and coordinate use of the system and standardization of metric units.

The intended goal was a complete changeover to the metric system in ten years. Some schools immediately converted to the metric system but many did not. In any case there will be a certain amount of confusion for some time. Even if the conversion were 100 percent, there would still exist all the surveys, plats, base sheets, section maps, etc., on record from prior to 1973 that must be converted. Conversion tables for changing from the U.S. to the metric and from the metric to the U.S. system are given in Appendix D.

There were two common methods of dimensioning in use prior to going metric. They are hereafter referred to as the *architectural* and *engineering* systems.

Building architects have used a dimensioning system based on feet, inches, and fractions of an inch. The inch is the twelfth part of a foot, and the fractions of the inch are always expressed with denominators which are multiples of 2, that is, ½, ¼, ⅛, ¹⁄₁₆, ¹⁄₃₂, ¹⁄₆₄, etc. The 12 in. to the foot used by the building architects is consistent with the system of measurement used for building materials and by the construction trades. Site maps that have been prepared in offices of building architects are often dimensioned in this manner, and it is therefore essential that the landscape architect be familiar with both this system and that used by the engineer and land surveyor.

Civil engineers and land surveyors have used a dimensioning system based on feet and decimals of a foot. This system breaks the foot into the tenth, hundredth, thousandth, etc., part of a foot rather than the twelfth part of a foot (inches) and fractions of an inch as used by the building architects. This decimal system is much more adaptable to the many computations required in surveyors' work. This is the system generally preferred and used by landscape architects.

It is important that the landscape architect to be able to convert easily and rapidly from one system to the other. It must be clearly understood that the foot is a basic unit of measure common to both systems. In any conversion the number of whole feet is never changed. The part that must be changed is that part of the dimension that is less than a whole foot. This is the part of the dimension which is stated as inches and fractions of an inch in the architect's system and as a decimal part of a foot in the engineer's system.

To convert from the architectural to the engineering system, express the fraction of an inch (if there is such) as a decimal of an inch. Then divide the inches (with its decimally expressed fraction) by 12 to obtain the decimal part of a foot.

Example B.1   Convert 12 ft 10⅜ in. to feet and decimals.

1. ⅜ in. = 0.375 in.

   Then

   10⅜ in. = 10.375 in.

2. 10.375 in. ÷ 12 = 0.8646 ft

   and

   12 ft 10⅜ in. = 12.8646 ft

Example B.2   Convert 100 ft 5¼ in. to engineering dimensioning.

1. ¼ in. = 0.25 in.

   Then

   5¼ in. = 5.25 in.

2. 5.25 in. ÷ 12 in. = 0.4375 ft

and

100 ft 5¼ in. = 100.4375 ft

To convert from engineering to architectural dimensioning, multiply the decimal part of the figure by 12 and convert the decimal part of the answer to a fraction by multiplying this decimal part by the desired denominator to obtain its numerator.

Example B.3   Convert 125.320 ft to feet and inches expressed to the nearest sixteenth of an inch.

1. 0.320 × 12 in. = 3.840 in.
2. 0.840 × 16   = 13.44

Then

$$0.840 = {}^{13}\!\!/_{16} \text{ in.}$$

and

125.320 ft = 125 ft 3${}^{13}\!\!/_{16}$ in.

Example B.4   Convert 12.389 ft to architectural dimensioning expressed to the nearest sixty-fourth of an inch.

1. 0.389 × 12 in. = 4.668 in.
2. 0.668 in. × 64 = 42.752

Then

$$0.668 \text{ in.} = {}^{43}\!\!/_{64} \text{ in.}$$

and

12.389 ft = 12 ft 4${}^{43}\!\!/_{64}$ in.

It may be found clearer to think of the decimal part of a foot as a percentage of 12 in.   In Example B.3, the 125.320 ft is 125 ft plus 32 percent of 12 in. 32 percent of 12 in. is 3${}^{13}\!\!/_{16}$ in., and the answer is 125 ft 3${}^{13}\!\!/_{16}$ in.   In example B.4, 12.389 ft is 12 ft plus 38.9 percent of 12 in.   38.9 percent of 12 in. is 4${}^{43}\!\!/_{64}$ in., and the answer is 12 ft 4${}^{43}\!\!/_{64}$ in.

B.2 VERNIERS

The vernier is a device that makes it possible to divide the smallest unit of a scale into far more accurate subdivisions than one could do by eye. Verniers are used on many measuring instruments, including protractors, planimeters, and transits.   Figure B.1 shows a simple form of vernier that adds one decimal place to the accuracy of the scale reading. All verniers work on this principle. The decimal vernier has 10 equal divisions, each division being nine-tenths of one division of the main scale, so that the total length of the 10 divisions is exactly equal to the length of nine divisions of the main scale. The zero graduation of the vernier is the index line for reading the main scale. When this is exactly opposite a mark on the main scale, no other graduation of the vernier will be opposite any other mark on the main scale except the tenth one. If the index (0) line of the vernier is moved forward one-tenth of a unit, the first line of the vernier will coincide with a graduation of the main scale since the unit divisions of the vernier are each equal to nine-tenths of a main-scale unit. Likewise, if the index line of the vernier is moved forward two-tenths, the second line of the vernier will coincide with a graduation of the main scale.

Fig.   B.1 A simple vernier.

The scale is read by reading the unit mark on the main scale at or immediately preceding the zero mark on the vernier and proceeding along the vernier upward from the zero index to read the first mark on the vernier that coincides with a unit mark on the main scale.

Example B.5 In Fig. B.2a the zero index of the vernier is just above 6.20. Following along the vernier in the same direction as the scale progresses, find the second graduation of the vernier coinciding with a graduation mark on the main scale, thus making the reading 6.22.

Examine Figs. B.2b and c to obtain readings of 10.00 and 12.26, respectively.

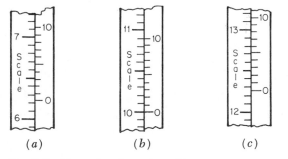

(a)   (b)   (c)

Fig. B.2 Examples of vernier settings.

Verniers on transits and protractors are for angular-measure reading in degrees, minutes, and seconds. The basic unit of the vernier is $^{29}\!/_{30}$ of each space on the main scale. Variations of verniers besides the 1-min vernier may be verniers reading to 30, 20, and 10 sec. The value of each vernier division can be determined by checking the number of divisions against the main scale with the vernier set at zero. Since transits are used to read angles to the left as well as angles to the right, the divisions of the vernier proceed from the zero index in both directions. In reading a vernier on a transit, always proceed along the vernier in the direction the angle is being measured.

B.3   THE PLANIMETER

The planimeter is an instrument used for making area takeoffs from plans or cross-section drawings.   It is particularly useful where the area boundaries are crooked and irregular, so that geometrical calculations of the area are not possible.   If the machine is operated carefully, accurate results are obtainable.

The planimeter is a precise instrument and should be given the best of care and handling.   The bearings at the ends of the measuring-wheel axle are very delicate and must be given the same care as a fine watch.   The rim of the measuring wheel must be kept absolutely true and clean.   It must not be touched by the fingers, to avoid causing rust or greasy spots on it.   The ball-and-socket joint must be kept smooth and clean.

The surface of the drawing over which the instrument is run will affect the accuracy of the answer.   The drawing must be smooth and clean, and the instrument should be so located on the drawing that the measuring wheel will not run off the edge of the paper.   If the drawing is on thick paper, sheets of equal thickness should be butted against the edges; if small, the draw-ing should be overlaid with a large sheet of tracing paper.

Figure B.3 shows a planimeter with an optical tracer lens.   Figure B.4 shows how the dials and vernier of a planimeter are read.   The reading shown is 3518, meaning 35.18 sq in.

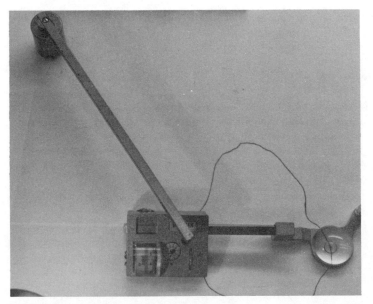

Fig. B.3   Compensating polar planimeter.

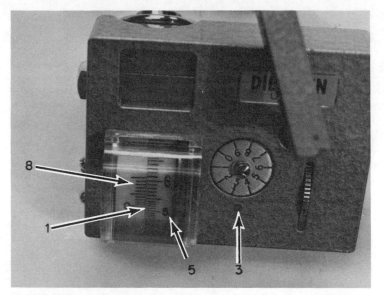

Fig. B.4 Closeup of planimeter dials. Read the dials to four places.

Some skill is required to guide the tracer point steadily along the area boundary line. With a little practice this becomes not too difficult, and if the following summary of rules is adhered to, fairly accurate measurements should result.

1. Test the instrument accuracy on the same type and condition of paper as that being measured in the problem.

2. Never operate the planimeter on other than a level surface.

3. Check the anchor location to make certain that the tracer point can be manipulated to reach comfortably all parts of the area boundary.

4. If there is difficulty in reaching all the area boundary with the tracer point, subdivide the area into smaller component parts.

5. Always move the tracer point to the right (in a clockwise direction) to obtain positive answers.

6. Make certain that the tracer point is returned to the exact starting point at the completion of a circuit.

7. Never touch the steel measuring wheel with your fingers.

8. Always record the readings as four figures even if the left-hand figures are zero.

9. Always check your reading with a second run.

10. Make a rough check with your scale to make sure your answers are realistic—that they are horse-sense-right.

To test the instrument for accuracy, use the testing rule furnished with the instrument, or very carefully draw a 2- × 2-in. square and measure this. The answer should read 0400, or 4 sq in. Make more than one trial, and if the answers do not average out to 4 sq in., work out a correction factor which, when applied to the instrument reading, will produce the correct answer; i.e., if the instrument reads 0389 (3.89 sq in.), divide 4 sq in. by 3.89 sq in. to obtain a correction factor of 1.029. Then all readings of areas measured on this kind of paper under these same weather conditions must be multiplied by 1.029 to obtain the correct number of square inches in the measured area. Figure B.5 shows a convenient form for tabulating planimeter recordings and calculations.

Areas can be measured with the anchor point inside the boundaries of the area being measured. The reading of the instrument must be increased by adding the *correction-circle area* to the instrument reading. The correction-circle area, including instructions for its application, is supplied with the instrument by the manufacturer. In most cases it is more convenient and less confusing simply to subdivide the large area into smaller components that can be measured by the planimeter with its anchor outside the boundary of the area being measured. Add the separate component readings together to obtain the total area of the large figure.

Planimeters having adjustable anchor arms and adjustable tracer arms are available. These can be set to the scale of the plan so that the areas can be read directly in square feet on the instrument. It is the author's experience that the bother of setting the instrument accurately and testing it each time a new scale is encountered completely offsets its advantages, and the most satisfactory planimeter for the landscape architect is the compensating polar planimeter with fixed arms that reads in square inches. Then, in each case, the answer in square inches is multipled by the number of square feet in a square inch; i.e., a 40-scale plan will equal 40 × 40 ft, or 1,600 sq ft per sq in.; a 50-scale plan will equal 50 × 50 ft, or 2,500 sq ft per sq in.; and a cross section having a horizontal scale of 1 in. = 40 ft and a vertical scale of 1 in. = 4 ft will equal 4 × 40 ft, or 160 sq ft per sq in. Note that the planimeter can be used to accurately measure areas of cross sections having exaggerated vertical scales.

AREA COMPUTATION BY PLANIMETER							
JOB_____ LOCATION _____ DATE _____ CALCULATED BY_____CHECKED BY_____ PAGE _____OF___							
Section or plane	First reading	Second reading	Average reading	Corr. factor	Corr. reading	Scale	Area, sq ft

Fig. B.5 A typical form for recording planimeter readings and converting to area quantities.

B.4   THE SLIDE RULE

The slide rule (Fig. B.6) is a useful tool for solving proportions and vertical-curve offsets and checking mathematical computations. It is rapidly being replaced in the latter capacity by the pocket-sized electronic calculators. Nevertheless, it is a very convenient instrument that provides a rapid method of obtaining approximate answers and checks.

The slide rule comes in a variety of types and sizes. The less complicated rule is easier to operate and involves less chance of error. The landscape architect has no need for a complicated rule and should be equipped with a simple one, about 10 in. long. This rule should have at least the four scales A, B, C, and D. It would be useful also to have a K scale and/or a DF scale, though these are not essential for doing most landscape architectural problems.

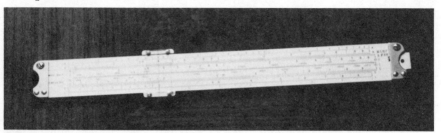

Fig. B.6 The slide rule in this picture is suitable for site-work calculations. This rule has sin and tan scales in addition to the L and K scales. These are convenient but not absolutely essential.

The slide rule has a center strip called the *slide* that can be moved back and forth. It also has a small glass or plastic runner that can be moved along the length of the rule. This has a fine hairline inscribed crosswise to the rule which is used as an indexing line. The various scales scribed on the rule and slide are accurately spaced proportionately as the logarithmic equivalents of the numbers they represent. Since these graduations are spaced as the logarithms of the numbers they represent, any two numbers can be multiplied by adding together the logarithms of the numbers they represent, and division can be performed by subtracting logarithmic graduations representing the two numbers.

It does take considerable practice to become adept in the operation of the slide rule. Reading the slide rule is somewhat difficult and requires care and patience at first. Some of the chapters in this book show slide-rule methods for solving problems pertinent to that chapter. The following examples show how to use the slide rule for solving general problems.

Multiplication

Use C and D scales. Multiply $4 \times 3 = 12$.

Set the index (1 on the C scale) of the C scale opposite 4 on the D scale. Move the runner along the slide rule until the hairline is over 3 on the C scale. Read the answer, 12, directly below on the D scale.

Division

Use C and D scales.   Solve $12 \div 3 = 4$.

Division is just the reverse of multiplication.   Set the hairline over 12 on the D scale, move the slide so that 3 on the C scale is exactly under the hairline, and read 4 on the D scale at the index of the C scale.

Combined Multiplication and Division

Use C and D scales.   Solve $\dfrac{414 \times 3}{9} = 138$.

Set the hairline over 414 on the D scale.   Place 9 on the C scale under the hairline.   Move the runner so that the hairline is over 3 on the C scale and read 138 on the D scale.

Percentages

Use C and D scales.   Solve 35% of $1,676 = 586.6$.

Set the hairline over 1,676 on the D scale.   Move the index of the C scale to the hairline.   Move the hairline to 35 on the C scale and read 5,866 on the D scale.   Mentally place the decimal point to obtain 586.6.

Proportional Ratios

Use C and D scales.   Solve $\dfrac{10}{40} = \dfrac{24}{x_1} = \dfrac{6}{x_2} = \dfrac{16}{x_3}$.

Place 10 on the C scale over 40 on the D scale.   Move the hairline to any number on the scale and find x immediately below on the D scale.   In this case find 96 on the D scale below 24 on the C scale, 24 on the D scale below 6 on the C scale, and 64 on the D scale below 16 on the C scale.

Squares and Square Roots

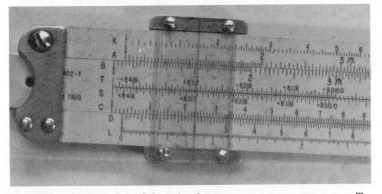

Fig. B.7   Closeup of a slide rule showing a square-root setup.   To obtain the square root of 144, place the hairline over 144 on the A scale.   Read the square root, 12, on the D scale.

Use A and D scales.   Solve $\sqrt{144} = 12$.

1. To find the square root of a number between 1 and 10 or between 100 and 1,000, set the hairline on the number on the left half of the A scale and read its square root under the hairline on the D scale.

2. To find the square root of a number between 10 and 100 or between 1,000 and 10,000, set the hairline over the number on the right half of the A scale and read its square root under the hairline on the D scale.

Reverse the process to square a number.

Cube and Cube Roots

Use K and D scales.   Solve $3\sqrt{216} = 6$.

1. To find the cube root of a number between 1 and 10, set the hairline on the number on the left third of the K scale and read the cube root under the hairline on the D scale.

2. To find the cube root of a number between 10 and 100, set the hairline on the number in the center third of the K scale and read the cube root under the hairline on the D scale.

3. To find the cube root of a number between 100 and 1,000, set the hairline on the number in the right third of the K scale and read the cube root under the hairline on the D scale.

Reverse the process to cube a number.

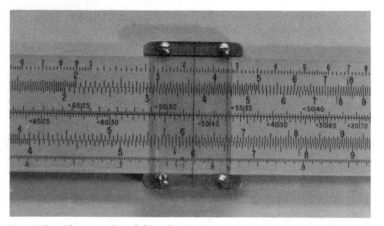

Fig. B.8   Closeup of a slide rule showing a cube-root setup.   To obtain the cube root of 216, place the hairline at 216 in the right third of the K scale.   Read the cube root, 6, on the D scale.

Note that in reading the slide rule, care must be taken to ascertain the value of each division, because they vary throughout the length of the rule. Note also that the slide rule does not show decimal places. The operator must round-figure the problem mentally to determine the magnitude of the answer, the number of decimal places, and the sign of the answer.

B.5 CALCULATORS AND DESK-TOP COMPUTERS

The essential difference between a calculator and a computer is that the computer can be programmed to do intricate mathematical problems step by step to completion, whereas the calculator must be operated step by step through the problem. The calculator is usually limited in its mathematical operations and is not able to make any selection.

The computer does not solve problems on its own; it only follows a program of carefully defined computational steps. It is faster and more accurate than a human being, but it cannot make decisions. It can be programmed to make a selection between numerical values of zero, less than zero, or greater than zero and, on the basis of this numeric readout, proceed along one of the three routes as directed by the programmed instructions given the machine.

There are leasing arrangements for time on large central computers, but for most landscape architects such an investment is unwarranted. There are other computers larger than the desk-top computer that can be individually owned, but generally these need a separate air-conditioned room and a specially trained operator. Considering the investment and the operational cost, most landscape architectural offices cannot afford such luxury. However, it does seem that no landscape architect can afford to operate his office without a desk-top computer.

Desk-top computers generally range in size from a hand-held instrument to about three times the size of a typewriter. These smaller machines lack the large storage and memory capacity of the larger machines, and they are much slower in operation. They do relieve landscape architects of the drudgery of tedious mathematical problems, freeing them for the more interesting and exciting facets of their profession. They do not relieve landscape architects of the need for a full and thorough understanding of the problem at hand nor for a thorough knowledge of the related mathematics. Some of the programs that an office could use are:

1. Converting degrees, minutes, and seconds to decimal degrees and/or radians and vice versa

2. Solving oblique triangles
   a. With three sides given
   b. With two sides and the included angle given
   c. With two sides and one angle (not included) given
   d. With one side and two angles given

3. Solving horizontal curves
   a. The intersection of two circles
   b. Circular curve, given the radius, internal angle, or arc length
   c. Circular curve, given the radius and chord
   d. Circular curve, given two tangent bearings and radius

4. Solving vertical curves
   a. Tangent elevations and vertical-curve elevations at stations
   b. Station and elevation for low or high point of vertical curve
   c. Station location of whole-foot contours on vertical curve

5. Solving traverse problems
    a. Area within a traverse
    b. Completion of traverse from end points
    c. Correction for angular error
    d. Calculation and sums of latitudes and departures from bearings and lengths
    e. Correction of latitudes and departures
    f. Computation of bearings
    g. Closing a traverse

6. Solving earthwork cut and fill
    a. Volume by using grid method
    b. Volume by using irregularly spaced cross sections
    c. Volume by using regularly spaced end areas

In addition to these programs there are programs for solving hydraulic problems, storm-water runoff, and irrigation, plus general office programs for bookkeeping and payroll.

Each year these small electronic marvels are being made more compact, more versatile, and less expensive. As more automatic programs are built into these machines, they become easier to program. Most manufacturers will supply any programs needed for a specific type of work, either included in the price of the machine or at an extra charge.

Weights and Measures

C.1 WEIGHTS

Apothecaries:

    1 pound = 12 ounces
    1 ounce = 8 drams
    1 dram   = 3 scruples
    1 scruple = 20 grains
    1 grain   =   0.0648 gram

Avoirdupois:

    1 ton   = 2,000 pounds
    1 pound =   16 ounces
    1 ounce =   16 drams
    1 dram =   27.34 grains
    1 grain =   0.0648 gram

Troy:

    1 pound   = 12 ounces
    1 ounce   = 20 pennyweights
    1 pennyweight = 24 grains
    1 carat   = 3.086 grains
    1 grain   = 0.0648 gram

Metric

```
1 metric ton  = 10 quintals
1 quintal     = 10 myriagrams
1 myriagram   = 10 kilograms
1 kilogram    = 10 hectograms
1 hectogram   = 10 decagrams
1 decagram    = 10 grams
1 gram        = 10 decigrams
1 decigram    = 10 centigrams
1 centigram   = 10 milligrams
```

C.2   LIQUID MEASURE

Apothecaries Fluid Measure

```
1 pint        = 16 fluid ounces = 28.875 cubic inches
1 fluid ounce =  8 fluid drams
1 fluid dram  = 60 minims
```

U.S. Liquid Measure

```
1 gallon = 4 quarts
1 quart  = 2 pints
1 pint   = 4 gills = 28.875 cubic inches
1 gill   = 4 fluid ounces
```

Metric Fluid Measure

```
1 kiloliter  = 10 hectoliters
1 hectoliter = 10 decaliters
1 decaliter  = 10 liters
1 liter      = 10 deciliters
1 deciliter  = 10 centiliters
1 centiliter = 10 milliliters
```

C.3   DRY MEASURE

U.S. Dry Measure

```
1 bushel =  4 pecks
1 peck   =  8 quarts
1 quart  =  2 pints
1 pint   = 33.6 cubic inches
```

C.4 LINEAR MEASURE

U.S. Linear Measure

1 league (land) = 3 miles
1 mile (statute) = 5,280 feet
1 furlong   = 40 rods
1 rod   = 5½ yards
1 yard   = 3 feet
1 foot   = 12 inches
1 inch   = 2.54 centimeters

Metric Linear Measure

1 myriameter = 10 kilometers
1 kilometer   = 10 hectometers
1 hectometer = 10 decameters
1 decameter   = 10 meters
1 meter   = 10 decimeters
1 decimeter   = 10 centimeters
1 centimeter = 10 millimeters
1 centimeter = 0.3937 inches

C.5 SQUARE MEASURE

U.S. Square Measure

1 square mile = 640 acres
1 acre   = 43,560 square feet = 160 square rods
1 square rod   = 30¼ square yards = 272¼ square feet
1 square yard = 9 square feet
1 square foot = 144 square inches

Metric Square Measure

1 square kilometer = 100 square hectometers
1 square hectometer = 100 square decameters
1 square decameter = 100 square meters
1 square meter   = 100 square decimeters
1 square decimeter = 100 square centimeters
1 square centimeter = 100 square millimeters

C.6   CUBIC MEASURE

U.S. Cubic Measure

1 cubic yard = 27 cubic feet
1 cubic foot = 1,728 cubic inches

Metric Cubic Measure

1 cubic meter   = 1,000 cubic decimeters
1 cubic decimeter =   100 cubic centimeters
1 cubic centimeter = 1,000 cubic millimeters

C.7   LAND AND SEA MEASURE

U.S. Land Measure*

1 township   = 36 square miles
1 square mile = 1 section = 640 acres
1 acre   = 43,560 square feet = 10 square chains
1 square chain = 16 square poles
1 square pole = 625 square links

Metric Land Measure

1 square kilometer = 100 hectares
1 hectare   = 100 ares
1 are   = 100 centiares
1 centiare   =   1 square meter

Chain Measure (Gunter's, surveyors')*

1 mile   = 80 chains
1 furlong = 10 chains
1 chain   = 100 links = 4 rods
1 rod   = 16½ feet
1 link   = 0.66 feet = 7.92 inches

Nautical Measure

1 degree longitude at equator = 60 nautical miles
1 nautical mile   = 1.15078 statute miles
1 fathom   = 6 feet

*Chains, poles, rods, and links are no longer used in land surveys. Acres and feet and decimals thereof are the units of measure used in land surveys since the thirties. Today, all land measure is being converted to the metric system as rapidly as possible.

Conversion Factors

D.1 CONVERSION FACTORS—MISCELLANEOUS

Knowing:	*Multiply by:*	*To obtain:*
Acres	43,560	Square feet
	0.0015625	Square miles
	4,840	Square yards
Acre-feet	43,560	Cubic feet
	325,851	Gallons
Atmospheres	29.92	Inches of mercury
	33.90	Feet of water
	14.70	Pounds per square inch
Cubic feet	1,728	Cubic inches
	7.48052	Gallons
Cubic feet per second	448.831	Gallons per minute
Cubic yards	27	Cubic feet
Degrees (angle)	0.01745	Radians
Fathoms	6	Feet
Feet	0.0001894	Miles
Feet of water (head)	62.43	Pounds per square foot
	0.4335	Pounds per square inch
Feet per minute	0.0113636	Miles per hour
Furlongs	660	Feet
	0.125	Miles

Knowing:	_Multiply by:_	_To obtain:_
Gallons	0.1337	Cubic feet
	231	Cubic inches
Gallons, imperial	1.20095	Gallons, U.S.
Gallons of water	8.3453	Pounds of water
Gallons per minute	0.002228	Cubic feet per second
	8.0208	Cubic feet per hour
Grains (troy)	0.0648	Grams
	0.0020833	Ounces (avoirdupois)
Grams	15.43	Grains
Horsepower	550	Foot-pounds per second
Inches	1,000	Mils
Inches of mercury	0.4912	Pounds per square inch
Inches of water	0.03613	Pounds per square inch
Knots	1	Nautical miles per hour
	1.15078	Statute miles per hour
Links (Gunter's)	7.92	Inches
	0.66	Feet
Microns	0.000001	Meters
Miles, nautical	6,076.1033	Feet
Miles, statute	5,280	Feet
Miles per hour	88	Feet per minute
Miles per minute	88	Feet per second
Ounces (avoirdupois)	16	Drams
	437.5	Grains
	28.349527	Grams
	0.9115	Ounces (troy)
Ounces (fluid)	1.805	Cubic inches
Pounds per square inch	2.307	Feet of water
	2.036	Inches of mercury
Pounds of water	0.01602	Cubic feet
Pounds (troy)	12	Ounces (troy)
	13.1657	Ounces (avoirdupois)
	5,760	Grains
Quart (dry)	67.20	Cubic inches
Quart (liquid)	57.75	Cubic inches
Quire	25	Sheets
Radians	57.29578	Degrees (angle)
Ream	500	Sheets
Rods	0.25	Chains (Gunter's)
	16.5	Feet
Square feet	0.00002296	Acres
Square chains (Gunter's)	16	Square rods
Square miles	640	Acres
Watts	0.05692	BTU per minute
	44.26	Foot-pounds per minute
	0.001341	Horsepower
Watt-hours	3.415	British thermal units
	2,655	Foot-pounds
Temperature, centigrade + 273	1	Absolute temperature, centigrade

Knowing:	Multiply by:	To obtain:
Temperature, centigrade + 17.78	1.8	Temperature, fahrenheit
Temperature, fahrenheit + 460	1	Absolute temperature, fahrenheit
Temperature, fahrenheit − 32	5/9	Temperature, centigrade

D.2   CONVERSION FACTORS—U.S. TO METRIC

Knowing:	Multiply by:	To obtain:
Acres	4,046.461	Square meters
	0.404646	Hectares
Acre-feet	1,233.49	Cubic meters
Atmospheres	76	Centimeters of mercury
	10,333	Kilograms per square meter
Cubic feet	28.316	Liters
	0.02832	Cubic meters
Cubic inches	16.39	Cubic centimeters
	0.01639	Liters
Feet	30.48	Centimeters
	0.0003048	Kilometers
	0.3048	Meters
Feet per minute	0.5080	Centimeters per second
	0.3048	Meters per minute
Feet per second	18.29	Meters per minute
Gallons	3.785	Liters
Gallons per minute	0.06308	Liters per second
Inches	2.54	Centimeters
	0.0254	Meters
	25.40	Millimeters
Knots	1.852	Kilometers per hour
Miles	1.6093	Kilometers
Ounces (avoirdupois)	28.349527	Grams
Pounds per cubic inch	27.68	Grams per cubic centimeter
Quarts	0.945	Liters
Square miles	2.590	Square kilometers
Yards	0.9144	Meters

D.3   CONVERSION FACTORS—METRIC TO U.S.

Knowing:	Multiply by:	To obtain:
Centimeters	0.03281	Feet
	0.3937	Inches
Centimeters per second	0.02237	Miles per hour
	1.969	Feet per minute
Cubic meters	35.31	Cubic feet
	1.308	Cubic yards
	264.2	Gallons (U.S. liquid)

Knowing:	*Multiply by:*	*To obtain:*
Grams per square centimeter	2.0481	Pounds per square foot
Hectares	2.4713	Acres
Kilograms	2.205	Pounds
Kilograms per square meter	0.0014223	Pounds per square inch
Kilograms per square centimeter	14.223	Pounds per square inch
Kilometer	3,280.87	Feet
	0.62137	Miles
	1,093.62	Yards
Kilometers per hour	54.68	Feet per minute
	0.9113	Feet per second
Liters	0.02838	Bushels (U.S. dry)
	61.02	Cubic inches
	0.03531	Cubic feet
	0.2642	Gallons (U.S. liquid)
	1.0567	Quarts (U.S. liquid)
Meters	3.281	Feet
	39.37	Inches
	1.094	Yards
Meters per second	2.237	Miles per hour
	0.03728	Miles per minute
Square centimeters	0.1550	Square inches
Square kilometers	0.3861	Square miles
Tons (metric)	2,205	Pounds

Index

Adjacent property:
  runoff from, 29
  topography, 14
Algebra:
  linear equations, 157, 158
  means and extremes, 158
  proportional statements, 158
  quadratic equations, 158
Allowable extreme fiber stress in bending, 150–153
Anchors, wall, 73
Angle:
  bearing, 4–10
  central (see interior below)
  interior, 35–36
Arc length, 36
Arc lengths, radius equals 1 ft, table, 183
Areas:
  by DMD, 10–11
  of geometric solids, 181
  of plane geometric figures, 179–180
  by planimeter, 10, 189–191
Average end areas, 81

Balancing:
  cut and fill, 29, 80
  latitude and departures, 4–10
Base lines, 23
Basins, catch, 109
Batter, 53, 56, 73
Beams:
  bending moment in, 141, 143, 146–149
  cantilever, 143, 148–149
  continuous, 143, 149
  dead loads, 141–143
  deflection in, 141
  design of, 143–145
  effective span of, 143
  fixed, 147–148
  horizontal shear, 141
  investigation of, 141, 143–145
  live loads, 141–143
  load-bearing capacity of, 141
  overhanging, 143, 149
  shear across the grain, 141
  simple, 143, 146–147
  solving for size, 143–145

Beams (*Cont.*):
types of, 143
Beams and stringers, 139, 150–153
Bearings of lines, 4–10, 23, 35
Bench mark, 12–13
Bending, allowable extreme fiber stress in, 150–153
Bending moment (*see* Beams, bending moment in)
Borings, test, 61
Brick facing on retaining walls, 65–66

Calculators, 195
Cantilever beams, 143, 148–149
Catch basin, 109
Cedar, 140, 150, 156
Center of gravity, 53, 55
Center post, 3
Central angle (*see* Angle, interior)
Centroids, illus., 55
Channels, flow capacity of, 113–118
Characteristics:
of contour lines, 19
of logarithms, 160
Charts:
circular pipe flow capacity, 110
ditch flow capacity, 115–118
pressure loss: in asbestos-cement pipe, 130
in copper pipe, 129
in polyethylene pipe, 132
in polyvinyl chloride (PVC) pipe, 131
in water meters, 127
rainfall intensity probability, 106, 107
swale flow capacity, 117, 118
Chord, length of, 38
Circular arc, 35
Circular curves, 35–38
Circular measure, 163
Closing a traverse, 4–10
Coefficient of runoff, 105
Coefficient of sliding friction, 62
Compass rule, 8
Compound curve, 38
Computer programs, 195–196
Computers, desk-top, 195–196
Contour interval, 14
Contour planes:
geometry of, illus., 91
parallel planes, comparison with, illus., 94
Contours:
characteristics of, 19
concentric, 19
definition of, 14

Contours (*Cont.*):
interpolation for (*see* Interpolation, for contours)
plotting, 14–16
Conversion:
of decimals to feet and inches, 187
of feet and inches to decimals, 186
Conversion factors:
metric to U.S., 203–204
miscellaneous, 201–203
U.S. to metric, 203
Coordinates, use of, 23–24
Correcting latitudes and departures, 6–10
Correcting traverse lengths and bearings, 10
Cosecant, 161
Cosine, 161
Cotangent, 161
Cross sections:
average end area, 81
parabolic, 48
scale exaggeration, 81
Cube roots, 164–179, 194
Cubes, 164–179, 194
Cubic measure, table, 200
Curves:
circular, 35–38
horizontal, illus., 39
parabolic (*see* Vertical curves)
reverse: with nonparallel tangents, 41
with parallel tangents, 40
vertical (*see* Vertical curves)
Cut and fill:
balancing, 79–81
computation of volume (*see* Earthwork)
Cypress, southern, 140, 156

Dam(s):
design of, 53–63
$h/3$ principle, illus., 59
illustration, 58
overturning, 56, 60
parallelogram of forces, illus., 58
settlement at toe, 61
sliding, 62
tabular calculation for weights, moments, and moment arms, illus., 58
Datum, 12–13
Dead load, 141–143
Deadmen, 73
Decimals:
conversion of, to feet and inches, 187
conversion of feet and inches to, 186
Deed descriptions, 3–4

Deflection in beams, 141
Deflection angles, 4–6, 35
Degree of curve, 35, 37, 163
Degree of slope, 20
Degrees, angular measure in, 37, 163
Departures (see Latitudes and departures)
Diagonal parking, illus., 50
Dimension lumber, 139
Dimensioning systems:
    architectural, 186
    engineering, 186
Ditches, flow capacity of, 115, 116, 118
Double meridian distance (DMD), 10
Drain inlets, 51
    illustration, 109
    ponding depths at, illus., 51
Drainage, storm: grading for, 29–30
    runoff, 102, 104–108
    (See also Rainfall)
Drainage channels (see Channels)
Dry measure, table, 198

Earth pressure, resultant, 63–66
Earthwork:
    cut and fill, 29, 79
    earth movement, 80
    shrinkage and expansion, 80
    volume calculation by: contour-planes
        method, 88–93
    cross-section method, 81–85
        cross sections, illus., 83
        tabular computations for, illus., 84
        tabular form for calculation, illus.,
            85
        topo map showing cross-section
            locations, illus., 82
    grid method, 85–88
    parallel-planes method, 93–98
Eighth lines, 3
End area, 81
Equilibrium, laws of, 141
    three forces in, 141
Excavation:
    computation of volumes (see Earthwork)
    shrinkage and compaction allowance
        (see Earthwork)
Exsecant, 162, 181

Fir, Douglas, 140, 150, 156
Fire hydrants, 100
Flow:
    in circular sewer pipes, chart, 110
    in ditches, 115, 116, 118
    in swales, 117, 118

Force, moment arm of, 52
French curve, 34
Functions of angles, trigonometric (see
    Trigonometric functions)

Geological survey, 12
Geometric figures:
    area of, 179–181
    centroids of, 55
    volume of, 180
Grades for surface drainage (see Grading, criteria)
Gradients:
    maximum and minimum, 30–31
    method of expressing, 20, 42
    positive and negative, 42
Grading:
    considerations, 28–29
    criteria, 30–31
    drawings, 33
Grading plan, 21, 28–33
    illustration, 32
Grading study, procedure for, 29–30
Gravity retaining walls (see Retaining
    walls)
Grid system:
    in determining earth volumes, 85–88
    in topographic mapping, 13–14

Hachures, 19
Hardwoods, 138–139
Hazen and Williams formula, 101
Hemlock, 151, 156
High point on vertical curve, 47
Horizontal curves (see Circular curves)
Horizontal equivalent, 20

Inches, conversion of, to decimals of a
    foot, 186
Inlet, drain, 109
Inlet time, 108
Intensity of rainfall, 105
Interpolation:
    for contours, 14–19
        using rubber band, illus., 17
        using scale and triangle, illus., 18
        using slide rule, illus., 16
    for parallel planes, 94–98
Inverts, 109
Irregular areas, measurement of, 10, 189
Irrigation:
    back-flow prevention, 136–137
    dividing system into sections (blocks),
        123–126

Irrigation (*Cont.*):
  prerequisites for designing system, 119–120
  pressure loss in system, 126–133
    plan of a portion of a sprinkler system, illus., 134
    plan of a simple feeder loop, illus., 135
    (*See also* Water distribution)
  spray heads: application rate, 121, 123–125
    (*See also* precipitation requirements *below*)
    arrangements, 122–123
    equivalent heads, 124
    precipitation rate (*see* application rate *above*)
    precipitation requirements: for golf courses, 124
      for turf and shrubbery, 124
    spacing, 122–123
    types of, 121

Joists, 139, 141

Land measure, table, 200
Land survey, 3–4
Larch, western, 140, 150, 156
Latitudes and departures, 6
  balancing of, 6
  computation of, 4–10
  corrections of, 4–10
  definition of, 6
Layout plan (*see* Staking plan)
Length:
  of arc, 36
  of chord, 38
  of radius, 35, 38
  of tangent, 35, 36, 39
Levels, taking, 12
Line of closure, 9
Linear equations, 157–158
Linear measure, table, 199
Lines, bearing of, 4–10
Liquid measure, table, 198
Loads:
  dead, 141
  live, 141–143
  snow, 141–142
  wind, 141–143
Logarithms:
  Briggs (common), 159
  characteristic, 160
  mantissa, 160
  Naperian (natural), 159

Low point on vertical curve, 46–47
Lumber:
  allowable stresses for, 150–153
  beams and stringers, 139, 150–153
  classification of, 139, 150–153
  dimension, 139, 150–153
  dimensions of, 154–155
  posts and timbers, 139, 150–153
  structural, properties of, 154–155

Manholes, 109–110
Manning's formula, chart, 110
Mantissa, 160
Maximum bending moments in beams, 146–149
Means and extremes, 158–159
Meridians, 3
Meters, water: maximum safe flow through, chart, 127
  pressure loss through, 126–128
Minutes (angular measure), 163
Moment:
  bending, 141, 143, 146–149
  of a force, 52
  resisting, 60–61, 66
Moment arm, 52

Numbers:
  exponents of, 159
  logarithms of, 159–160
  powers of, 164–179
  roots of, 164–179

Oblique triangles, 163, 182
Overhanging beams (*see* Beams, cantilever)

Parabolic cross section, 48
Parallel planes, 93–98
  comparison with contour planes, illus., 94
Parallelogram of forces, 53, 54
  horizontally loaded cantilevered wall, illus., 70
  horizontally loaded gravity wall, illus., 66
  surcharged cantilevered wall, illus., 72
  surcharged gravity wall, illus., 69
Parking areas:
  dimensions of, 49–50
  grading of, 49–51
  layout for, illus., 50

Percent of slope, 20
Pine, southern, 151–152
Pipe:
    pressure losses: in asbestos-cement,
        130
    in copper, 129
    in polyethylene, 132
    in polyvinyl chloride (PVC), 131
    sizing of: for irrigation, 133–135
        for sanitary sewers, 102–103, 110
        for storm sewers, 108–114
        for water mains, 100–102
Pipe slopes:
    hydraulic gradients, 108–109
    self-cleaning velocity, 102, 108
Planimeter:
    care of, 189
    compensating polar, illus., 189
    correction circle area, 191
    operation of, 189–191
    typical form for recording calculations,
        illus., 191
Plat, portion of surveyor's record, illus.,
    5
Plat book, 4
Plotting contours, 14–16
Point:
    of compound curvature, 38
    of curvature, 35
    of intersection, 36
    of tangency, 35
    of vertical intersection, 42
Posts and timbers, 139
Properties of structural lumber, 154–155
Property descriptions, 3
Proportional statements, 158, 193
Pumps, irrigation, 136
    intake chamber, 136
    nonoverloading motor, 136
    submergence, 136
    suction screen, 136

Quadratic equations, 157–158
Quarter line, 3
Quarter post, 3

Radians, 163, 202
Rafters, 139, 141
Rainfall:
    duration of, 105
    intensity of, 105
    probability curves for, 105–107
    runoff coefficients, 105
    storm frequency, 105–106
Rate of slope, 20

Rational formula, 108
Redwood, 140, 152, 156
Reinforced concrete retaining walls, 53,
    66
Resultant of wall and earth pressures,
    52–54
Retaining walls:
    design of, 53, 63–66
    illustration, 56
    investigation of, 60–63
    stability of, 57–60
    wood (see Walls, wood)
Reverse curves, 40–41
Right triangles, 161–162, 181
Rise, 20
Roads:
    alignment: horizontal, 34–41
        vertical, 41–48
    plan of, 25, 33, 43
    plan and profile of, illus., 25, 43
    profile of, 42–43
    stationing, 23–25, 27
    tangent sections of, 35
Roof runoff, 102
Roots, square and cube, 164–179
Run, 20
Runoff coefficients, 105

Sag curves, 46
Sanitary sewer lines, 102
    house connections, 103
    lift stations, 102
    pumping stations (see lift stations
        above)
    "Ten States Standards," 102
Sea measure, table, 200
Secant, 161, 181
Section of land, 3
Settlement of earth (see Earthwork)
Sewage, 103
Sewer(s):
    inverts, 109
    manholes, 27
    sanitary, 102–103
    staking out, 27, 102, 103, 109–110
    stationing, 24–27
    storm, 107–114
    wye-branch centerline, 27
Sewerage, 103
Shrinkage allowance in earthwork, 80
Sight distance, 46
Sine, 161, 163, 181, 182
Slide rule, operation of: arithmetical,
        192–194
    cube-root setup, illus., 194
    finding offsets on vertical curves, 46

Slide rule, operation of (*Cont.*):
    locating whole-foot contours, 16
    square-root setup, illus., 193
Slope(s):
  criteria, 30–31
  longitudinal, 19
  maximum, 30–31
  method of expressing, 20, 42
    degree of, 20
    horizontal equivalent, 20
    percent of, 20
    rate of, 20
  transverse, 20
Specifications, unit price, 80
Sprinkler irrigation (*see* Irrigation)
Square measure, table, 199
Staking plan, 21–27
  coordinates, 23–24
  dimensioning, 21–23
  scale, 21
  stationing, 24–27
Stationing, 23–27
Storm drainage (*see* Drainage, storm)
Storm sewers, 107–114
Subdivision plat, 4
  portion of record plat, illus., 5
Summit curves, 45
Surcharge, 64
Surface drainage, establishing grades for, 30–31
Survey:
  computations: area from DMDs, illus., 11
    correcting latitudes and departures, illus., 7
    correcting length and bearing of lines, illus., 8
    DMDs for each line of traverse, illus., 11
  descriptions, 3–4
  land, 3–4
  public lands, 1–3
Surveyor's level, 12
Surveyor's transit, 12
Swales, 113–118

Tables:
  allowable extreme fiber stress in bending, 150–153
  arc lengths, radius equals 1 ft, 183
  areas: of plane geometric figures, 179–180
    of surface of geometrical solids, 181
  bearing capacity of soils and rock, 61
  coefficients of rainfall runoff, 105
  coefficients of sliding friction, 62

Tables (*Cont.*):
  combined wind and snow load, 142
  conversion factors: metric to U.S., 203–204
    miscellaneous, 201–203
    U.S. to metric, 203
  cubic measure, 200
  dry measure, 198
  flow velocity in ditches, maximum allowable, 118
  guide piles and posts, depth of set, 76
  land measure, 200
  linear measure, 199
  liquid measure, 198
  live floor loads commonly used, 142
  maximum bending moment in beams, 146–149
  nautical measure, 200
  pipe capacities: polyethylene, 134
    polyvinyl chloride (PVC), 134
  properties of structural lumber, 154–155
  square measure, 199
  squares, cubes, square roots, and cube roots, 164–179
  weight of wood, 156
  weights, 197–198
  wind loads on vertical surfaces, 142
Tabular forms:
  for area computation by planimeter, 191
  for correcting latitudes and departures, 7
  for earthwork calculations: by cross-section method, 85
    by parallel-planes method, 96
  for storm-drainage design summary, 114
  for vertical-curve computations, 44
Tangents:
  definition of, 35
  length of, 36, 39
Test borings, 61
Tier, 3
Timber:
  allowable stresses for, 150–153
  properties of standard sizes, 154–155
Time of concentration, 107–108
Topographic map:
  from grid survey, illus., 13
  from stadia survey, illus., 15
Topographic mapping:
  by grid method, 13–14
  by stadia method, 14–15
Town, 3
Township, 3

Transit rule, 8
Transverse slope, 20
Traverse:
    closing a, 4–10
    as corrected for closure, illus., 9
    from field survey, illus., 6
Triangles:
    area of, 179, 182
    centroids of, 55
    oblique, 163, 182
    right, 161–162, 181
Trigonometric functions, 161–163
    oblique-triangle formulas, 163, 182
    right-triangle formulas, 161, 181

Unit-price specifications, 80
Utilities, 99–103
    codes and ordinances, 100
    definition of, 99
    electricity, 99
    regulations, 100
    sanitary sewers, 102–103
    storm sewers, 103
    underground, 100
    water distribution, 100–102
        fire hydrants, 100
        mains, 100
        reservoirs, 100
        standpipes, 100
Utility plan, 23

Verniers, how to read, 187–189
    examples of vernier settings, illus.,
        188
    a simple vernier, illus., 188
Versed sine, 162, 181
Vertical curves, 41–48
    elevation on, 44
    form for setting up calculations, illus.,
        44
    high and low points, 46–47
    illustration, 42
    road plan and profile, illus., 43
    rule for solving, 44
    sag curves, 46
    summit curves, 45
Volume:
    of cut and fill, 29, 79
        contour-planes method, 88–93
        cross-section method, 81–85
        grid method, 85–88
        parallel-planes method, 93–98
    of geometrical solids, 180

Walks, recommended slopes for, 30–31
Walls:
    concrete, 52–73
        cantilever, 53
            horizontally loaded, illus., 65, 70
            surcharged, illus., 65, 72
        counterfort, 55
        gravity, 53
            horizontally loaded, illus., 64, 66
            surcharged, illus., 64, 69
        reinforced, 53
        section of: showing key to prevent
            sliding, illus., 63
            showing sloping bottom to pre-
                vent sliding, illus., 63
    earth pressure on, 64–66, 74–75
    wood, 73–78
        anchors for, 73
        deadmen for, 73
        depth of set, 75
        horizontal earth pressure, 75
        horizontal planking, 73, 77
        railroad ties, 73
        retaining, illus., 74
        sheet pile, 73, 76
Water distribution:
    head losses, 101, 126
    pressure losses: in loops, 135
        in meters, 126–127
        in pipes (see Pipe, pressure losses)
    (See also Irrigation)
Water pressure, 100–102
Weights, table of, 197–198
Wind load:
    on roofs, 141–142
    on vertical surfaces, 141–142
Wood:
    beams (see Beams)
    cedar, 140, 150, 156
    classification of lumber, 139
    cypress, southern, 140, 156
    Douglas fir, 140, 150, 156
    hardwoods, 138
    heartwood, 139
    joists, 141
    larch, western, 140, 150, 156
    preservatives, 139
    rafters, 141
    redwood, 140, 152, 156
    sapwood, 139
    softwoods, 138
    weight per cu ft, 156
    (See also Lumber; Wood construc-
        tion)
Wood construction:
    allowable extreme stress in bending,
        150–153

Wood construction (*Cont.*):
  beam design (*see* Beams)
  beams and stringers, 139, 150–153
  dead loads, 141–143
  decking, floors, and roofs, 141–145
  dimension lumber, 139, 150–153
  equilibrium, 141
  live loads, 141–143
  maximum bending moments, 146–149

Wood construction (*Cont.*):
  plan and elevation of pedestrian
    bridge, illus., 144
  posts and timbers, 139, 150–153
  properties of structural lumber,
    154–155
  snow and wind loads, 142
  walls (*see* Walls, wood)
  (*See also* Lumber)